Michael Bloch is a freelance historian and writer who has had privileged access to the Windsor files in Paris for over ten years. He is the author of *The Duke of Windsor's War, Operation Willi* and *The Secret File of the Duke of Windsor*, and the editor of *Wallis & Edward: Letters 1931-1937*.

From the reviews of *The Secret File of the Duke of Windsor*:

'It is perhaps the most moving, intimate Royal story to be revealed in modern times'
Daily Mail

'Michael Bloch has undoubted gifts as an historian and marshalls his material with considerable skill'
Spectator

'Throws new light on the Abdication settlement'
New Statesman

'Well presented . . . likely to evoke a measure of sympathy for the Windsors'
Sunday Telegraph

'Serious and scholarly'
Financial Tim

The Reign
and Abdication
of Edward VIII

Michael Bloch

BLACK SWAN

THE REIGN & ABDICATION OF EDWARD VIII
A BLACK SWAN BOOK 0 552 99472 3

Originally published in Great Britain by Bantam
Press, a division of Transworld Publishers Ltd

PRINTING HISTORY
Bantam Press edition published 1990
Black Swan edition published 1991

This book is set in 11/12 Melior by
Falcon Typographic Art Ltd

Black Swan Books are published by Transworld
Publishers Ltd, 61-63 Uxbridge Road, Ealing, London
W5 5SA, in Australia by Transworld Publishers
(Australia) Pty Ltd, 15-23 Helles Avenue, Moorebank,
NSW 2170, and in New Zealand by Transworld
Publishers (NZ) Ltd, Cnr Moselle and Waipareira
Avenues, Henderson, Auckland.

Printed and bound in Great Britain by
Cox & Wyman Ltd, Reading, Berks

To Andrew Best

Contents

List of Illustrations
From the King's Private Collection

Acknowledgements

I should like to thank the following for helping me in various ways: Caroline Belgrave; Dr B. S. Benedikz; Andrew Best; Peter Bloxham; Maître Suzanne Blum; Bethsabée Blumel; Mark Brockbank; Vincent Brome; Matthew Bryant; Dr John Charmley; the late Philip Core; the late Professor Michael Crowder; John Curtis; Maître Jean-Pierre Dagorne; the late Dudley Danby; the Rev. Neil Dawson; Michael Day; Robert Egerton; Tom Graves; Inga Haag; Hugo Haig-Thomas; Richard Hough; the late H. Montgomery Hyde; David Irving; Dora Irwin; the late Professor Christopher Jackson; Alison Joynson; Trevor Langford; James Lees-Milne; Maître Jean Lisbonne; the staff of the London Library; Frances McCurtain; Professor R. B. McDowell; Ursula Mackenzie; K. C. Malaker; Philip Mansell; Brian Masters; Thomas Moraitis; the Hon. Lady Mosley; Steve Nelson; Raymond de Nicolay; Robert B. Payn; Stuart Preston; John Raish; Annette Remond; Andrew Roberts; Kenneth Rose; Michael Rubinstein; the late Gaston Sanègre; Anne Seagrim; Judith Wardman; Philip Ziegler; and my parents. My apologies to anyone whom I may inadvertently have omitted.

Introduction

In September 1979, while I was pupil to the late John Phillips at the Middle Temple in London, I received an unexpected invitation from Maître Suzanne Blum, the venerable French *avocat* who had for some thirty years represented the Duke and Duchess of Windsor, to work in her office in Paris. She wanted me to help with the enormous English correspondence which had arisen out of her guardianship of the Duchess, and also to write a number of historical works based on important archives which had been deposited with her by her royal clients. To join this fascinating and formidable figure in order to undertake such a project was indeed exciting for a trainee barrister of twenty-five whose private ambition was to make a professional career in the writing of history; and it is difficult for me to express my gratitude for the kindness shown to me during the past ten years by Maître Blum, who as I write is still lucid and vigorous and preparing to celebrate her ninety-first birthday.

My task in Paris was to edit the private correspondence of the Windsors from the time of their first meeting, and to write about their years of exile which witnessed the ex-King's unhappy relations with his country and family. But there were two other books I wanted to write, which came outside the scope of Maître Blum's commission and of the main archives she put at my disposal, though regarding which I always had her support. One was an account of the Nazi plot to kidnap the Duke in July 1940, which

13

appeared in 1984 under the title *Operation Willi*. The other was an account of the Abdication: I began work on this in 1985, and my then publisher, the excellent John Curtis of Weidenfeld & Nicolson, wanted to bring it out in time for the fiftieth anniversary of the Abdication in December 1986. But the final illness and death of the Duchess in the early months of 1986 meant that I became preoccupied with other duties and that the anniversary itself promised to be little noticed; and the unfinished manuscript went into the drawer for a period.

Though hardly a year goes by without the publication of some gossipy work about the Windsors, there are in fact few serious accounts of the Abdication. The last, which appeared more than fifteen years ago, was Frances Donaldson's *Edward VIII* (1974). This was justly admired for the way it brought together the various materials which were then available; but Lady Donaldson had an obvious 'down' on her royal subject and was determined to award him low marks. In this account I have tried to redress the balance; and I have been able to make use of those new sources which have appeared during the past decade and a half. Possibly the most important of these is my edition of the intimate correspondence of the King and Mrs Simpson, which was published after the Duchess of Windsor's death in 1986 and must lead to a major reassessment of her role in the Abdication. Also to have appeared in recent years are the personal records of two persons closely involved in the crisis, Sir Winston Churchill and Lord Reith, as well as of such interesting contemporary observers as Lord Crawford, Lord Ponsonby, Victor Cazalet and Leo Amery.

A problem which has hitherto faced all who have written about the Abdication is that the public records on the subject are officially closed to general scrutiny until the year 2037. This problem, however, has been greatly lessened since the publication in 1969 of the massive biography of Baldwin by Keith Middlemas and John Barnes, which succeeded in telling much

14

of the official story; and I have had the good fortune to be able to make use (in many cases for the first time) of the personal records of three cabinet ministers who were in the thick of the crisis – Duff Cooper (thanks to the kindness of his official biographer, John Charmley), Sir Samuel Hoare (by kind permission of the Royal Librarian), and Ramsay MacDonald (whose excellent diary, somehow escaping the 2037 ban, may be perused by all in the Public Record Office).

I have also been able to see a number of interesting unpublished documents at Maître Blum's office, including copies of most of the important letters addressed to Edward VIII. Immediately after the Duke of Windsor's death in 1972, the originals of these letters were transported under irregular circumstances from the Bois de Boulogne to Windsor Castle; but the Duke had made typed transcripts of them at the time he wrote his memoirs, and these were among the papers which he prudently deposited with his lawyer. It is also thanks to Maître Blum that I have been able to use photographs from the King's private collection.

This book is by no means a comprehensive account of the reign of Edward VIII; but it does put forward two views which are in my opinion vital for a proper understanding of the Abdication and which are at variance with almost everything previously written on the subject.

The first concerns Mrs Simpson. Historians such as Lady Donaldson seem to assume as a matter of course that she was happy to divorce her husband, wanted to marry the King, and envisaged becoming Queen of England. Following the publication of her correspondence with the King and others, it is difficult to sustain this view. The truth seems to be that the King dragged her unwillingly into divorce, bewildered her with his marriage project, and chose a future with her in preference to the throne very much against her wishes. It was her reluctance to go along with his plans that imposed such a strain on Edward VIII, and accounts for so much of his erratic behaviour during his reign.

The second point is that Edward VIII never in any sense fought for his throne. On 16 November 1936, he told Baldwin that he was determined to marry Mrs Simpson, even if it meant abdicating; and he in fact abdicated on 11 December, almost a month later. During that month, he is generally portrayed as desperately seeking some solution which would enable him, contrary to the wishes of conservative England, both to marry and remain King. This, indeed, is how he portrayed himself in his own memoirs, in which Baldwin appears as the enemy. But it is not a true picture. There was never any real confrontation between King and Government; and when the King spoke of abdication in mid-November it was (in the view I shall put forward) already his firm intention to abdicate. Thus the whole 'Abdication Crisis' may be regarded as a fiction, since it was in effect resolved before it had even started – though of course it did not look that way at the time to those (both on the King's side and the Government's) who could not be absolutely sure what the sovereign was going to do.

On election day in June 1987, long after I had conceived and begun this book and made arrangements for its publication, it was announced that Philip Ziegler had been commissioned by the Queen to write the official biography of Edward VIII. It is indeed good news that the Royal Archives and the Public Records should at last be releasing some of their treasures on this hitherto restricted subject, and to so fine an historian as Mr Ziegler, with whom I have always had very happy relations. I am most grateful to him for reading my manuscript and making many helpful suggestions.

MICHAEL BLOCH
September 1989

Chapter One

Edward VIII

At a quarter to midnight on Monday 20 January 1936, George the Fifth, King of Great Britain and Ireland and the British Dominions Beyond the Seas, Defender of the Faith, Emperor of India, died in his sleep at Sandringham. He was succeeded by his eldest son, Edward Albert Christian George Andrew Patrick David, who took the style of Edward the Eighth.

The new King was a youthful-looking forty-one. Among his subjects, and indeed all over the world, he was an adored and legendary figure. His romantic good looks, his gallant service in the First World War, his spectacular overseas goodwill tours, his modernity, his common touch, his sympathy with the unfortunate – all combined to make him the most popular English sovereign to reach the throne since the similarly glamorous 'Prince Hal' had become Henry V in the fifteenth century. The old King, with his blameless private life and staid unvarying routine, had been admired as a symbol of continuity and tradition in an age of change; but people now thought less of the past than the future. After the failure of old-fashioned statesmen to avert the miseries of the First World War and Depression, men looked to the Prince Charming who was now their monarch as the usher-in of a new age of peace and hope.

Amid expressions of mourning for George V, tributes to the qualities of his successor were lavish. *The Times* wrote in its leader:

His winning smile, 'the smile that conquered Canada',

17

his laughter-loving boyishness, sometimes nervous, but always self-possessed, his attractive habit of identifying himself with the different nationalities of the United Kingdom and the Empire, his thoughtful tact, his kindness and sympathy, his affection for children, his delightful sense of humour, his bodily activity and love of sport, his ready memory for faces, his freedom, for all his dignity, from personal or official side, his powers of conversation, and his remarkable talents of voice, memory and quick resourcefulness as a speaker . . . have endeared him to all . . .

In the House of Commons, the Prime Minister, Stanley Baldwin, declared:

Congratulations to our new King as he takes his place in the long line of his distinguished ancestors. No two sovereigns in that long gallery had the same countenance nor served their people in identical fashion . . . King Edward VIII in his turn brings to that same altar a personality richly endowed with experience of public affairs, with the fruits of travel, with universal goodwill. He has the secret of youth in the prime of age. He has a wider and more intimate knowledge of all classes of his subjects . . . than any of his predecessors . . .

In his memoirs, the King later modestly reflected that 'such official eulogies should not be taken too literally'. But private letters which he received on his succession, copies of which exist among his papers in Paris, were equally glowing in their prediction of a brilliant reign.

Winston Churchill was sure he would bring 'peace and true glory' and that 'Your Majesty's name will shine in history as the bravest & best-loved of all the Sovereigns who have worn the island Crown'. The Archbishop of York found it 'difficult to exaggerate' how the King was worshipped by the working people of the country on account of his 'constant and understanding sympathy'. Lord Dawson, the royal physician, spoke of 'how deep is the confidence that a great reign has opened . . . It will be a new chapter in which opportunity, health, content and happiness will all be more widely based.'

Sir Edward Grigg, who had been his principal aide during his early overseas tours, wrote: 'You begin your reign from a position made by yourself which no King of England has ever had on his accession before.' 'We all know', wrote Lady Minto, a Viceroy's widow, 'that the Empire is safe in your hands.' From the Cabinet, Walter Elliot, the Agriculture Minister, who was forty-seven, wrote:

> You, Sir, come into power as one of the younger generation, and your own generation will serve you in the years that lie ahead as loyally as any generation ever served a King

while Sir Samuel Hoare, a veteran Conservative politician who had lately resigned as Foreign Secretary, wrote to Sir Godfrey Thomas, one of the King's closest aides, to say

> how confidently I wish the new King every success . . . He must not feel nervous or despondent about the future. He will make a great King.
>
> And those of us who know something of his work and his worth have no anxiety for the reign that is now beginning.[1]

Though the admiration of the King's qualities was sincere, there was perhaps something a little too insistent in the protestations of confidence. In fact, those who knew him well were deeply troubled. For all his virtues, he had always been an impulsive and dissatisfied character, impatient of his royal role. Lonely and inclined to melancholy, he had sought comfort throughout his adult life in the maternal affections of mature and married women. Since 1934 he had been deeply in love with Mrs Ernest Simpson (née Wallis

Warfield), the wife of a London businessman; she was American and already once divorced. His devotion to her had become total and obsessive, and her company and support had become for him so essential that without it he felt he could scarcely function. At some point before his accession he had formed the intense secret desire to marry her. And – as the King himself frankly tells us in his memoirs – he was always aware that this might involve his having to give up his rights to the throne.

> The hope formed that one day I might be able to share my life with her . . . It was all quite vague but none the less vivid, the dream of being able to bring into my life what for so long had been lacking, without which my service to the State would seem an empty thing . . . *I could not discount the possibility of having to withdraw altogether from the line of succession if my hope were ever to be fulfilled.* However, I took comfort from the fact that my brother Bertie, to whom the succession would pass, was in outlook and temperament very like my father . . .[2]

He had hoped to discuss his marriage project with his father during the autumn of 1935; but no opportunity arose during the last months of the old King's life.

Yet George V sensed what was in his son's mind. He confided his fears to Cosmo Gordon Lang, the Archbishop of Canterbury, who found the King's last days 'clouded with anxiety for the future'.[3] 'When I am gone', the old sovereign is reported to have told Baldwin, 'the boy will ruin himself in six months.' The apprehension felt in royal circles was communicated by senior courtiers to the Prime Minister. Clement Attlee recalled:

> As a Privy Councillor I attended the meeting in St James's Palace of the Accession Council . . . I thought King Edward looked very nervous and ill-at-ease. I remember Baldwin expressing to me his anxiety for the future and

his doubts as to whether the new King would stay the course.[4]

On the eve of the new reign, Tom Jones had already found the Prime Minister 'distinctly nervous'. Baldwin told him:

> You know what a scrimshanker I am. I had rather hoped to escape the responsibility of having to take charge of the Prince as King. But perhaps Providence has kept me here for that purpose. I am less confident about him than Lucy [Mrs Baldwin] is. It is a tragedy he is not married. He is very fond of children . . . The subject [of Mrs Simpson] is never mentioned between us. Nor is there any man who can handle him. I have seen Halsey* and Godfrey Thomas† . . . When I was a little boy in Worcestershire reading history books I never thought I should have to interfere between a King and his Mistress.[5]

And Lord Crawford,‡ a Lancashire grandee and former Conservative Chief Whip who was at the centre of the political, intellectual and social life of London, wrote in his diary on 2 February 1936:

> The King again spends the weekend at [Fort] Belvedere [his private house near Windsor] and one assumes Mrs Simpson is there. If the emotions of the past fortnight have not been strong enough to bring that liaison to an end, we must contemplate its continuance until she is supplanted by some younger rival . . . Criticism may become insistent, bitter; then he may do something fatuous by talking of abdication: he has done so en *famille* before now . . . [6]

---

* Admiral Sir Lionel Halsey (1872–1949), Comptroller and Treasurer to the Prince of Wales 1920–36.

† Sir Godfrey Thomas (1889–1968), career diplomat, Private Secretary to the Prince of Wales 1919–36, Assistant Private Secretary to King Edward VIII, 1936.

‡ David Lindsay, 27th Earl of Crawford and 10th Earl of Balcarres (1871–1940).

One of the best accounts of the personality of the new monarch was written in 1936 by Geoffrey Dennis, a novelist and League of Nations official who had had the opportunity of studying the then Prince of Wales at Oxford during the years 1912–14 and again in France during the First World War.* Dennis summed up the King's virtues as follows:

> Common sense. In dealing with men, uncommon sense. Humour, over underlying sadness. The usual kingly qualities of tact, tolerance, physical courage. Moral courage. The quality, not more usual in kings than other people, of pure goodness of heart. Generosity: pity. Inability – moral incapacity – to be mean or cruel. Intelligence above the average in some directions: where men and their motives were concerned; where memory played a part; regarding machinery and all mechanisms. A clear-cut charming individuality. An absence absolute of insincerity.

These were the defects:

> The ineradicable royal one of dislike of opposition and remonstrance. Impatience of excuses and delays; a nervous irritated quality in the impatience. Obstinacy, which sometimes skirted danger: wanting his own way, and put out when he did not get it; getting it, sometimes, when better not to. Nervous youthful need of perpetual distraction. Pleasure in any kind of company that provided it. Ordinary failings of flesh and spirit . . . Without base flattery, nobody I think could have called him artistically or intellectually gifted, or have attributed to him a subtle, remarkable or especially interesting mind.

---

* Geoffrey Pomeroy Dennis (1892–1963), at this time Chief of Document Services at the League of Nations. Most unfortunately, the Duke of Windsor was to sue Dennis in 1937 for suggesting that Mrs Simpson had been his mistress before their marriage.

The concerns of one ardent minority of his subjects – in books, art, music, the passion of ideas – no-one imagined him to share.

And Dennis went on to describe the former Prince of Wales as a man

> who would never have chosen the destiny of ordered duty in the glare and glitter, under millions of staring eyes; to whom, alike highly-strung and humble-minded, un-royal peace and freedom would have been peculiarly dear. He hated the fuss and the fawning; the monotony of majesty. He hated the clicking cameras. He longed for the right to live his own life which every one of the King's subjects but himself possessed and, in hours of depression, longed for escape from fate and the throne ahead. 'It was the devil.'[7]

A controversy which may never be settled is whether Edward VIII, coming to the throne after twenty-five exhausting years as Prince of Wales, really intended to remain King of England. Dennis was correct in stating that he had often cursed the inexorable destiny that would carry him to the lonely pinnacle of kingship. 'I was not made to be Prince of Wales', he lamented to Alan Lascelles in the twenties.[8] But there can be few heirs to thrones who have not regretted, at some time or other, their lack of freedom to choose their own futures. There are some aspects of his reign – his reluctance to discuss his coronation, to install himself in Buckingham Palace – which might be taken to imply that he did not think he would be staying very long. And there was a widespread belief afterwards in informed circles that he had never meant to stay very long, that he had come to the crown with the actual intention of giving it up. A number of independent but strikingly similar views may be quoted. Sir Samuel Hoare (who had protested in January 1936 that he had had 'no anxiety for the reign that is now beginning') afterwards wrote that the King's fatal weakness, more serious than his personal affections, was that he did not like being King. The ritual and tradition of a historic office made no appeal to him . . . Even without the affair of the marriage, whilst I hoped against hope that the interests of a King's life would gradually reconcile him to kingship, I doubted whether he would ever like the part sufficiently to make a success of it.[9]

Leo Amery, leader of the imperialist wing of the Conservative Party, concluded in December 1936: 'The real explanation . . . is, I believe, that he never really wanted to be King . . . and that consciously or unconsciously Mrs Simpson represented escape from the prison house . . . '[10] And Sir Donald Somervell, who as Attorney-General in 1936 was deeply involved in the crisis, wrote:

I think the King had always had a claustrophobic repugnance to the throne. He is a man I imagine with few spiritual resources in religion or imagination. He is happy if the passing moment is fair — otherwise and therefore generally very unhappy. Such a character would be more than most at the mercy of an infatuation such as he had for Mrs Simpson. Semi-consciously it may have been a bolt-hole . . . To surrender a kingdom because it's a bore is unimpressive, to surrender it for Love seems on a bigger scale . . . I think the explanation may be that for years he had got into the centre of his being the very natural feeling that it was unjust that the accident of birth should so inexorably determine his life and limit the scope of his inclinations.[11]

The King himself, while admitting that he had considered giving up the throne for personal reasons even before he had reached it, always vigorously denied that he had not wished to rule. In his memoirs he wrote:

It was even said that I did not want to be King at all. No doubt as I had grown older, maturing as I had in the world of action, it is entirely possible that, had the choice been left to me, I might not have conspicuously chosen the Throne as the most desirable goal of all my aspirations. But not to wish to be King was something else. Only my death or some precipitous action on my part could have prevented my becoming King when my father died. Now that he was dead I *was* the King. And what was more, I wanted to be a successful King, though a King in a modern way.[12]

As far as the question of his marriage to Mrs Simpson was concerned, he was determined but resigned:

I have always been something of a fatalist. I believe that man is seldom master of his own fate. When great issues are invoked, forces are let loose that are beyond the limited powers of personal decision. There was no way of telling then [at the outset of the reign] how my private problem could be resolved on the Throne, if it could be resolved at all . . . Yet I continued to hope with all my heart that time would produce a solution . . . [13]

The truth seems to have been that he was prepared to rule – but only on his own terms. He well knew that those terms might not be acceptable; but meanwhile he was prepared to give the thing a try. 'What was at stake', he wrote, 'was the question of my right to make a life on the Throne in terms of my own philosophy.'[14] The marriage he craved was the main test; but it was perhaps only the most important manifestation of a more general need.* As he told Walter Monckton early in the reign:

They must take him as he was – a man different from his father and determined to be himself. He would be available for public business and public occasions

---

* In May 1938 Baldwin told Lord Ponsonby that Edward VIII 'had wanted to abdicate much earlier when George V was ill. But once he became King he liked it but gradually found he was caged and his arcane infatuation gave him the spur to break through . . . ' (Ponsonby's diary, quoted in R. A. Jones, *Arthur Ponsonby*, p. 218).

when he was wanted, but his private life was to be his own . . . [15]

The reign therefore began with Edward VIII in a mood of pessimistic experiment, and under the strain of a deep personal problem.

At the Accession Privy Council which took place within hours of his succeeding, the King declared:

> When my father stood here twenty-six years ago, He declared that one of the objects of his life would be to uphold constitutional government. In this I am determined to follow in My Father's footsteps and to work as He did throughout His life for the happiness and welfare of all classes of My Subjects . . .

'Fine scene & everything passed off well', wrote the former Prime Minister Ramsay MacDonald, who presided over the occasion as Lord President of the Council. '"How will he do?" passed from mouth to mouth, but his first appearance as King was decidedly promising – a little nervous & slight in his ways but already with an increased steadiness & self-possession.'

In spite of fears expressed in high places, the reign began auspiciously. Edward VIII's dignity, piety and self-control during the obsequies of the late King – and his decision that he and his three brothers should watch by night over the catafalque in Westminster Hall – created a moving impression. Many were surprised at the intensity of his grief; some attributed it to a sense of guilt at the passing of a parent with whom he had never been able to communicate, least of all towards the end on the most pressing of personal issues. But the strain under which he laboured did not prevent him from a perfect discharge of his ceremonial functions, and from receiving and impressing the many foreign dignitaries who attended the funeral.

His senior aides grumbled about his new tone and style, his dependence on Mrs Simpson, and his habit of disappearing with her every week-end to Fort Belvedere ('the Fort'), his private house in Windsor Great Park which was 'off limits' to courtiers. But for the first few weeks of the reign, the general verdict was that he was behaving well. 'The Court . . . have been delighted by King Edward's whole attitude to the Queen and to themselves', wrote Amery in the early days.[16] When the Privy Council held its first regular meeting on 31 January, Ramsay MacDonald (who had been close to George V) noted: 'What a difference! King young, lively, talkative. But though more informal & conversational, promising & nothing really essential lost.'[17] The King seemed to be mastering his dislike of official paperwork – 'those d—d red boxes full of mostly bunk to read', as he described it to Mrs Simpson.* He took especially seriously his role as head of the armed forces, making early visits to those units and regiments with which he was particularly associated; and he received all whom he was required to receive with his usual charm. The Secretary of State for War, Duff Cooper, was surprised soon after the accession to receive a visit from Deverell, the Chief of the Imperial General Staff, who had come from a royal audience. Deverell was a blunt Yorkshireman, but 'his tongue was loosened and his eyes were rolling' and he had found the interview 'really inspiring'.[18]

Later, as the spring wore on, the King would be accused of being neglectful, ill-humoured, inconsiderate, disorganized, unpunctual; but then he was under the strain of a crisis in his personal affairs.

One of his earliest decisions was to broadcast to

---

* 'At the outset, King Edward had thrown himself wholeheartedly into his official work. He had read his way through the red boxes; and in order to prove his industry to his staff, he used to initial every piece of paper he read', wrote Helen Hardinge, who went on to lament that such perseverance did not last long, as was shortly revealed by a lack of initials.

the peoples of the Empire: he was impatient when he learned that it would not be convenient for him to do so until the first of March, St David's Day. In accordance with practice, a speech for him to read was submitted to him by the Home Office – a long discourse in formal language on the virtues of the late King and the intention of his successor to carry on his work. King Edward insisted on rewriting this 'painstakingly . . . in my own simple style' and on adding a paragraph of his own:

I am better known to you as the Prince of Wales – as a man who, during the war and since, has had the opportunity of getting to know the people of nearly every country of the world, under all conditions and circumstances. And though now I speak to you as the King, I am still that same man who has had that experience and whose constant effort it will be to promote the well-being of his fellow men.

He also tried to interpolate a sentence expressing sympathy with Indian nationalist aspirations – but the Home Secretary, 'not without difficulty', persuaded him to remove this. 'All goes to show', commented Crawford, 'that we have to deal with a very opinionated man who probably feels much more resentment than anybody knows at the restraints and restrictions which have surrounded him hitherto.'[19]

The day of the broadcast arrived. Sir John Reith, the formidable Scot who headed the BBC, a man essentially republican in sentiment, noted in his diary:

The King arrived [at Broadcasting House] at 3.40. There was a great crowd and much cheering . . . He was in very good form, read over his speech; asked if I thought he should say 'Ladies and Gentlemen' or anything like that and I advised definitely not. He said he felt happier coming to Broadcasting House than doing it in Buckingham Palace. I made the announcement myself . . . When he was finished I went back and he asked if I minded his having a cigarette despite studio regulations . . . He stayed for about 25 minutes. We played back the whole performance to him and he was awfully pleased to hear it.[20]

Edward VIII was a thinking man. The thoughts did not always run very deep, and in 1936 they tended to take place in the intervals of an overpowering personal obsession; but he nevertheless thought more about his times and his role in them than any English sovereign since George III. In his memoirs, he gave a miscellany of his views on coming to the throne:

> I believed, among other things, in private enterprise, a strong Navy, the long week-end, a balanced budget, the gold standard, and close relations with the United States. At the same time, while regarding with misgivings the continued encroachments by government on private prerogative, I had become convinced that it was their duty to intervene in the economic system whenever the failure of the free play of the market brought distress to the working classes or impeded the rational development of housing . . . I must admit that I was not a supporter of the League of Nations . . . I was all for Mr Winston Churchill in his campaign to rearm Britain.[21]

There is evidence that he had in fact thought about these matters and held these views. He also felt deeply about the problems of unemployment and economic depression. There was little he could do about this in 1936, other than to follow and encourage the Government's efforts and to make the best of his visits to the distressed areas of Clydeside in April and South Wales in November to raise working-class morale; but his Governorship of the Bahamas four years later, when he was responsible for finding solutions to acute local problems of poverty and unemployment, illustrates that he had reflected upon such problems and had practical ideas.[22]

He was more active as King in the realm of foreign affairs: he had studied these carefully and was unusually well-acquainted with London's diplomatic community, being on terms of personal friendship with both the Foreign Secretary, Anthony Eden, and the permanent head of the Foreign Office, Sir Robert Vansittart. A few days before he came to the throne, Harold Nicolson, meeting him at a theatre party, noted:

> He talks a great deal about America and diplomacy. He resents the fact that we do not send our best men there. He knows an astonishing amount about it all.[23]

And Eden told Victor Cazalet that Edward VIII was 'very good about seeing people. Kept them waiting at times, but always did what was asked willingly and well'. Eden gave a humorous example of his disarming charm with foreign statesmen. He asked Maisky, the Soviet Ambassador: 'Why did you kill my cousin?' — whereupon the Russian burst into apology, regretting the incident and insisting that he personally had nothing to do with it.[24]

Marshal Mannerheim, who represented Finland at the funeral of George V, has left an interesting account of the conversation he had with the King afterwards on the subject of European affairs:

> . . . the King led the conversation to Germany, and asked me if I had been there recently and what my opinion was about political developments. I expressed the personal opinion that whatever one might think of the Nazi movement, it could not be denied that it had put an end to communism in Germany to the advantage of Western civilization. The King said that he was of the same opinion, and further indicated that one must not allow sentimental considerations to influence one's attitude to that country, for one day the Nazi system would be replaced by another, and the fact remained that meanwhile the power of the communists in Germany had been crushed. The King saw in communism

a danger to the world and said . . . that the thought of a reconciliation between the Western Powers and Germany was not foreign to him, but he added: 'It is difficult to approach Germany because it can only be done together with France.'[25]

Much has been written about Edward VIII's naive pro-German views, partly the result of his consciousness of his own German ancestry,* which were to find expression in March 1936 when he urged his ministers not to act (as they had little intention of doing anyway) against Hitler's remilitarization of the Rhineland contrary to the Treaty of Versailles. Two popular myths may be discounted. The first is that his attitude towards Germany outraged the Government and intensified their desire to see him go. This is what Hitler and Ribbentrop wanted to believe; but in fact the King's notions, inspired not so much by love of the Nazis as by fear of communism and the desire to avoid a future war, were mild and commonplace, widely shared at this time by public opinion (especially among ex-servicemen) and in the Government and the Foreign Office, which were already actively pursuing a policy of appeasing the dictators. The second is that he exceeded his constitutional limits in attempting to push the Government in a pro-German direction. For what they were worth, he was in fact entitled to press his views: only a few months earlier, George V had violently opposed the idea of breaking off relations with Italy over Abyssinia and is even reported to have threatened to abdicate in the event of such an outcome. The Foreign Office thought the King occasionally indiscreet and meddlesome, but they were if anything relying on his influence to sell their views to the Government. We know that Vansittart assiduously

---

* Fourteen out of his sixteen great-great-grandparents had been born into German royal houses. See the family tree on p. 25 of the present writer's *Operation Willi* (1984).

paid court to Mrs Simpson in the hope that she might enlist the King's personal support for his pro-Italian policy, designed to keep Mussolini out of the arms of Hitler.

It is unfortunate that Edward VIII should be remembered as the King who was taken in by Hitler. In so far as he thought about the matter, his successor – who stood on the balcony of the Palace with Neville Chamberlain after Munich to receive the cheers of the London crowds – can scarcely be accused of less. King Edward might equally well be thought of as the sovereign who knew how to charm foreign statesmen; who had been instrumental, in 1934, in founding the British Council, which gave his country its first organized overseas cultural relations; who was the first monarch to be deeply interested in relations between Great Britain and both North and South America.

Edward VIII came to the throne filled with reforming intentions. Years later, a view arose that he had wished to cast off the constitutional restraints of kingship altogether and become the ruler of his realm not just in name but in fact – as his cousin Carol was to do when he took dictatorial charge of Rumania the following year. This theory is largely based on two comments as to his intentions which were made at the time, both from pro-Nazi sources which must be regarded as frivolous and unreliable. His German cousin the Duke of Coburg, who had an audience on the first day of the reign, wrote in a self-serving report destined for Hitler's eyes:

> The King is resolved to concentrate the business of government on himself. For England, not too easy . . . [26]

And in November 1936, Chips Channon similarly noted:

> The King . . . too is going the dictator way, and is pro-German, against Russia and against too much slipshod democracy. I shouldn't be surprised if he aimed at making himself a mild dictator, a difficult enough task for an English King.[27]

This was wishful thinking, or at least an absurd exaggeration of his attitude. There is no doubt that he was irked by some of the constraints on what he could say and do; that he wished to be more than a mere figurehead; that he exercised freely his right 'to be consulted, to encourage and to warn' on matters concerning which he had firm views. But politics interested him little. He had been trained for one role and did not seek another. Far from intending to behave unconstitutionally, he finally accepted the harshest constitutional advice tendered by a British Government to a British sovereign in modern times – that he could not pursue his heart's desire and remain on the throne. Those who seriously imagine that he harboured an ambition to become England's Mussolini should read the long letter he wrote to Winston Churchill on becoming Governor of the Bahamas in 1940, complaining that his education had never prepared him for a post in which he was required to take responsibility for executive decisions.[28]

He did not wish to transform the monarchy's constitutional role – but he certainly had it in mind drastically to reform its image and style. Under George V, the Court and the royal way of life had made few concessions to rapidly changing social ideas and conditions. Edward VIII sought to simplify and modernize. He was a king who disliked courtiers and hated palaces. He also hated debutantes, large official receptions, superfluous paperwork, elaborate ceremonies and the Established Church. He regarded the whole world of his father with distaste – the stultifying routine, the unvarying traditions, the ancient hierarchical apparatus, the attendant bishops, the seasonal peregrinations between the royal palaces and estates.

As the Archbishop of Canterbury ruefully noted on the old King's death, the new reign also promised to be a new régime.[29]

In his memoirs, the King tended to play down his efforts to produce change. He wrote in the late forties, a time of drabness in England when people were on the whole glad that the monarchy had retained its old panoply and style. As he said:

> I had no desire to go down in history as Edward the Reformer. Edward the Innovator – that might have been more to the point. Yet I had no notion of tinkering with the fundamental rules of the Monarchy, nor of upsetting the proud traditions of the Court. In truth, all I ever had in mind was to throw open the windows a little and to let into the venerable institution some of the fresh air that I had become accustomed to breathe as Prince of Wales. My modest ambition was to broaden the base of Monarchy a little more, to make it a little more responsive to the changing circumstances of my times . . . [30]

He went on to say, half-humorously, that the only lasting changes attributable to him were the inauguration of the King's Flight and the scrapping of the rule that the Yeomen of the Guard at the Tower of London should wear square beards.

But in fact he did or tried to do far more. Many of the changes were small – but all were symbolic and took place within a few months. He banished the frock coat at Court, and introduced other informalities of dress. He opened the Royal Victorian Order and other honours to women. He dispensed with the 'humble submissions' – the customary handwritten letters sent by the Prime Minister to the sovereign after each cabinet meeting, which had become a superfluous chore for the premier since the introduction of cabinet minutes. He tried (unsuccessfully) to get rid of the 'loyal declaration' – the undertaking by the sovereign, read by him at the opening of his first parliament, to uphold Protestantism, which was 'repugnant' to him as 'wholly inappropriate to an institution designed to shelter all creeds'. He refused to hold Courts for the presentation of debutantes, who were presented instead at a series of garden parties (one of which, to his embarrassment, was a wash-out); no doubt, given his own way, he would cheerfully have abandoned the whole business of courts, levées, presentations and investitures.

More visible at the time were the considerable differences in the King's personal lifestyle between the old reign and the new. Edward VIII was not unconscious of the dignity of his office: but after the intense conservatism of his father, his ways seemed astonishingly informal. On the first morning of his reign, as John Betjeman wrote, he arrived in London 'hatless from the air' – the first time a sovereign had ever flown in an aeroplane. He caused a sensation on one occasion by walking on foot the few hundred yards from his old bachelor rooms at York House, St James's Palace, where he continued to live until the autumn, to Buckingham Palace where he had his office, carrying an open umbrella; and because it was raining, he drove to the State Opening of Parliament in November not in a state coach but a motor car. He spent his week-ends not at Windsor Castle with the Court but at Fort Belvedere with Mrs Simpson and their friends (he was in fact the only sovereign in recent centuries never to spend a night at Windsor); he made only brief appearances at Sandringham and Balmoral, where his parents had spent half their year; and it was only with reluctance that he finally moved into Buckingham Palace in October. He was seen at fashionable luncheon and dinner parties in the capital – wherever Mrs Simpson was to be found. The mourning for his father spared him the duty of appearing at such royal events as Ascot and Cowes Week – but all the signs are that it was a duty he would gladly have ditched. The sort of life he wanted, informal, middle-class, intensely domestic, was not very different from what he would later have in France – a life in which he was looked after in a comfortable house by a devoted mothering wife, entertaining his friends, gardening, golfing, smoking his pipe and walking his dogs.

If he could not abide pomp and side, he also hated extravagance and waste. His reign was remarkable for his insistence on economy. In 1935, George V and his Court had been living in much the same style as when he had come to the throne in 1910 – which was not only socially inappropriate but could no longer be afforded financially. The Privy Purse accounts for 1936 among the Duke of Windsor's papers in Paris reveal that the private royal estate of Sandringham was losing annually the staggering sum of £40,000 (worth well over a million pounds in the values of fifty years later); Balmoral and the other Scottish estates ran less lavishly, but still managed to lose over half that sum. Edward VIII instituted a drastic review of the management of these properties; while in London he immediately began looking into the extravagance of the Royal Household. In 1937 he gave his friend the historian Philip Guedalla

a superb account of his digging into the sinecures and wastage at Court. He said that he never took lunch, and used to have a good look round when they were at theirs. He described finding in the bowels of the earth at Buckingham Palace an enormous room packed with candles, also a troglodytish individual who seemed to sleep there. When he asked about this he was told he was a pensioner: and when he asked why he was there he was told that 'he helps with the candles'. He hated this sort of exploitation and never forgave the people who determined to go on with their pickings and had enormous amounts of provisions sent to Bognor Regis. He said that those people never forgave him either.[31]

There were other things that were not forgiven. In 1932, Civil Servants had been required in view of the economic crisis to take a modest cut in pay. Edward VIII enforced a similar cut on officials of the Royal Household. He himself was accorded, aside from the diminished revenues of the Royal Duchies of Lancaster and Cornwall, a Civil List allowance of £410,000 – smaller than that allowed to his father in 1911. (Critics pointed to the large sums he spent buying jewellery for Mrs Simpson: but this came out of his own private money and was his own affair.)

Such reforms were applauded by at least one important representative section of his subjects. In the debate on the Civil List in the House of Commons that spring, the opposition Labour Party called for 'such changes as would result in increased simplicity' seeing that

> . . . great and numerous residences, an army of attendants, a titled entourage and the habitual observance of elaborate ceremonies are today hindrances to that right understanding which unites the King and his people . . .

The day after the debate, the Labour leader Clement Attlee dined with the King, and discovered to his surprise 'not only that what I had said met with no resentment, but a complete understanding of the point of view expressed'.[32]

Changes may have been welcomed by working-class parliamentarians; but they were greeted with dismay by the old guard of George V's courtiers, who saw in them the beginning of the end of their privileges and their world. They blamed his relationship with Mrs Simpson, who had an American passion for informality and thrift and who was at the centre of the private life which the King sought to lead away from the Court. Through his reforms, Edward VIII aroused the suspicion and hostility of many of the reactionaries who surrounded him. The question was – would he keep them on?

During the first six months of his reign, Edward VIII's immense public popularity appeared if anything to increase. As memories of the old King faded, the excitement of having a glamorous and modern sovereign made itself felt. His deportment at his father's funeral in January, his broadcast in March, his visit to the workers of Clydeside in April – all captured the public imagination. The British press, respecting the privacy of royalty, wrote nothing of Mrs Simpson; and no more than a few dozen people can have known of any problem.

On 16 July 1936 an attempt was made to assassinate the King as he rode with his entourage along Constitution Hill after presenting new colours to certain Guards battalions in Hyde Park. This has never been recognized for what it was; in order to allay panic, the story which was officially released at the time spoke only of a pistol being tossed by a malcontented spectator at the King's horse. But the private report sent to the King by the Home Secretary, Sir John Simon, told another story. The culprit (who was subsequently charged with a relatively minor offence and sentenced to one year's imprisonment) was an Irishman who went under the assumed name of McMahon, suffered from persecution mania, and harboured some obscure grievance against the British Government which he had elaborated in a deranged letter received by the Home Secretary's office that same morning.

> While standing in the crowd near Wellington Arch, before the Royal Procession reached the spot, he asked a mounted policeman to move so that he could obtain a better view. A special constable saw him draw a revolver as the King approached and was able by his prompt action to knock the weapon out of McMahon's hand. The revolver was picked up by another mounted policeman and was found to be loaded in four of its chambers.[33]

This was how the King recalled the experience:

> Just as we emerged from the Arch at the top of the Hill, I noticed a slight commotion in the crowd on my left. A man pushed himself through the police line, and an

instant later something bright and metallic flew through the air. It was well aimed, for it struck the pavement close by me, skidding first under my horse, then under the General's.

For one icy moment I braced myself for the blast that never came. There was a convulsive stir in the crowd as several policemen threw themselves upon the man . . . Turning to [General Sergison-Brooke, General Officer Commanding London District], I said: '"Boy", I don't know what that thing was, but if it had gone off it would have made a nasty mess of us.' The General gave a smile of relief and we rode on as if nothing had happened . . . [34]

The King made light of the affair, which he referred to jocularly as the 'dastardly attempt' – a phrase used by an outraged elderly courtier. There was great public relief and rejoicing at his escape. A headline in *The Times* praised *The King's Calm*; and Sir John Simon was cheered in the House when he expressed their thankfulness 'that the risk to which His Majesty was exposed was so promptly averted'. The King received many hundreds of letters, the Archbishop of Canterbury rejoicing in an event 'which only served to show Your Majesty's calm and courage', and the Prime Minister expressing the relief 'of all your Majesty's servants'.

It is interesting to speculate on how the six-month reign would have gone down in history had Special Constable A. G. Dick not seen McMahon raise his pistol, and 'the dastardly attempt' succeeded.

Chapter Two

The Growing Unease

'No-one will ever understand the story of the King's life', wrote Walter Monckton, who was to be his principal adviser in the Abdication Crisis, 'who does not appreciate . . . the intensity and depth of his devotion to Mrs Simpson.' He continued:

> To him she was the perfect woman. She insisted that he be at his best and do his best at all times, and he regarded her as his inspiration. It is a great mistake to imagine that he was merely in love with her in the ordinary physical sense of the term. There was an intellectual companionship, and there is no doubt that his lonely nature found in her a spiritual comradeship . . . He felt that he and Mrs Simpson were made for each other and that there was no other honest way of meeting the situation than marrying her.[1]

Others who knew him well explained the King's infatuation in similar terms. Thus Lord Dawson of Penn, the famous Royal Physician and a seasoned student of human nature, writing after the Abdication to the Princess Royal:

> A *first* absorbing love coming after forty is apt to take possession. To have abandoned it would have spoilt life and work and therefore worth . . . [2]

And thus Winston Churchill, who had known him from the King's boyhood:

40

He delighted in her company, and found in her qualities as necessary to his happiness as the air he breathed. Those who knew him well and watched him closely noticed that many little tricks and fidgetings of nervousness fell away from him. He was a completed being instead of a sick and harassed soul. This experience which happens to a great many people in the flower of youth came late in life to him, and was all the more precious and compulsive for that fact . . . [3]

Many were puzzled as to what he saw in her; for she was a rather ordinary woman – already thirty-nine in 1936, chic but by no means beautiful, witty but by no means brilliant in conversation, uneducated, unathletic and frequently unwell. She hailed from Baltimore, only child of a mother widowed when 'Wallis' was five months old, the poor relation of genteel Southern families. An early marriage to a dashing but alcoholic airman had come to grief, and after a short period of enjoying life as a single woman on a small income, she had come to London in 1928 to marry Ernest Simpson, a somewhat dull shipping agent of Anglo-American parentage who offered her devotion and security. A remote social connection with Thelma, Viscountess Furness, the Prince of Wales' current favourite, had fortuitously brought the Simpsons into the princely orbit in the years 1931–3; and in 1934 the Prince lost interest in Thelma and fell seriously in love with Wallis. By the autumn of the following year he had no doubts that here was the human being with whom he wished to spend the rest of his life. Her marriage to Ernest continued; throughout her fairy-tale idyll with the Prince, she clung to it as something real; but by 1936 he had become exasperated by the situation and was seeking comfort elsewhere.

The full intensity of his passion for her, and the true nature of their relationship, is revealed in their intimate correspondence published soon after her death in April 1986, in which they write of themselves as a composite being represented by their joint initials WE.

It was in the nature of a mother–son affair. He wrote to her in 1935:

> I love you more and more every minute and no difficulties or complications can possibly prevent our ultimate happiness. WE are so strong together in our purpose which is our very life. I do hate and loathe the present situation . . . and am just going mad . . . that you are alone there with Ernest. God bless WE for ever my Wallis. You know your David will love you and look after you so long as he has strength in this eanum [little] body.[4]

And she to him, rebuking him after an incident:

> I was and still am terribly upset. You see my dear one can't go through life stepping on other people. I know you aren't *really* selfish or thoughtless at heart but your life has been such that quite naturally you only think of what you want and take it too without the slightest thought of others . . . Sometimes I think you haven't grown up where love is concerned and perhaps it's only a boyish passion . . . Your behaviour last night made me realise how very alone I shall be some day – and because I love you I don't seem to have the strength to protect myself from your youthfulness . . . God bless WE and be kind to me in the years to come for I have lost something noble for a boy who may always remain Peter Pan.[5]

Before coming to the throne, he had talked to her of marriage. On New Year's Day, 1936, he wrote to her: 'Oh! my Wallis I know we'll have *Viel Glück* to make us *one* this year. God bless WE.'[6] And on 18 January, from Sandringham, he wrote her

> a line to say I love you more and more and need you so to be with me at this difficult time. There is no hope whatsoever for the King it's only a matter of time and I won't be able to get up to London tomorrow if he's worse. But I do long to see you even for a few minutes my

Wallis it would help so much. Please take care of yourself and don't get a cold. You are all and everything I have in life and WE must hold each other so tight. It will all work out right for us. God bless WE.[7]

There is no evidence that she encouraged his idea of marrying her, which she seems to have regarded as a fantasy. Soon after his accession she wrote to him in sombre vein, dropping the 'WE':

Some day of course I must learn to be always alone for I will be in my heart also I must develop strength to look at papers containing your photographs and accounts of your activities – and perhaps you will miss the *eanum* in your scheme. One can be awfully alone in crowds – but also perhaps both of us will cease to want what is hardest to have and will be content with the simple way . . . God bless you and above all make you strong where you have been weak.[8]

To her closest confidante, her Aunt Bessie Merryman in Washington, she wrote of the new King: 'It's a very lonely job – and it's a tragedy that he can't bring himself to marry without loving.'[9] She was fully aware of his dependence on her:

I have had to be at the new King's beck and call [she wrote on 30 January], being the only person he has to talk things over with normally . . . The King has lost six pounds and the strain has been tremendous . . . Last week-end we went to the Fort and go again tomorrow where he will get the needed rest. Everyone including some of the cabinet ministers have been too divine to me . . . I am implored on all sides not to leave him as he is so dependent on me and I am considered to be a good influence believe it or not and right in the things I try to influence him to do. Of course I am very fond of him and proud and want him to do his job well and he is so lonely and needs companionship and affection, otherwise he goes wrong. Ernest has of course been marvellous about it all . . . How things will work out now I can't say . . . [10]

She was not flattering herself when she wrote that she was generally regarded as good for the King. Almost all who saw them together remarked that her influence was strong but benevolent. Even his mother noted with approval that she had stopped him drinking heavily.[11] Harold Nicolson found her 'virtuous and wise' and 'clearly out to help him'.[12] Victor Cazalet thought her 'the one friend he has ever had. She does have a wonderful influence over him.'[13] Robert Bruce-Lockhart was impressed that he 'definitely has more confidence in himself' since she had taken over.[14] Chips Channon saw him as 'Mrs Simpson's absolute slave, and she . . . is behaving well. She encourages him to meet people of importance; above all she makes him happy. The Empire ought to be grateful.'[15] But none of these people yet realized that he meant to marry her.

During the course of his brief reign, there were times when the King did very well indeed, times when he did remarkably badly. The whole record may loosely be summarized as follows. During the first month or so he was thought to do well. Throughout the spring he was erratic and volatile in his behaviour and intermittently neglected his duties. In late June and July he appeared to do well and was in high spirits. In August he was on holiday: such royal functions as he was called upon to perform on his travels he performed very well indeed. In September and October he was at his worst; and in the first half of November – before the crisis came home to him – he was at his best.

Only now, with the appearance of their intimate letters, is it possible to understand that these ups and downs coincided exactly with the course of his relationship with Mrs Simpson. When he was sure of her, when she was standing by him, he was a good king; otherwise he was hopeless. For he was not always sure of her. In the early autumn she talked of leaving him for his own good, and was reluctant to go through with her divorce. In the early spring she was forced to choose between the King and Ernest Simpson – and it was uncertain how she would choose.

The crisis came barely a month after his accession, in late February or early March. There was a personal interview between the King and Ernest Simpson at York House, recorded by Simpson's friend Bernard Rickatson-Hatt, the editor-in-chief of Reuters. Rickatson-Hatt, whom Simpson had brought to the meeting as a witness, began at one moment to leave; but Simpson asked him to stay, and then

> told the King that Wallis would have to choose between them, and what did the King mean to do about it? Did he mean to marry her? The King rose from his chair and said: 'Do you really think I would be crowned without Wallis at my side?'[16]

Mrs Simpson was at that moment in Paris, from where she confessed to her aunt her mood of 'exhaustion, rage and despair.'[17] She was reluctant to put an end to her marriage; but the determining factor was the attitude of her husband. He had had enough of sharing his wife with another man, albeit his sovereign; he was willing to abandon her to the King, who was evidently going to look after her; he himself was in love with another woman, his wife's American schoolfriend Mary Raffray. By the end of April the Simpsons had agreed that shortly they would go their separate ways. Wallis prepared to leave behind her the old life she had led with Ernest and chance her future with the King. But she did not do so without reservations. She wrote to Aunt Bessie in a remarkable letter of 4 May:

> I have always had the courage for the new things that life sometimes offers. The K on the other hand has another thing only on his mind [i.e. marriage]. Whether I would allow such an action depends on many things and events and I should never allow him if possible to prevent a rather stubborn character to do anything that would hurt

the country and help the socialists [sic]. In any case there is a new life before me whereas I can't go back to the old . . . My nerves are fast going, the demands on me are heavy from every quarter . . . I have discussed all this with Ernest. Naturally he is sad but sees my point, he knows HM's devotion to me is deep and of the right sort. His only fear is that He will go through with His idea. I feel however these things sort themselves out. May and June means that Ernest and myself will be working all this out . . . [18]

There followed, in the early summer, the carefully stage-managed preliminaries to divorce. The King was the stage-manager. He wrote to her in June:

My talk with Ernest was difficult this evening but I must get after him now or he won't move. It's all so unsatisfactory until it's all settled and WE are really one and I can't bear your having to hear unpleasant things said as I'm just as sensitive as you are you know that. I know you will approve of A[llen]'s plan but of course won't do a thing until WE can discuss it. It's the only way. I must make own drowsy [sleep] now which I expect you are doing too and I only hope a girl is missing a boy as much as he is missing her . . . God bless WE.[19]

George Allen was the London solicitor who dealt with the King's private affairs. He had found a suitable divorce solicitor for Mrs Simpson, Theodore Goddard. Towards the end of the Abdication Crisis, Goddard confirmed to Ramsay MacDonald that, right from the beginning, it was the King who had pressed for and masterminded the divorce;[20] and Ernest Simpson's friend Rickatson-Hatt has recorded that, 'but for the King's obstinacy and jealousy, the affair would have run its course without breaking up the Simpson marriage'.[21]

As the spring of 1936 progressed, and these problems and manoeuvres weighed heavily upon the King, his general behaviour tended to confirm the predictions of his critics, and there were increasing fears and hostile murmurings. He seemed to want to spend more and more of his time with Mrs Simpson, was habitually unpunctual or unavailable for business, exhibited moodiness and indiscretion and neglected paperwork. It was the courtiers who suffered most; and, disturbed as they already were by his plans for economy and simplification, they tended to take a perhaps exaggeratedly uncharitable view of his shortcomings. But he allowed none to approach him on the subject of Mrs Simpson.

Lord Wigram, the veteran and ailing Private Secretary inherited from George V, was deeply worried. As early as 13 February he spoke to Ramsay MacDonald of his deep suspicions that the King's 'mind was made up' to marry Mrs Simpson and 'get rid of her husband'. He regarded Mrs Simpson as a security risk: '[The King] takes down his papers [to Fort Belvedere] & leakages easy; she is said to be consulted on everything; believed to be the kind of person who would sell secrets.'[22] This was hysterical prejudice and there is no evidence that Mrs Simpson had any such inclinations: but the King's own casual attitude to papers did not inspire confidence, and it is even claimed that top-secret documents on foreign political matters were gradually withheld from him.

Wigram meant to retire before Edward VIII appointed his new Court at the end of the six months' period of mourning for his father; but he first asked Baldwin — this was in early April — to see the King to warn him about his 'conduct' (though 'at the same time he made it clear', notes Baldwin's biographer, 'that against a passion so overmastering it was very doubtful whether any words of reasons would prevail'[23]). There was a plan, conceived by Wigram together with Sir Warren Fisher, the head of the Civil Service, that the Prime Minister should lead a delegation to the King for this purpose, including the Speaker of the House of Commons and Lord Halifax, the Lord Privy Seal. But

Baldwin, who was close to a nervous breakdown after a year as premier during which Edward VIII had been merely one of many anxieties, instinctively declined to interfere.

The mood of criticism spread from the courtiers to the politicians. ''Ere we 'ave this little obstinate man with 'is Mrs Simpson', was the verdict of the Colonial Secretary, the earthy Jim Thomas, before he fell from office that spring for leaking budget secrets. 'Hit won't do . . . I know the people of this country . . . They 'ate having no family life at Court.' Ramsay MacDonald complained to Harold Nicolson about the King's 'appalling obstinacy', which was 'making a bad effect' in the country. 'The people do not mind fornication, but they loathe adultery.'[24] Crawford found Lord Hailsham, the Lord Chancellor, frightened:

> He seems to fear [wrote Crawford on 8 April] that something must happen sooner or later which will produce an open scandal. For my part I feel certain that a crisis must occur and without much delay as our newspapers will not long forgo their claim to discuss what is already the subject matter of articles in France and America, probably in Australia too. And then what is the little man going to do – how can he face that storm?[25]

Neville Chamberlain drafted a memorandum for the Cabinet, urging that the King should 'settle down', wear dark clothes, work at his 'boxes' and refrain from making remarks in public on such subjects as slums and unemployment. Baldwin 'thought it wise to suppress this memorandum'.[26]

On 27 May Baldwin had the chance of meeting Mrs Simpson, when he and his wife were invited to dine with the King at York House, the bachelor residence in St James's Palace which the sovereign continued to occupy. ('Sooner or later', the King had told a nervous Mrs Simpson, 'my Prime Minister must meet my future wife.'[27]) Among the other guests were the Louis Mountbattens, the Wigrams, the Duff Coopers and both Mr and Mrs Simpson. 'My wife and I were well placed,' Baldwin told his future biographer, 'but I own it surprised me to see Mrs Simpson at one end of the table and Lady Cunard at the other.' Mrs Baldwin was more acerbic: she thought Mrs Simpson 'had stolen the fairy Prince'.[28] The King directed that the names of the Simpsons appear with the other guests in the following day's Court Circular: this caused some sensation among the limited newspaper readers to have heard of her. 'The Times today had the most serious news that it has had for many years', wrote Sir John Reith, Director-General of the BBC. ' . . . It is too horrible and it is serious and sad beyond calculation.'[29]

Six weeks later, on 9 July, when the King gave his next party, the name of Mrs Simpson was published without that of her husband. There was now endless talk. 'The Simpson scandal is growing,' wrote Chips Channon, 'and she, poor Wallis, looks unhappy. The world is closing in around her, the flatterers, the sycophants, and the malice.'[30]

In high social and official circles, many now suspected the King's intentions. But he had unburdened himself to no-one; the British newspapers, respecting the private life of royalty, did not mention her; and her coming divorce remained a well-kept secret. One of the few who knew of it and were consulted about it was the King's close friend and adviser Walter Monckton, who as holder of the post of Attorney-General to the Duchy of Cornwall had been the principal legal counsellor of the former Prince of Wales. Disturbed by the implications, Monckton in turn consulted another old friend of the King, Winston Churchill, who advised

that such a divorce would be most dangerous; that people were free to believe or ignore gossip as they chose; but that court proceedings were in another sphere. If any judgment were given in court against Mr Simpson it would be open to a Minister of Religion to say from the pulpit that an innocent man had allowed himself to be divorced on account of the King's intimacies with his wife. I urge most strongly that every effort should be made to prevent such a suit.[31]

These views were communicated to the King; but he did not listen.

More than ever the King had need of sympathetic advisers – if he would eventually consult them. The legacy of George V was a Court which was old-fashioned, old of years, and conservative, filled with men who mistrusted and disapproved of Edward VIII – and not only on account of Mrs Simpson. But the new King had the task of setting up a new Court – to be installed in July 1936 at the end of mourning for his father. There were many who expected a clean sweep. When Alexander Hardinge, George V's long-serving Assistant Private Secretary, 'very much criticised the Prince of Wales and his entourage' in December 1935, Chips Channon remarked: 'It is high time such dreary, narrow-minded fogies were sacked, as, indeed, they will be, in the next reign.'[32]

In the event, what was remarkable about the Court appointed by Edward VIII was that he kept things so much as they were. The two pillars of the old guard – Wigram the Private Secretary and Cromer the Lord Chamberlain – were both invited to stay on, though Wigram chose to leave, suffering from a weak heart and sensing trouble ahead. (He was to reappear in the autumn as the Duke of York's principal adviser in the Abdication Crisis.) Three of his old staff as Prince of Wales achieved significant positions: Godfrey Thomas became Assistant Private Secretary; Piers Legh was earmarked as Master of the Household; Lionel Halsey was appointed his senior equerry. Nor did he forget his family. His cousin-by-marriage the Duke of Beaufort became Master of the Horse; his uncle the Earl of Athlone, Gold Stick; Lord Louis Mountbatten, his Honorary Naval ADC, a post once held by Mountbatten's father. Officers and peers among his friends became equerries and lords-in-waiting: but there were no appointments from outside traditional court circles.

It is one of the mysteries of the reign of Edward VIII that he did not get rid of the disapproving men who stood in the way of his new vision of the monarchy and were hardly likely to give him much support in his coming trials. Cromer, who was astonished by his own reappointment, had an uncharitable explanation, recorded by Crawford:

> ... he [Cromer] knows that war was in effect declared on the old gang; but it is possible that HM is beginning to realise the paucity and meagreness of his own entourage – perhaps he now sees how small is their fund of experience and *savoir-faire* – hence a reaction in favour of King George's staff.[33]

And yet, during the crisis, the King found men of talent and goodwill to serve him, even if they were unable to dissuade him from his decision – Walter Monckton, George Allen, Edward Peacock, Perry Brownlow.

None of the appointments was controversial. They included none of his Falstaffs – men such as 'Fruity' Metcalfe or Brigadier Trotter. Some accused him of high-handedness in getting rid of a few obviously superannuated relics; but he was evidently not high-handed enough for his own good.

What was astonishing, however, was his choice of Hardinge to succeed Wigram. Hardinge was efficient; but the King can have had no possible personal liking for or trust in this cold and arrogant individual, whose disloyal remarks about his new master just a month before he came to the throne had provoked Chips Channon's sharp comment. And the appointment began with a row, as two letters of Hardinge among the Duke of Windsor's papers testify. Hardinge had heard – he wrote to the King on 20 July – 'from a roundabout source' that the Private Secretary's salary was to be reduced from £1,500 to £1,000. His Majesty had, 'not unnaturally, little idea of the responsibilities and complexity of work' of the Private Secretary's office, continued the new incumbent with amazing lack of tact. The proposed reduction would reduce him to the level of a mere functionary like the Keeper of the Privy Purse.

The following day Hardinge wrote again, but scarcely redeemed himself. He was 'very sorry' that his Majesty had been 'put out' by the first letter, which had been couched in terms which ought not to have caused 'the slightest annoyance'. He assured the King that £500 a year made no particular difference to his circumstances, but that he had personally been 'very hurt' by the decision and the way it had come to his knowledge: it amounted to a devaluation of the great office he was about to assume and a lowering of its 'great traditions'.[34]

This bizarre contretemps might have been thought to have killed any trust which existed between sovereign and servant: but Hardinge stayed on. He would remain until 1943, when George VI would dismiss him as a result of an incident which occurred during the royal visit that year to North Africa. 'What did I tell you and warn you?' the Duke of Windsor is said to have remarked subsequently to his brother.

Even stranger was the King's decision to allow Alan Lascelles to stay on as Assistant Private Secretary. This highly gifted but inflexible courtier had been appointed to that post (under Wigram and as Hardinge's colleague) in the last weeks of George V's reign; but earlier, in the twenties, he had been Assistant Private Secretary to the Prince of Wales; and he had resigned from that post on account of his deep disapproval of the Prince's personality and private life. He continued to regard Edward VIII in the light of the feelings formed in the earlier period.

When the abdication was announced, Harold Nicolson found Lascelles jubilant. He declared that the late King was like the child in the fairy story who was given every gift except a soul. There was nothing in him which understood the intellectual or spiritual sides of life . . . Even nature meant nothing, and his garden at the Fort nothing beyond a form of exercise. He enjoyed nothing at all except through the senses. He had no real friends for whom he cared a straw . . . He was without a soul, and this made him a trifle mad . . . He never cared for England and the English. He rather hated his country . . . and did not like being reminded of his duties . . . [35]

Whether or not there is any justice in such views, one must marvel at the King's decision to have had their author in his high service.

Following his erratic behaviour between late February and June, Edward VIII, who with the end of Court mourning began to undertake his regular ceremonial duties, showed himself during July to be on the whole an excellent King. This may be related to the fact that, after some hesitations, the preliminary stages of Mrs Simpson's divorce were going smoothly and secretly ahead. These took the traditional form (dictated by the ludicrous laws of the time) of the husband being divorced allowing himself to be 'discovered' at a hotel with a woman who was not his wife; of these facts being 'established' by detectives hired by the wife's solicitors; and of the wife consequently breaking off relations with the 'offending' husband in a letter which might be read out in court. In accordance with this ritual, on 21 July Ernest Simpson booked into the Hotel de Paris at Bray – not, as was usual, with a hired companion, but with the woman he was eventually to marry as his third wife. Something of a crisis then followed, as the hotel management, who had got wind of the identity of this particular client and the reasons for his visit, dismissed and tried to send away the servants who would have to be called as trial witnesses. But Mrs Simpson's resourceful solicitor Theodore Goddard caught them in time, and kept them in comfort at a neighbouring hostelry until they would be required to give evidence.[36] If all went well with their testimony, Mrs Simpson would receive a provisional divorce decree during the autumn, leading to a final dissolution of her marriage six months later, in the spring of 1937.

On 8 August, the King left England on his summer holiday. He was attended by Mrs Simpson, various of their friends, a cabinet minister (Duff Cooper) and a private secretary (Thomas and Lascelles in rotation). At Sibernik in Yugoslavia the party joined the Steam Yacht *Nahlin* which the King had chartered, and began a pleasant month-long cruise along the Yugoslav, Greek and Turkish coasts; from Istanbul they proceeded by train to Austria, where they spent a further five days. Edward VIII did good work for England, arousing great public enthusiasm everywhere and paying useful and successful visits to the senior statesmen of the countries on his way – Paul of Yugoslavia, Metaxas of Greece, Atatürk, Boris of Bulgaria, Schuschnigg of Austria. The British Minister in Vienna, Sir Walford Selby, reported to the Foreign Office that

> the visit has been *invaluable* from the point of view of our position here. The impression made by His Majesty was reflected in the send-off He had last night. The Ringstrasse was a seething crowd and He was cheered again and again. His Majesty has certainly caught the imagination of the Austrians to a quite remarkable degree. I was informed last night by the Foreign Minister that it was reacting to the benefit of the Government . . . Though His Majesty's visit was incognito and this was generally observed, His Majesty met all official needs to a degree which would satisfy His greediest servant.[37]

and similar reports confirming the excellent political effect of the unofficial royal progress were received from Sir Sidney Waterlow, the Minister in Athens, and Sir Percy Loraine, Ambassador to Turkey.

The holiday therefore – which constituted the only foreign travel undertaken by Edward VIII, with the exception of a day-trip to France in July to inaugurate the Canadian War Memorial at Vimy Ridge – provides an indication of his outstanding potential as a representative of his country abroad. But it had another and more baleful significance: it exposed his relationship with Mrs Simpson to the gaze of the international press. The British newspapers continued to say nothing on the subject; but American and continental journals were quick to publish sensational photographs of the King and his favourite, sometimes scantily clad, at the *Nahlin*'s various ports of call, where the couple were frequently recognized and mobbed by delighted crowds. Thus the press outside of England was building up the story of his romance to a scandalous pitch at the very moment – in the weeks prior to the divorce – when it would have been most in the King's interest to calm it down.

The King, Mrs Simpson and the remains of their party left Vienna on 13 September. Mrs Simpson continued to Paris, where she meant to spend a few quiet days. The King meanwhile returned by air to England, 'to resume my duties and to deal with a personal problem which it had become increasingly clear could not be held much longer in abeyance'.[38]

Chapter Three

The King at his Worst

14 September–27 October

For the King, the six weeks between his return from his European trip on 14 September and Mrs Simpson's decree nisi hearing at Ipswich on 27 October were a time of torment. It is during this period that we see him at his most tense and morose, his most thoughtless and reckless. In comparison, the following six weeks – the latter half of which comprised the Abdication Crisis – found him charming and punctilious, considerate and serene. The reason for his dark mood in September and October (which can now be properly appreciated thanks to the publication of his private correspondence with her) was his intense anxiety that Mrs Simpson might not succeed in obtaining her divorce decree, and that he would thus be unable to marry her; or that she would simply refuse to go ahead with proceedings which she had always regarded with a measure of reluctance and distaste – in effect, that she would leave him.

For Mrs Simpson had now woken up. Lying ill in bed at the Hotel Meurice in Paris, suddenly depressed after the excitement of her royal holiday, horrified by the American press cuttings, which had been forwarded, of the *Nahlin* cruise, she decided that the time had come to put a halt to a liaison which had got out of hand and was leading towards catastrophe. On 16 September she wrote to the King:

This is a difficult letter to write . . . I must really return to Ernest . . . I feel I am better with him than with you – and so you must understand. I am sure dear David that in a few months your life will run as it did before and without my nagging. Also you have been independent of affection all your life. We have had lovely beautiful times together and I thank God for them and know that you will go on with your job doing it better and in a more dignified manner each year . . . I am sure you and I would only create disaster together . . . I want you to be happy. I feel sure that I can't make you so and I honestly don't think you can me . . . I am sure that after this letter you will realise that no human being could assume this responsibility and it would be most unfair to make things harder for me by seeing me . . . [1]

It is hard to doubt the sincerity of this letter. Had it been written a year or even six months earlier, one might take the view that Mrs Simpson was 'playing hard to get'; but by September 1936 the King's attachment to her was the one thing she could be absolutely certain of.

The King's reply to her plea for release was a letter from the Fort beginning with the immortal line: 'Why do you say such hard things to David . . . ?' He felt 'hurt' and 'terribly unhappy' and 'bursting with love and such longing to hold you tighter than I ever have before'. Their separation – 'every moment' of it – was unendurable to him. He was dismayed by the thought of leaving for Balmoral without her – 'and not knowing when you will join me there'.[2] Faced with this letter (and incessant telephone calls to the same effect), Mrs Simpson weakened in her resolve and decided to follow the King to Scotland. He arrived on Deeside on 18 September; accompanied by her friends Herman and Katherine Rogers, she joined him there five days later.

This was to be the first of several abortive attempts which Mrs Simpson would make to escape from the King that autumn. Why did she allow herself to be deflected in her intention to terminate a relationship which, as she put it, could 'only create disaster'? In her memoirs she gave two reasons: that she was too fond of the King simply to abandon him in the face of his passionate entreaties; and that she always hoped his great popularity would ultimately protect him from the consequences of his actions.[3] At the time she gave, as we shall see, a third reason to close friends: that the King was so dependent on her that her disappearance might put him in an altogether desperate state.* 'The easy view is that she should have made him give her up', wrote Walter Monckton. 'But I never knew any man whom it would have been harder to get rid of.'[4]

Edward VIII had his faults; and he was occasionally guilty of indiscretions. But those faults and indiscretions were later magnified by commentators to the point of absurdity. The eleven days he spent in Aberdeenshire – seven of them with Mrs Simpson – are a case in point. Osbert Sitwell wrote in his poem *Rat Week* of

> That nameless, faceless, raucous gang
> Who graced Balmoral's Coburg towers . . .

The 'raucous gang' consisted (with their wives) of the King's brother Prince George and second cousin Lord Louis Mountbatten; his old shipmate Commander Colin Buist; the Dukes of Marlborough, Sutherland and Buccleuch; the Earl of Rosebery; and the Hon. Esmond Harmsworth, heir to Viscount Rothermere's press empire. They were different, no doubt, from the usual complement of ministers and bishops who had stayed in his father's time, but hardly a list which disgraced the Court Circular. They were all personal friends and contemporaries of the King from whom he had received recent hospitality.

---

* See below, pp. 86–8.

He later wrote that 'life within the castle was extremely pleasant and by present day [1951] house party standards entirely normal. My guests enjoyed themselves as much as I did.'[5] In the daytime they walked and stalked; in the evening he played the pipes after dinner, and they amused themselves with bridge and the latest motion pictures from London, the ballroom having been turned into a cinema. Balmoral under Edward VIII was a more informal place than in the late King's day: how could it have been otherwise?

Mrs Simpson – who, judging by her recent escape effort, would rather have been elsewhere – made the best of this new milestone in her now tarnished royal idyll. Gossip that she behaved as mistress of the house, that she occupied Queen Mary's bedroom, was wide of the mark. She was there as the King's friend; she already knew most of her fellow-guests personally. Her only influence on the household was in the help she gave with the menus and evening entertainments – including her introduction, as a late-night snack, of the club sandwich. 'Have you thought of changing the film as all the nuts have seen it?' she scribbled to the King. 'WE can see it in London.'[6]

But he had been unwise to bring her there, for her presence – on the eve of the divorce case – was sure to excite comment and rumour. In July Winston Churchill, consulted by Monckton, had 'deprecated strongly Mrs Simpson going to such a highly official place upon which the eyes of Scotland were concentrated and which was already sacred to the memories of Queen Victoria and John Brown'.[7] The King had ignored such advice; and, predictably, he gave instructions that her name was to be included with the other guests in the Court Circular. When she arrived, on 23 September, he compounded matters by driving personally in his motor to meet her at Aberdeen station, where he was recognized. By an unfortunate coincidence, the Duke and Duchess of York were also in Aberdeen that day, to perform the opening of a new wing of the Aberdeen Royal Infirmary; headlines about this official visit, and the King's private visit to pick up his guests, appeared side by side in the Aberdeen evening newspapers.

For this thoughtless action the King was criticized in the city and county of Aberdeen. Two stories earned him further criticism. It was said that, when the Duke and Duchess of York came from nearby Birkhall to dine at Balmoral on 26 September, Mrs Simpson tried to 'receive' the Duchess and was snubbed: as to whether anything of the sort actually occurred, there is conflicting evidence from those present.[8] And it was said that the King had been heavy-handed in his attempts, during his brief stay in Scotland, to introduce reforms and economies into the administration of his estates. After decades in which nothing had altered, any changes were bound to arouse some resentment; but changes were absolutely necessary, for by 1936 the Scottish estates were losing the large sum of £19,800 annually (£600,000 in the values of fifty years later). In carrying out the reforms he considered overdue, the King did not consult the Duke of York – 'which I might say made me rather sad', as the Duke wrote afterwards to Lord Wigram.[9]

The heir presumptive, the Aberdeen Corporation, and some old retainers may have had their feathers ruffled; but the effect on Scottish opinion as a whole was not great. Two months later, at the Scottish Conservative Conference in Glasgow, Katherine Elliot, wife of the newly appointed Secretary of State for Scotland, was surprised that almost no-one there appeared to have heard of Mrs Simpson. But the gossip which filtered through to London society was terrific. Marie Belloc Lowndes wrote in her diary that the King and Mrs Simpson had wandered around the moors in shorts, that outraged Scottish peers planned to boycott the Coronation, and other absurdities.[10] Chips Channon bemoaned that the King had 'chucked' the infirmary visit at Aberdeen to meet his friends – whereas he had never in fact undertaken the engagement at all.[11] Two eminent Scotsmen living in London

– Sir John Reith and Sir James Barrie – independently remarked that some Scottish minister might attack the King from the pulpit, as John Knox had thundered against the vices of Mary Queen of Scots.[12]

Perhaps such wild talk was inevitable after Mrs Simpson's sojourn at Balmoral. The King's mistake had been to ask her in the first place, at a time when he was anxious to spare her hurtful rumour and publicity: it was ironic that he also invited Esmond Harmsworth, probably with a view to his helping restrain the press comment on the forthcoming divorce. But in his state of mind the King was apt to make mistakes.

Accompanied by Mrs Simpson, the King returned to London in the Royal Train, arriving on the morning of Thursday 1 October. It was the day Queen Mary was due to complete her move from Buckingham Palace to Marlborough House; and the King, with his usual punctilious attentiveness towards his mother, gave her lunch at the Palace and then spent the afternoon with her, inspecting her new residence.

The Queen, with her huge collection of *objets d'art* and her passion for making inventories, had taken longer than anticipated making her move – and the King probably wished she had taken even longer. For now she was gone, he had to move into the Palace himself. This he did not relish. As he wrote in his memoirs:

I took up residence in that vast building without pleasure; the dank, musty smell I had always associated with the building assailed me afresh the instant I set foot inside the King's Door. Out of respect for my father's memory, I was reluctant to occupy his rooms on the second floor. At my mother's suggestion, I moved into the 'Belgian suite' on the first floor . . . kept for visiting foreign monarchs. This five-room suite had tall french windows opening on the gardens . . . A curious presentiment induced me to leave the rooms as they were. Somehow I had the feeling that I would not be there very long. About the only changes I made were to add a shower to the bath-tub and to replace the ornate four-poster bed with a single one of my own. I installed a small extra switchboard to handle my personal calls, and added a private line to the Fort. During the two months that I lived in Buckingham Palace, I never got over the feeling of not quite belonging there.[13]

To the King, the Palace was a symbolic royal prison. Earlier in the year he had confided to Walter Monckton:

He could not bear to feel that he would be cooped up in Buckingham Palace all the time within the iron bars. They must take him as he was — a man different from his father and determined to be himself. He would be available for public business when he was wanted, but his private life was to be his own and was, as far as possible, to be lived in the same way as when he was Prince of Wales.[14]

At the outset of his reign he had hoped not to have to live there at all; but Wigram had warned him that 'that would be the beginning of the end of the British Empire, as Buckingham Palace was the centre of it'.[15]

Mrs Simpson was staying at Claridge's while a furnished house in Regent's Park was being prepared for her. On Friday 9 October she went with the King to the Fort for the week-end; she did not return to London from there but moved to a rented house on the seafront at Felixstowe. For her divorce case had been set down for trial at Ipswich Assizes on 27 October; and for this she needed a Suffolk residence.

Why had Ipswich been chosen? Once again, it was a result of the King's manoeuvres. When Mrs Simpson received her decree *nisi*, it would be at least six months before she could apply to have her divorce made absolute; and the King was determined that she should be free to marry him before his Coronation, due to take place on 12 May 1937. The London lists were full for October and November: the only prospect of an early hearing was on one of the provincial circuits. It was the King who arranged it all: throughout October he consulted Mrs Simpson's divorce solicitor, Theodore Goddard, and her senior counsel, the celebrated advocate Norman Birkett KC.

At this time, therefore, the King still believed that Mrs Simpson might be crowned as his wife by his side. He was not yet thinking of abdication. One other significant fact supports this view: he devoted his spare time at the Fort, that early autumn, to planting his garden for the following spring.

Installed at the hated Palace, deprived for the time being of Mrs Simpson's company, the King was wretched. That October he fulfilled no public duties, apart from routine audiences at the Palace; and he broke several appointments. 'One hears these stories of engagements being chucked, or of outrageous examples of tardiness', wrote Lord Crawford. 'He doesn't yet realise how much trouble is taken on his behalf nor what inconvenience is caused by his forgetfulness and vacillation. Somebody . . . said that the King would be blackballed from any respectable London club and I see what the man meant – the all-absorbing egocentricity.'[16]

At Court – the new Court set up by the King before his summer holiday – chaos and suspicion reigned. Absorbed in his problem, he had not bothered to define the duties of his new courtiers, none of whom appeared to trust each other or command the attention of their now elusive and unpredictable master. All thought about one subject; none dared mention it. Fear was in the air.

A chilling account of the Palace régime that October is that of Charles Lambe, a gifted naval officer, then thirty-five, who arrived at the beginning of the month to take up his duties as one of the King's equerries. Lambe was a friend of Lord Louis Mountbatten, to whom he owed his new post; he venerated the King, and had met and liked Mrs Simpson. What he found was not, however, what he had expected.

Atmosphere very 'unhappy' in naval sense. A great deal of whispering and secrecy. One courtier was always bleating, a centre of discontent. Everything an effort and done with a shrug of the shoulders. Another ancien régime — outraged, pompous and ineffectual. Godfrey Thomas — forbearing, overworked and tired but always loyal and patient . . .

There was no welcome. I was an outsider like a guest in a Guards Mess. Tolerated but suspect. This suspicion was not confined to me. Everyone whispered . . .

From the first the organisation seemed wrong. The nominal Executive Head was the Lord Chamberlain [Cromer] but inside the Palace there was no Chief of Staff. Consequently the good old atmosphere of competition for the King's ear prevailed . . .

Lambe was nervous of his first official encounter with his royal master; and the King seemed nervous too. Emerging hastily from his car at the King's door, dressed in a tight overcoat, followed by a torrent of despatch boxes, he noticed the new arrival with the exclamation: 'Hello, you've taken over, have you?', shook hands with a forced smile, and disappeared into his private apartments. Of his first spell of duty, Lambe wrote:

I went out to dinner every evening, but not until the King had gone. It was almost impossible to find out what his movements were even inside the Palace. This . . . meant no peace for anyone. For as much as an hour sometimes, the car would wait outside the Garden Entrance while a porter, & two footmen and I waited inside, sometimes talking feebly to relieve the monotony and gloom . . . It never seemed to occur to him that his lack of routine and impulsiveness entailed all this hanging about.

One of the many problems was that the King forbade his staff from giving any directions to the police about his movements. On one occasion the Duke of York, who had called to take his brother to the station, was furious to discover that his instructions to have a way cleared through the traffic had been countermanded on the King's orders. 'Why *does* he do that? It's so stupid and makes things more difficult for everyone concerned.'

Lambe found his first week 'very wearing' and 'full of doubting moments'. It was difficult to know how or when to approach the King when he was needed. But men such as Lambe – and indeed most of his superiors – still knew nothing about the Ipswich divorce.[17]

The divorce and the state of mind of the petitioner were now the total preoccupation of the King. From Felixstowe, Mrs Simpson was sending him further doubting letters, indicating that she was thinking of dropping the proceedings. 'Do you feel you still want me to go ahead', she wrote on 14 October, 'as I feel it will hurt your popularity in the country.' She wondered whether it was not best for her to 'steal quietly away'. She predicted 'that you will have trouble in the House of Commons etc and may be forced to go. I can't put you in that position.' She was far from sure that the judge would grant her decree *nisi*; and she feared that a physical assault might be made on her as she drove to the courthouse.[18]

To these sensible pleas and warnings the King's reply was typical:

These three gardenias are eanum [little] but they say enormous ooh and that a boy loves a girl more and more and is holding her so tight these trying days of

65

waiting. Far the hardest is not being able to be together and one is so lonely and cut off. But it will all be over soon now my sweetheart and it will be so lovely and exciting when it is.

I know it sounds easy to say don't worry but please don't too much Wallis. I'm doing half the worrying and looking after things this end . . . [19]

The King was indeed doing his best at his end. He was in almost permanent communication with her lawyers; and he had summoned Walter Monckton, the lawyer in whom he had the greatest trust, to return from India by air to advise on the progress of the divorce. Meanwhile, in the course of Monday 12 October, the day Mrs Simpson had installed herself at Felixstowe, the press had started to become aware of the Ipswich proceedings. The *Evening Standard* was the first to get the news; its editor, Percy Cudlipp, consulted his proprietor, Lord Beaverbrook, who in turn consulted Theodore Goddard with whom he was on friendly terms. Goddard reported to the King, who called Beaverbrook to the Palace. Beaverbrook later recalled the interview, which took place on the 16th.

The King asked me to help in suppressing all advance news of the Simpson divorce, and in limiting the publicity after the event. He stated his case calmly and with great cogency and force.

The reasons he gave for his wish were that Mrs Simpson was ill, unhappy, and distressed by the thought of notoriety. Notoriety would attach to her only because she had been his guest on the *Nahlin* and at Balmoral. As the publicity would be due to her association with himself, he felt it his duty to protect her.[20]

These arguments satisfied Beaverbrook, who, together with Esmond Harmsworth and Monckton, engaged in complicated but successful negotiations with other newspaper owners (not only in the United Kingdom but also in France and Eire) to confine the publication of the news to a formal report of the divorce hearing, no mention being made of Mrs Simpson's friendship with the King. This was a considerable achievement, and from this moment the King treated Beaverbrook, whom he had known very little, as a friend and ally. But as yet he had taken no-one into his confidence about his plan to marry Mrs Simpson – though it was a plan which many now suspected.

Even before news of the impending divorce came through, the mood in the circles of power was one of intense nervousness. The British press might maintain its reserve; but the American press (which had startled Mrs Simpson into appreciating the reality of her position) had run wild. Cuttings of sensational American articles dealing with the *Nahlin* cruise and the Balmoral gossip, speculating on the King's marriage plans, spreading every sort of rumour, had reached the desks of influential people, often accompanying outraged letters from British citizens resident in North America who demanded that some action be taken either to prove the untruth of the stories or restrain the King. Among the recipients of such mail were Queen Mary; the Archbishop of Canterbury, Dr C. G. Lang; the editor of *The Times*, Geoffrey Dawson; and the Prime Minister, Stanley Baldwin.

Having been ordered to eschew all work for three months to avert a nervous breakdown, Baldwin had returned to London on 12 October – the day Mrs Simpson arrived in Felixstowe. Before his rest cure, his staff had kept the American letters and cuttings from his gaze; but now he saw them all, and was gravely alarmed – though he instinctively shrank from having to confront the King about the matter. When Eden called to discuss the situation in Spain, Baldwin cut him short with the words: 'Have you had any letters about the King? . . . I fear we may have difficulties there. I hope that you will try not to trouble me too much with foreign affairs just now.' Eden was astonished by these remarks; but, upon examining his own mail, he began to appreciate the Prime Minister's anxieties.[21]

On 14 October Baldwin had an audience with the King. This was to discuss the forthcoming royal visit to the Fleet, and the problem of Mrs Simpson was not mentioned; but before leaving the Palace, Baldwin had a conversation with Hardinge, who warned that 'a day would come when the Prime Minister would have to intervene'.[22] Baldwin agreed, but hoped that the confrontation could be avoided until after the Coronation. Surprisingly, neither the Prime Minister nor the King's Private Secretary knew of Ipswich at this time, though the news had been in the hands of newspaper editors for two days. It was only the following day that Hardinge heard of it – and then only through the medium of a press agency. He lost no time in informing Baldwin, whom he urged 'to see the King and ask if these proceedings could not be stopped', since the danger in which they placed the King was 'becoming every day greater'.[23] Baldwin meanwhile saw Sir Samuel Hoare, First Lord of the Admiralty, who called to ask if he might miss the following week's cabinet meeting in order to accept the King's invitation to shoot at Sandringham. The premier told the alarmed minister (who as yet knew nothing) to accept the royal invitation, so that he might try to persuade his host 'that the divorce proceedings which are due at Ipswich at the end of the month must be dropped' and 'to give up the idea of marriage altogether'.[24]

But Baldwin was not to be allowed the luxury of deputing this task to another. On Friday 16 October – the day the King saw Beaverbrook – he went to spend the week-end with Lord Fitzalan, a former viceroy of Ireland and leading Roman Catholic layman who lived at Cumberland Lodge, a grace-and-favour residence in Windsor Great Park. The other guests were Fitzalan's nephew the Duke of Norfolk (who as hereditary Earl Marshal was responsible for the Coronation), the Conservative elder statesman Lord Salisbury and the press magnate Lord Kemsley.* All four men expressed alarm at the divorce; Kemsley warned the Prime Minister that 'the non-conformist conscience is not dead'.[25] On Saturday Hardinge joined them for lunch, and insisted, with the support of the others, that the Prime Minister seek an immediate audience with the King to warn him of the consequences if he failed to put a stop to the divorce and continued to flaunt his association with Mrs Simpson.

This was no mere personal intervention on Hardinge's part. That a plot was afoot among not only senior courtiers but also senior civil servants is clear from a letter written by Neville Chamberlain to his wife Annie on Sunday the 18th.

> Warren [Sir Warren Fisher, Permanent Secretary to the Treasury] tells me that this morning S.B. instead of having a peaceful laze in an armchair was to have imparted to him a piece of news which will completely upset him because he will be told that he must take action. It is in fact of a very alarming kind, viz that a certain lady, egged on by a particular friend of hers, is going no later than Friday next to institute proceedings against her husband for divorce!!! Here's a how-de-do. If this doesn't upset S.B.'s sleep I'm a Dutchman. Warren is in a very grim state of mind – talks of writing himself to the lady – which I doubt the wisdom of. But though there are features about the situation which are amusing, au fond it is pretty serious. I can't believe that S.B. will do anything. But perhaps it is better that things should come to a head now than later when the month of May gets nearer.[26]

Reluctantly, Baldwin agreed to broach the subject of the divorce with the sovereign and asked Hardinge

---

* Owner of the *Sunday Times* and – in partnership with his brother Lord Camrose – of the *Daily Telegraph*.

to arrange an immediate audience. This was easier said than done, for on Sunday 18 October the King vanished. Due at Sandringham, where the first and last shooting party of the reign was about to assemble, he left the Fort in the morning after leaving word that he was not to be expected in Norfolk until late at night. Undoubtedly he spent the day with Mrs Simpson – possibly at Felixstowe, more probably in London, not getting to Sandringham until 4 a.m. the following morning, where Hardinge's message awaited him. The King rang Hardinge at breakfast time; he agreed to receive the Prime Minister at ten o'clock the following morning, Tuesday 20 October; and he accepted Hardinge's suggestion that, so as not to excite speculation, the meeting take place at the Fort.[27]

The King spent the morning going round the park at Sandringham, ordering many changes; in the afternoon he visited the Estate flax factory. His first guests arrived, including Lord Harewood and Sir Samuel Hoare. After dinner he excused himself in order to drive to the Fort, where he hoped to have a good night's rest before the Prime Minister's call.[28]

Baldwin's meeting with the King on 20 October 1936 – the first of eight historic interviews between them that autumn on the subject of the sovereign's intentions towards Mrs Simpson – is unusually well documented. The Prime Minister gave circumstantial accounts of it to the House of Commons, to his wife and son, to Tom Jones, to the trade-union leader Walter Citrine and to various political colleagues.[29] The Duke of Windsor's account in his memoirs is less detailed as regards the talk, but tallies in all material respects.[30] At this first meeting, Baldwin set out, without much enthusiasm, to get the King to put an end to the divorce and discover his intentions with regard to Mrs Simpson; and to warn him that criticism was mounting, that the press could not be held for much longer, that a scandal threatened.

The King for his part was determined that Mrs Simpson should receive her decree *nisi* – at this moment, almost nothing else mattered to him – and was not prepared to come clean about his plans, or address himself to criticism, until she had safely obtained it. He therefore received the Prime Minister warily, playing the part of an innocent; but though it was far from obvious to Baldwin, the King in fact heard all that was said.

Baldwin motored over from Chequers, feeling 'like a physician'. The King was talking to one of his gardeners, which gave Baldwin the opportunity to remark on the loveliness of the grounds, a subject on which he dwelt for some minutes. 'Friendly, casual, discursive, he might have been a neighbour who had called to discuss a dispute over a boundary fence.' But once in the King's octagonal drawing room, the Prime Minister's affability gave way to an attack of nerves; he helped himself to whisky and began to smoke his pipe.

He opened by reminding the King of an old promise made as Prince of Wales that Baldwin could always approach him on any subject. Did that still hold good? The King nodded. Baldwin assured the King that he liked him as a man, as well as regarding him as an admirable monarch for an age of change. 'You have all the advantages that a man can have. You are young . . . You are fond of your house and you like children. You have only one disadvantage. You are not married and you should be.' The Prime Minister paused; but the King did not rise to the bait, and so Baldwin continued: 'You may think my views out of date, but I believe I know how to interpret the minds of my own people; and I say, although it is true that standards are lower since the war, it only leads the people to expect a higher standard from their King.' When the King still said nothing, he carried on: 'People are talking about you and this American woman Mrs Simpson.'

Still the King made no comment, so Baldwin produced a file of letters and cuttings he had been receiving. He had been inundated with correspondence from people 'who don't like the way you are going on'. The

American press was full of 'stories about your behaviour', as were even the Chinese vernacular papers. Such comment would 'sap the position of the throne in the world' unless stopped. The King not yet having uttered, the Prime Minister said bluntly: 'I don't believe you can go on like this and get away with it.'

'What do you mean, not get away with it?' said the King, suddenly stung to speech. Baldwin had used the phrase intentionally, knowing it to be one of the King's favourites. 'I think you know our people', continued the Prime Minister. The nation would tolerate much in private life which they would not accept in a public figure, and when they saw Mrs Simpson's name in the Court Circular they resented it. The King seemed displeased at this remark. 'The lady is my friend and I do not wish to let her in by the back door but openly.' After a pause, he continued: 'I hope you will agree that I have carried out my kingly duties with dignity.' Baldwin said that he did agree, all the more since he knew that royal duties were not much to his liking. 'I know there is nothing kingly about me,' the King said pathetically, 'but I have tried to mix with the people and make them think I was one of them.'

Baldwin was touched by this, but came to the point of his visit. He spoke of the divorce: 'Must this case really go on?'

As to the King's reply, his own account and all accounts derived from Baldwin agree. 'I have no right to interfere with the affairs of an individual', he said. 'It would be wrong were I to attempt to influence Mrs Simpson just because she happens to be a friend of the King.' Since the King meant to marry her, and had been influencing her in the matter of the divorce from the beginning, this reply was disingenuous to say the least; as Baldwin later remarked, it was the one lie the King ever told him.

Baldwin persisted that the divorce was dangerous for the King. If Mrs Simpson were granted her decree, 'everyone would be talking . . . and there might be sides taken and factions grow up in a matter where no faction ought ever to exist'. The King replied that he had received assurances from the press. 'But you cannot keep them quiet for long,' added Baldwin, 'and when they do start to give tongue it will be a grave situation for the country. It will be an even graver situation for you, Sir.' Could not Mrs Simpson leave him and go away for at least six months?

In his account, the Duke of Windsor says that the Prime Minister 'seemed to be sounding the depths of my feelings, trying to decide whether this was just a fleeting attachment or the real thing'. If so, Baldwin was left under no misapprehension, for (as he told his younger son) whenever the King spoke of Mrs Simpson his face wore 'such a look of beauty as . . . might have lighted the face of a young knight who had caught a glimpse of the holy grail'.* But the subject of marriage was not mentioned on either side. The King was clearly determined to evade the issue; and Baldwin 'pressed him for no kind of answer', merely asking him to reflect on all that had been said.

The audience had lasted an hour. Leaving his file of letters behind for the King to look through, Baldwin rose to leave, glad the 'the ice had been broken'. In his memoirs, the King commented sarcastically that the only ice that had been broken was that which had melted in the Prime Minister's drink. But though the circumstances of the moment caused him to assume an attitude of unconcern, one cannot avoid the conclusion – observing the events of the next four weeks – that the King had profoundly comprehended and been affected by all that the Prime Minister had said. 'You and I must settle this matter together', were the King's parting words, as if he already saw clearly what was to come. 'I will not have anyone interfering.'

---

* According to the son, the King declared that he could not live without Mrs Simpson; but this statement clearly belongs to their next meeting on 16 November (A. W. Baldwin, *My Father* (1955), pp. 299–300).

*

The interview of 20 October had impressed on the King that his affair with Mrs Simpson was now a matter of acute political moment; it had impressed upon Baldwin the King's depth of feeling and immovability on the subject. Meanwhile the date of the divorce hearing at Ipswich drew closer.

The King returned to Sandringham for dinner in good spirits. (Where had he spent the hours between?) That evening, and during the two days of shooting that followed, he was an excellent host: Charles Lambe, who had been given such a hard time as equerry, felt a surge of devotion for him.[31] On the 23rd he returned to London to meet the visiting Crown Prince of Denmark. He would never see Sandringham again.

On Friday the 24th, the King was at the Fort, where Norman Birkett and Walter Monckton lunched with him to discuss the conduct of the case. Monckton noted that Birkett 'was deeply impressed by the King's straightness and kindness and devotion to Mrs Simpson, and was captivated by his charm'.[32] Walking in the grounds of the Fort alone with Monckton, the King suddenly exclaimed, as he later recalled:

Listen, Walter, one doesn't know how things are going to turn out. I am beginning to wonder whether I really am the kind of king they want. Am I not a bit too independent? As you know, my make-up is very different from that of my father. I believe they would prefer someone more like him. Well, there is my brother Bertie.

It was the first time Monckton had heard such remarks from the King, who — four days after his talk with Baldwin — had evidently started to visualize abdication.[33]

Right up to the last, efforts were made in official circles to stop the divorce, efforts in which Hardinge continued to be involved. As Neville Chamberlain

74

anticipated in the letter which has been quoted, Sir Warren Fisher, the chief civil servant, tried to get in touch with Mrs Simpson to persuade her to drop the proceedings. The King heard of this initiative and angrily put a stop to it; and Fisher had to be content with an assurance from Theodore Goddard that she did not appear to be contemplating marriage to the King.[34]

The last days before Ipswich must have been supremely uncomfortable ones for both Mrs Simpson and the King. He desperately tried to reassure her. He told her nothing of Baldwin's audience. He wanted to visit her on the eve of the hearing – but Goddard warned him urgently of the disastrous consequences of such an action, with the house at Felixstowe besieged by reporters and photographers.[35] Mrs Simpson passed a sleepless night, 'wondering whether I was doing the right thing, whether my recklessness of consequences would not betray me, whether I was right in my confidence that what I would do would bring no harm to the King'. But 'it was too late for me to turn back'.[36]

Tuesday 27 October was the day of the hearing. The courthouse at Ipswich was surrounded by a mob of journalists; but special police measures were in force and the courtroom was virtually empty, entry having been forbidden not only to the public but to solicitors and clients involved in other cases. This was the result of secret consultation between the King and the Chief Constable of Suffolk.[37] The judge, Mr Justice Hawke, who had not been forewarned, was taken aback by these circumstances and barely troubled to conceal his hostility: by a coincidence, he was Monckton's predecessor as Attorney-General to the Duchy of Cornwall. The proceedings lasted nineteen minutes. The evidence was presented in the usual form of fabricated letters and the testimony of hotel servants – the servants who had so nearly disappeared the previous July. Mrs Simpson, exhausted by lack of sleep and intimidated by the judge, answered the few questions which were put to her with an understandable nervousness. Norman

Birkett asked for a decree *nisi* with costs.* The judge, after an outburst of irritation, granted it with obvious reluctance. 'I suppose I must', he concluded, his begrudging words to be reported in every American newspaper, 'in these unusual circumstances. So you may have it, with costs.'

---

* The costs were later reimbursed to Ernest Simpson.

Chapter Four

The King at his Best

27 October–13 November

On the morning of Tuesday 27 October – the morning of the hearing at Ipswich – Edward VIII held a Privy Council at Buckingham Palace to swear in some of his new courtiers as Councillors and prorogue Parliament, the new session of which he would be opening the following week. Ramsay MacDonald, the Lord President, found the King more than usually abstracted. He hardly seemed to be aware of the proceedings; his mind was obviously elsewhere. (Always behind with his news, MacDonald only discovered two days later where it had in fact been.[1]) After the Council, the King gave an audience to the visiting Prime Minister of Canada, W. L. Mackenzie King. The latter had spent a night at Chequers on 23 October; and both Hardinge and Dawson, the editor of The Times, had tried to put pressure on Baldwin to get the Canadian to deliver an oblique warning to the King on the effect his friendship with Mrs Simpson was having in the dominions. In the event, he merely spoke of the great respect with which the Crown was held in Canada and the King's personal popularity there.[2]

It was after lunch that the message arrived for which the King had been anxiously waiting – a telephone call from the office of Theodore Goddard to say Mrs Simpson had received her decree. That evening, the King dined with her at the furnished house in Cumberland Terrace, Regent's Park, into which she had finally moved on her return from Suffolk. He presented her with a magnificent emerald ring, inscribed with the words *WE are ours now, 27.X.36*: this was intended as her engagement ring.[3]* He also told her of Baldwin's audience at the Fort a week earlier. This gravely alarmed her; but he assured her (as she recalled in her memoirs) that he would be able to 'fix' things.[4]

The King greeted the divorce (provisional as it still was) with joy and relief. One cannot understand the extent of his relief unless one bears in mind the terrors which had been obsessing him over the preceding weeks – of a press scandal, of a hitch in the proceedings, above all that Mrs Simpson might back out of those proceedings, as she had been threatening to do. Only if one realizes this can one appreciate that 27 October 1936 was perhaps the greatest day of the King's life – more of a turning point for him than his accession or abdication or even the day of his marriage the following June. It represented the triumphant conclusion of his efforts to ensure that Mrs Simpson would be his for life and would marry him; for she had now burnt her boats, and there was no going back to the old life with Simpson which she had with such reluctance put behind her. The nervous state which had engulfed him in the early autumn now left him and gave way to a state of euphoria – a euphoria which not even the political crisis of November and December, nor his renunciation of the throne, nor his long separation from Mrs Simpson was able wholly to dispel. Henceforth his mind was fixed on a future of nuptial bliss.

---

* This magnificent stone did not derive, as people imagined, from the jewels of Queen Alexandra, but had been obtained for the King by Cartier, who had made the ring. It was reputed to be part of the largest emerald in the world, formerly in the possession of the Mogul Emperors, which had been purchased by Cartier from a seller in Baghdad but broken up by them on the grounds that there was no-one in the world rich enough to buy the complete stone.

If the King was relieved by Ipswich, however, there was nobody (with the possible exceptions of Theodore Goddard and the Suffolk police) who shared his relief – certainly not Mrs Simpson, who henceforth lived in a state of permanent fear as to what was going to happen. For the divorce raised to fever-pitch the speculation as to whether he intended to marry her. Such speculation was still more or less confined to London society and high official and professional circles; but diaries of the moment show that the concern among such people was now obsessive. They also show that even in the last days of October – some three weeks before the King raised the marriage question with Baldwin – people were already talking both of abdication and a possible morganatic solution.

Harold Nicolson, 28 October: Mrs Simpson has now obtained her divorce, and there are very serious rumours that the King will make her Duchess of Edinburgh and marry. The point is whether he is so infatuated as to insist on her becoming Queen or whether the marriage will be purely morganatic . . . I gather . . . there is considerable danger . . . [5]

Ramsay MacDonald, 29 October: Waiting for the Coronation is to be destruction to my reputation. Mrs S divorced her husband on Tuesday by a stretch of law and justice . . . Privy Council concerned with next move . . . I hope someone can be found who would move him to see what he is doing to the country . . . [6]

Sir John Reith, 29 October: Lunched with Harley [a film tycoon] . . . He told me that Coronation insurance risks had risen from four to twenty-one per cent in two-and-a-half months. This is all due to the wretched Simpson affair and it is most significant . . . [7]

Robert Bruce-Lockhart, 29 October: Talk, as usual, mostly about the King and Mrs Simpson . . . Everyone . . . is convinced that the King will marry her. Only doubt is whether he will do so before the Coronation or wait until afterwards.[8]

Lord Ponsonby, * *29 October*: It is certainly extraordinary that the King with his undoubted intelligence, character and charm should flaunt [sic] public opinion with this second rate American woman who has now divorced her husband.[9]

Victor Cazalet, early November: King and Mrs Simpson only source of conversation. Everyone has ideas, nearly everyone is miserable about it . . . Some think he will have to abdicate, others think he will marry her, still again some think he may do it morganatically . . . The divorce business was v. unfortunate and quite unnecessary.[10]

Chips Channon, 2 November: Of course all the world is saying that the King intends to marry Wallis, now that her divorce is over. Personally I suspect that this is true, and that we shall live to see a great dénouement . . . [11]

Tom Jones, 3 November: [The divorce] is the news . . . the scandal doing no end of harm to this country's prestige . . . He may insist on marrying the lady, but he can't insist on having her crowned Queen of England . . . [12]

Lord Crawford, 3 November: The King and the Lady – the source of endless talk and speculation. It seems to be the only thing that counts and we are paying small heed to matters of terrible moment abroad. At the same time the papers never breathe a word about the subject . . . [13]

The British press remained silent for the time being; but (as Baldwin had warned at the Fort) they could hardly do so indefinitely. The American papers had now

---

* Arthur Ponsonby, 1st Baron Ponsonby (1871–1946), son of Queen Victoria's Private Secretary Sir Henry Ponsonby and leader of the Labour Party in the House of Lords, 1931–5.

become hysterical. 'King's Moll Renoed in Wolsey's Home Town', ran one celebrated headline; and the Hearst press, prompted by its chief who followed events from his castle in Wales, declared everywhere that the King would 'Wed Wally'. The pressure on the Government to act was becoming intense; it was a time of hectic consultations.

How far was the King aware of the endless talk, the growing pressure? He may not have been aware of its full extent. The press continued to say nothing. His position shielded him from gossip. No-one yet dared confront him and warn him (for he himself had indicated that he was unapproachable on the subject). 'I cannot believe that H.M. has any notion of this universal tongue-wagging', wrote Tom Jones.[14] And yet, in general terms, the King cannot have failed to sense what was happening. The significance of Baldwin's visit to the Fort had not been lost on him. Concerning that event, he wrote in his memoirs: 'A friendship which had so far remained within the sheltered realm of my private solicitude was manifestly about to become an affair of state.' Already, before the divorce, he had mentioned the possibility of abdication to Walter Monckton; and this possibility (as he later admitted) had been in his mind ever since, before becoming King, he had made up his mind to marry Mrs Simpson. As for the talk, he may not have been directly exposed to it; but Mrs Simpson, who moved among the social parliamentary set, caught the full force of it, and the time would soon come when she would urgently warn him of it.

One must conclude that the King in his heart knew what was coming – but that he did not wish to know. The file of letters which Baldwin left with him on 20 October, the articles from the American press, the pleas of Mrs Simpson – these for the moment he ignored. His attitude was not so much that of a weak and foolish man as of an extraordinarily fatalistic man, and a man so deeply obsessed with a particular plan that, until forced to do so, he did not wish to think

81

about anything which might interfere with that plan. He would just drift along, as it were, until the inevitable crisis came.

A key to understanding the King's state of mind lies in the fact that, between the divorce hearing on 27 October and the arrival of what amounted to an ultimatum on 13 November, he carried out his duties superbly well. Previously depressed, he was now in high spirits, unusually charming in private as well as public life. Previously neglectful of his obligations, he now fulfilled them with flair. Perhaps a realization that there might be little time left to him filled him with an unusual determination to do his best. Or perhaps (as he wrote of his mood while opening Parliament) a consciousness of the growing disapproval filled him with a spirit of defiance. During these three weeks, we see him at his best as King.

On the evening of 30 October, the King gave his first diplomatic reception at Buckingham Palace – a dinner in honour of the Argentine Foreign Minister, Dr Carlos Savedra Lammas, who was in the process of concluding a trade agreement in London. Anglo-Argentine relations were a special interest of Edward VIII; according to Philip Guedalla, present as head of the Ibero-American Institute, the sovereign carried off the evening 'effortlessly and with admirable effect', putting his guests at their ease, getting the conversation going and charming Dr Lammas, to whom he spoke in Spanish.

The evening had opened as a rather nervous ceremonial. By end of dinner it turned into an enjoyable men's party . . . They stood about in the next room and argued about the news from Spain . . . The King was sitting with his guest from Argentina and signalled one or two of them in turn to join the little group. There was a long session with the Governor of the Bank of England . . . In the big drawing room their host marshalled his little party and brought each of them to bear upon the chief guest . . .

Guedalla saw the King as a brilliant stage-manager at an event like this; he gave no sign of strain and never let his attention wander.[15]

Four days later, on Tuesday 3 November, the King opened Parliament. As it was raining, he decided to cancel the traditional carriage procession and drive to Westminster in a Daimler – which disappointed the spectators, as well as Charles Lambe who had been due to ride in the cortège. As he entered the House of Lords, dressed in the uniform of an Admiral of the Fleet and carrying a cocked hat,* the assembled parliamentarians and dignitaries were struck by the dramatic atmosphere engendered by the King and his extraordinary serenity and youthfulness. He 'looked like a boy of eighteen', wrote Harold Nicolson to his wife[16]; while Channon found him 'looking exactly as he did in 1911, at the investiture at Caernarvon. Not a day older, a young, happy Prince Charming, or so he seemed. He walked with dignity and calm and took his place on the throne.'[17]

Conscious of an overpowering smell of mothballs, the King asked the peers to be seated and then read aloud the Loyal Declaration, whereby he promised to uphold the Protestant faith and succession. This act was deeply repugnant to him as 'wholly inappropriate to an institution supposed to shelter all creeds': but he had been informed that it was constitutionally obligatory for a new monarch under the Bill of Rights of 1689. The Lord Chancellor then handed him the Gracious Speech, the annual declaration of the Government's programme; he took it, placed the cocked hat on his head, and began to read. ('It was all very solemn and

---

* The uniform was the King's own idea. Normally the sovereign wears a crown at this ceremony: but Edward VIII had not been crowned.

not a word was mine.') For an instant he was seized by nerves; but he quickly reasserted himself, and read in a strong, confident voice. He was all the more determined to do well, knowing that those present would be comparing him to his father, and some of them 'measuring me with more curiosity than the occasion normally warranted'.[18]

The verdict on his performance was unanimous. 'He . . . did it well', wrote Harold Nicolson, delighting in the King's idiosyncratic pronunciations of 'Almoighty God' and 'the Amurrican Government'.[19] 'He was not nervous, not fidgety,' wrote Channon, 'but supremely dignified . . . The whole scene was like a six-no-trumper at bridge.'[20] Even Ramsay MacDonald, worried to a state of deep bewilderment by the King's conduct, thought that he 'looked graceful, slender and handsome . . . & went through the ceremony perfectly'.[21] The Times commented that 'his whole Royal demeanour made one feel that "in himself was all his state"'. Charles Lambe found it all 'such good theatre . . . He took ample time and did it with great dignity and authority. My only regret is that more people could not have been there to be as impressed as I was.'[22]

There was much gossip about Mrs Simpson having been present in the diplomatic gallery during the ceremony. This was invention: she had in fact been shopping in Harrods at the time.[23] She did, however, accompany the King to a reception at Londonderry House that afternoon.

We have a picture of the King in more intimate and relaxed surroundings two nights later, 5 November, when he and Mrs Simpson dined at the London house of his Lord-in-Waiting, Perry Brownlow. Among the guests was Beaverbrook, who had never before met Mrs Simpson.

> She appeared to me to be a simple woman . . . Her smile was kindly and pleasing, and her conversation interspersed with protestations of ignorance of politics

and with declarations of simplicity of character and outlook . . . I was greatly impressed by the way the other women greeted her . . . All but one of them greeted Mrs Simpson with a kiss. She received it with appropriate dignity, but in no case did she return it . . .

The King 'spoke very plainly about some of his Ministers, making blunt criticisms of this man or that', talk which Beaverbrook enjoyed; no mention was made of the divorce, although the King did remark that he would like to consult Beaverbrook soon about a certain matter.[24] After dinner Chips Channon joined the party, and found the King looking 'well, bronzed, flecked, fair, and in a very good temper'. The King made them all play an 'innocent and enjoyable' game with an empty bottle and matchsticks. His attention to Mrs Simpson was 'very touching. He worships her, and she seems tactful and just right with him . . . ' They discussed Anthony Eden, whom Channon described as an idealist. 'Heaven spare us from idealists, they cause all the trouble', said the King with a laugh. Beaverbrook agreed.

'I like the King very much', Channon concluded his account of the evening. 'He is so manly, so honest and far shrewder than people pretend.'[25]

With the beginning of the parliamentary year, the political hostesses resumed their salons in London; and they were quick to seek out Mrs Simpson. Some of them, such as the kindly Sibyl Colefax, had become her personal friends; others she regarded as remote and formidable figures. They begged her to warn the King of the dangerous gossip that was building up and threatened to do such damage to him; and they asked her two questions. Had the King proposed marriage to her? And why did she not leave England and so put an end to the scandal which surrounded the throne?

To the first of these questions, she could not answer

the truth. The King's marriage plan, suspected though it so widely was, remained a secret which he had revealed to no-one: she could not talk of it without both betraying him and intensifying gossip and rumour. Besides, she herself did not yet believe in the marriage: if it was going to harm him, it was something she desperately wished to avoid. She therefore felt she had to deny that he had proposed to her; and the need to dissimulate in this way made her miserable. 'I long to be gay and open with everybody', she wrote in a depressed note to the King early that November. 'Hiding is an awful life.'[26] To the second question, she replied what was undoubtedly the truth: that she longed to go away, but that the King would not hear of it, and there was no telling what might happen if she simply abandoned him.

In this respect, Friday 6 November, the day after the Brownlow dinner, was an unsettling day for Mrs Simpson. She spent the afternoon having a long, distressed talk with Lady Oxford, Asquith's widow, who afterwards wrote to her:

> There was not one word you said to me this afternoon wh I did not understand, my dear, & with which I did not sympathise . . . I love him also & wd do anything to help him . . . To stand criticism is a sign of greatness, as sometimes criticism comes from a real desire to warn him of public opinion. He must be patient & elastic & not too set . . . There is no one I wish him to marry. I see no reason why he shd marry . . . He can go on with his present life perfectly well . . . [27]

That evening, dining with Lady Cunard, Mrs Simpson met Lady Londonderry, the socially influential wife of a prominent Conservative politician, with whom she had a similar private talk. The next morning, Saturday 7 November, she wrote to Lady Londonderry from Cumberland Terrace in terms which show that the appeals which had been made to her had not been without effect:

I have been thinking over all you told me last night. I have come to the conclusion that perhaps no-one has been *really* frank with a certain person in telling him how the country feels about his friendship with me; perhaps nothing has been said to him at all. I feel that he should know however and therefore I am going to tell him the things you told me . . . [28]

That week-end — from Saturday 7 to Monday 9 November — the King and Mrs Simpson gave what was to be their last house party at Fort Belvedere. The guests included Sibyl Colefax; the Paul Bonners, Americans who lived in Chelsea; and Charles Lambe, who left a record of the occasion. The King was relaxed and cheerful and, in his attitude towards Mrs Simpson, 'like a child'. He was a solicitous host, and spent much time showing his guests around the house and gardens. The conversation was easy and trivial and 'never flagged'. After dinner, the King played the bag-pipes; Lambe was a good pianist, and there were also songs at the piano.[29] There was only one moment of embarrassment: returning to the house after a walk in the grounds with his party, the King insisted on taking off Mrs Simpson's galoshes, in spite of her protests and in front of his guests, of whose astonishment he seemed quite oblivious.[30]

That Sunday at the Fort, it was Sibyl Colefax's turn to have a long talk alone with Mrs Simpson, which she later reported with great excitement to Harold Nicolson, Leo Amery and Robert Bruce-Lockhart, all of whom recorded it in their diaries. She found Mrs Simpson

really miserable. All sorts of people had come to her reminding her of her duty and begging her to leave the country. 'They do not understand', she said, 'that if I did so, the King would come after me regardless of anything. They would then get their scandal in a far worse form than they are getting it now.'

Indeed, according to the account Lady Colefax gave Bruce Lockhart, ' . . . Mrs Simpson wanted to leave him and clear out, but the King threatened to quit, to follow her, even to commit suicide'. Like everyone else, Sibyl asked if the King had proposed to her, receiving a reply firmly in the negative.[31]

We may assume that, as she had promised Lady Londonderry, Mrs Simpson remonstrated with the King at the end of that week-end, pointing out the mounting tide of criticism, begging him yet again to let her leave, warning him that the marriage could no longer be kept secret. But such remonstrance did not have the effect she would have wished. The King had not yet frankly disclosed his marriage intentions to any man; but on the following evening, Monday 9 November, sitting in the Empire drawing room at Buckingham Palace, he decided to make a frank confession of those intentions to Walter Monckton. He did so, moreover, making it clear that his resolve to marry was unalterable, and that he believed an issue with the Government could not, indeed should not, be long delayed. Monckton recorded:

> The King told me . . . that he intended to marry Mrs Simpson when she was free . . . I suggested that he might wait before taking any steps to act on a determination which could not in any event be given effect until the end of April 1937 [when Mrs Simpson could apply to have her divorce made absolute]. But I could see at once that he did not agree with this advice because he felt that he could not go forward to the Coronation on 12 May 1937 meaning in his heart to make the marriage whatever happened and, as he felt, deceiving the government and the people into imagining that he had dropped the association or, at any rate, did not intend to marry.[32]

The King continued his official work. On Tuesday 10 November, he presided over what was to be his last official reception – a lunch at the Palace for the visiting Polish Foreign Minister, Colonel Ludwig Beck. He ate almost nothing and talked charmingly, asking Beck about the problems of Polish miners. The Polish Ambassador, Count Edward Raczyński, had heard talk of the growing crisis but now found it difficult to believe, observing the monarch's relaxed and confident form.[33]

The next day was Armistice Day. The King laid a wreath at the Cenotaph, remembering 'how often I had seen my father's bearded figure stoop over in this same gesture of reverence'.[34] After spending the afternoon with his mother he went secretly and unnoticed to the Field of Remembrance at Westminster Abbey to plant a cross in memory of his father – 'looking for all the world as if he meant it', wrote Lambe. In the evening, as was his custom, he went to the Albert Hall to join the British Legion in community singing of songs of the Great War. He read the celebrated passage from Binyon's *The Trust*: 'They shall not grow old as we that are left grow old . . . ' The occasion was broadcast by the BBC, but for some reason the King's reading of these lines was not. The reception of the veterans was tremendous, though several faces looked up when the band played 'Hallo! Hallo! Who's your lady friend?'[35]

That night the King left to conduct a two-day review of the Home Fleet at Portland. 'They were good days', he wrote in his memoirs. 'Engrossed in inspecting the ships, talking to sailors and reminiscing with old shipmates, I was able to put aside for a few hours the burning issue that was pressing for decision.' [36] The weather was terrible; but he carried out his duties with his usual tireless energy.[37] Sir Samuel Hoare, who as First Lord of the Admiralty was Minister in attendance, recalled in his memoirs:

The King seemed to know personally every officer and seaman of the Fleet. On one of the evenings there was a smoking concert in the aircraft carrier *Courageous* . . . The vast underdeck was packed with thousands of seamen.

In my long experience of public meetings I never saw one so completely dominated by a single personality. At one point he turned to me and said: 'I am going to see what is happening at the other end.' Elbowing his way through the crowd, he walked to the end of the hall and started community singing to the accompaniment of a seaman's mouth organ. When he came back to the platform, he made an impromptu speech that brought the house down. Then, a seaman in the crowd proposed three cheers for him, and there followed an unforgettable scene of the wildest and most spontaneous enthusiasm. Here, indeed, was the Prince Charming, who could win the hearts of all sorts and conditions of men and women and send a thrill through great crowds.

The whole visit had been one long series of personal triumphs for the King. When I travelled back with him, I was amazed at his liveliness after two days of continuous inspections in the worst possible weather. As we sat down together in the very shaky and noisy royal saloon on the return journey to London, his bright and vivacious conversation never flagged.[38]

The royal train was stopped at Slough; and from there the King, after two weeks in which he had performed his role perfectly and appeared in excellent humour, drove directly to the Fort that evening of Friday 13 November.

Chapter Five

The Decision to Abdicate

13 November–16 November

As soon as the King entered the Fort that Friday evening, he was told by his butler, Osborne, that an official
despatch box had arrived containing an important
communication from Major Hardinge, who had also
telephoned to urge that the King read this immediately upon his return.[1] Before attending to the matter,
the King went to greet Mrs Simpson and her Aunt
Bessie, the latter of whom had arrived in England on 9
November to be with her niece at this testing time.[2] He
appeared to them to be 'in high good spirits', stimulated
by 'the enthusiastic reception' he had received from
the Fleet.[3] He longed for a bath after his tour (he was
in fact incubating a cold from which he would suffer
severely the following week), but thought it better to
open Hardinge's letter first. It read as follows.

Buckingham Palace
13 November 1936

Sir,

With my humble duty.
As your Majesty's Private Secretary, I feel it my duty to
bring to your notice the following facts which have come
to my knowledge and which I *know* to be accurate.
(1) The silence of the British Press on the subject of Your
Majesty's friendship with Mrs Simpson is not going to be

maintained. It is probably only a matter of days before the outburst begins. Judging by the letters from British subjects living in foreign countries where the Press has been outspoken, the effect will be calamitous.

(2) The Prime Minister and senior members of the Government are meeting today to discuss what action should be taken to deal with the serious situation which is developing. As Your Majesty no doubt knows, the resignation of the Government – an eventuality which can by no means be excluded – would result in Your Majesty having to find someone else capable of forming a government which would receive the support of the present House of Commons. I have reason to know that, in view of the feeling prevalent among members of the House of Commons of all parties, this is hardly within the bounds of possibility. The only alternative remaining is a dissolution and a General Election, in which Your Majesty's personal affairs would be the chief issue – and I cannot help feeling that even those who would sympathise with Your Majesty as an individual would deeply resent the damage which would inevitably be done to the Crown, the corner-stone on which the whole Empire rests.

If Your Majesty will permit me to say so, there is only one step which holds out any prospect of avoiding this dangerous situation, and that is for Mrs Simpson to go abroad *without further delay*, and I would beg Your Majesty to give this proposal your earnest consideration before the position has become irretrievable. Owing to the changing attitude of the Press, the matter has become one of great urgency.

I have the honour, etc., etc.,

ALEXANDER HARDINGE

PS I am by way of going after dinner tonight to High Wycombe to shoot there tomorrow, but the Post Office will have my telephone number, and I am of course entirely at Your Majesty's disposal if there is anything at all that you want.[4]

When the King rejoined Mrs Simpson and her aunt for dinner an hour later, he said nothing; but they noticed that his high spirits had gone.

In his memoirs, begun some twelve years later, the King wrote of his reactions to this letter. It presented him, he said, with 'the most serious crisis of my life'. It made him 'shocked and angry – shocked by the suddenness of the blow, angry because of the way it was launched with the startling suggestion that I should send from my land, my realm, the woman I intended to marry'. He was 'puzzled' by Hardinge's motive in writing it. He did not doubt his Private Secretary's right – indeed duty – to inform him that a political crisis was developing; 'but what hurt was the cold formality with which so personal a matter affecting my whole happiness had been broached'. He did not know whether to interpret the letter as 'a warning' or 'an ultimatum'. The phrase 'I have reason to know' seemed to suggest that Hardinge had had previous contacts with the Prime Minister on the subject, of which he had told the King nothing.[5]

Writing of his shock and bafflement, the King was not, perhaps, being entirely frank. For there can have been nothing in the least 'startling' to him about the suggestion that Mrs Simpson should leave England: it was what she herself had been suggesting for some time, and (as she had made the King aware) it was also the course being urged upon her by almost all of her own and the King's friends. Nor can he have been surprised to learn of an imminent explosion in the Government and the press. Baldwin had warned him of both on 20 October; and the King's actions since that date point to his belief that an issue with the Government could not be long delayed.

In truth, what outraged the King was not that such a broadside had come – everything indicates that he expected something, and was prepared to act immediately – but that it derived from Hardinge. The appointment of this man, so critical of the King and so completely outside his sympathy, had been an extra-ordinary mistake; and it is probable that the King immediately regretted it. Hardinge's secretaryship had begun with the quarrel about salary, in which he expressed himself in a manner which can have left his master in little doubt of his hostility. Any lingering respect which the King may have had for him would have been dispelled by Hardinge's evident intrigues against the divorce: his hand was clear, for instance, in the efforts of the senior civil servant, Sir Warren Fisher, to influence Mrs Simpson before Ipswich. Had a message of this kind come from Baldwin, or from a man such as his faithful old courtier Godfrey Thomas, the King would have received it without resentment. That it should come, in such frigid style, from Hardinge made more difficult and painful the step the King felt he now had to take.

Many historians (including the Duke of Windsor himself) advance the view that Hardinge's letter marked the turning point of the reign; that it forced the King, after nine months of evasion, finally to confront the Government on the subject of his marriage; that it set in motion the chain of events which led, exactly four weeks later, to abdication. This is to give it too much importance. At most it hastened developments by a few days – and ensured that the offending Hardinge would take no further part in them. For by the evening of 13 November, two factors had entered the situation. First, the pressure on Baldwin himself to take issue with the King had become irresistible. Secondly, as the present writer believes, the King had already virtually made up his mind to abdicate.

The King had only been waiting for a signal upon which to move: now that the signal had arrived (albeit from a quarter he found distasteful), he moved rapidly. On Saturday, after a night of reflection, he resolved to consult the two men who had helped him manage the divorce in October, Lord Beaverbrook and Walter Monckton. Beaverbrook turned out to have sailed for New York two days previously: the King telephoned him on his ship and urged him to return as soon as possible. With Monckton he arranged a secret meeting at Windsor Castle on Sunday afternoon. It will be remembered that the King had seen Monckton the previous Monday to take him into his confidence about the marriage; but that he had rejected as dishonourable Monckton's suggestion that he might keep his plan a secret until after the Coronation.

Of the meeting at Windsor on 15 November, which lasted less than an hour, we have the King's account and Monckton's. They differ in one vital particular.

Monckton was shown Hardinge's letter. 'His expression', wrote the King, 'left me in no doubt that it had shocked him as much as it had me.' And indeed, Monckton – who knew Hardinge moderately well, since they had been contemporaries at Harrow – sympathized with the King's annoyance.

> I . . . think that Hardinge took too pessimistic and critical a view of the King's conduct; I am sure that he expressed his opinion too emphatically and widely to have any hope of retaining the King's confidence when the crisis came . . .

The King was minded to dismiss Hardinge; but Monckton advised him not to do so 'as this would at once indicate a breach over Mrs Simpson'. The King then asked if Monckton himself would take over unofficially from Hardinge as the liaison officer between himself as sovereign and the Prime Minister. 'I realised that I was asking for a good deal. With a gallantry consistent with his generous spirit, he immediately volunteered to serve me.'

According to the King, he and Monckton were of one mind that the letter called for some immediate action, that 'time would not wait'. He claims to have told Monckton: 'The first thing I must do is to send for the Prime Minister – tomorrow. I shall tell him that if, as would now appear, he and the Government are against my marrying Mrs Simpson, I am prepared to go.' Monckton said that Baldwin would not like to hear that; to which the King replied that he would not find it easy to say.

In his own account, however, Monckton implies that he advised against any immediate action. As on the previous Monday, he counselled the King to be patient and do nothing precipitate: 'but [the King] discussed the matter with Mrs Simpson after leaving me and decided to send for Mr Baldwin and tell him of his intention to marry'.[6]

What was the substance of this discussion with Mrs Simpson? From her memoirs we learn that, until that Sunday afternoon, the King had told her nothing. When he set out for Windsor Castle, he merely said that the purpose of his visit was to supervise the hanging of some pictures. An hour later she joined him there, and they drove together to have tea with the Duke and Duchess of Kent at their country house in Buckinghamshire. On the drive back to the Fort, however, the King told her about the meeting with Monckton; and as soon as they returned, he asked her to read Hardinge's letter. Her account continues:

I was stunned . . . Clearly, there was only one thing for me to do: it was to leave the country immediately as Hardinge had implored . . .

Almost peremptorily [the King] said, 'You'll do no such thing. I won't have it. This letter is an impertinence.'

'That may well be. But just the same I think he's being sincere. He's trying to warn you that the Government will make you give me up.'

'They can't stop me. On the Throne or off, I'm going to marry you.'

Now it was my turn to beg him to let me go. Summoning all the powers of persuasion in my possession, I tried to convince him of the hopelessness of our position. For him to go on hoping, to go on fighting the inevitable, could only mean tragedy for him and catastrophe for me. He would not listen. Taking my hand, he said, with the calm of a man whose mind is made up, 'I'm going to send for Mr Baldwin to see me at the Palace tomorrow. I'm going to tell him that if the country won't approve our marrying, I'm ready to go.'

I burst into tears . . .[7]

She adds that this was the first time that the possibility of abdication had been mentioned between them. This may not have been strictly true; a month earlier, on 14 October, waiting for the Ipswich proceedings, she had written to him: 'I can't help but feel you will have trouble in the House of Commons and may be forced to go.'[8] But it is hard to doubt her real distress, and her desire to follow Hardinge's advice and disappear from the scene. As her letters show, this had been her main desire for the past two months. One week earlier, at the Fort on Sunday 8 November, she had confided to Sibyl Colefax her 'misery', saying that she longed to leave the King but feared he would follow her or go insane. No doubt she harboured a momentary hope, on reading the letter, that it would finally reconcile the King to her departure; but he was not to be moved.

The following day, Monday 16 November, the King, still at Fort Belvedere, telephoned Hardinge in the early afternoon. Making no mention whatever of the letter or its contents, he asked that Baldwin call at Buckingham Palace that evening, adding that he would be glad if the Prime Minister brought with him four other members of the Cabinet, Lord Halifax and Neville Chamberlain (who were the leading Conservatives in the National Government) and Duff Cooper and Sir Samuel Hoare (whom the King regarded as his friends). Baldwin replied that he would rather come alone. The King agreed to this; and Hardinge spoke again to Baldwin, fixing the appointment for half past six and telling him to expect 'something dramatic'.[9]

Following the events of the week-end, the King

had arranged to see Baldwin at the earliest possible moment, contrary to the advice of Walter Monckton, who was now his principal counsellor and agent, and in spite of the passionate entreaties of Mrs Simpson. But had the King not taken the initiative, Baldwin himself would have come to him for the same discussion within a matter of days. For he was now being driven to action from every quarter.

Baldwin's instinct was to continue to wait; but since the divorce at Ipswich he had been given little peace. It has been seen how that event at the end of October had provoked widespread and for the most part alarmed speculation that the King meant to marry Mrs Simpson. This tide of speculation − largely confined as it still was to fashionable and official circles − coincided with the return of the political world to London for the opening of Parliament. Meeting the nation's statesmen reassembling for the new session, the Prime Minister was urged from every side to join issue with the King on a matter which threatened to become an open scandal.

On Sunday 1 November, Baldwin had been at Hatfield House, where he had discussed the crisis with Lord Salisbury and the Archbishop of Canterbury. He was left in no doubt as to the attitude of conservative circles; and soon he also learned the attitude of the political opposition. Attlee, the leader of the Labour Party, sought him out and expressed the view 'that while Labour people had no objection at all to an American woman becoming Queen, I was certain that they would not approve of Mrs Simpson for that position . . . '[10] Walter Citrine, the trade-union leader, who had recently been in America, came to Chequers on 7 November, and assured the Prime Minister that Attlee

was undoubtedly interpreting the minds of the Labour

movement. We were republican at heart but we realised that the limited monarchy, as it had operated in Great Britain during the life of the late King George V, was probably the safest system in present circumstances . . . I said that most people were prepared to smile indulgently while the King was Prince of Wales, but now I thought it was a different matter. It was impossible to contemplate, without a feeling of humiliation, the fact that the newspapers in other countries were carrying discreditable stories about the King.[11]

Baldwin confided to Citrine that he did not believe the British newspapers could be held for much longer; and the events of the next days confirmed this view. Dawson, editor of The Times, came to see him on 11 November to ask pointedly whether press silence ought to be carried on. Baldwin declared that he was unable to offer any advice[12]; but the following day he was warned by Gwynne, editor of the conservative Morning Post, that 'the Press could not continue to keep silent unless assured that the Government had the matter in hand'. To this Baldwin replied that, though the matter was not yet before the Cabinet, he and certain senior colleagues were 'keeping a close watch on the situation'.[13]

On the morning of Friday 13 November Baldwin presided at a Cabinet, after which five senior ministers stayed behind with him to discuss the crisis: Ramsay MacDonald of the National Labour Party, Simon and Runciman of the National Liberals and Chamberlain and Halifax of the Conservatives; Baldwin had already taken this inner group briefly into his confidence after the armistice service on the 11th. In his diary, MacDonald summed up the mood of the meeting: 'Agreed that the scandal should be ended & HM brought right up against it.'[14] To Baldwin's surprise, Chamberlain produced two letters which it was proposed the Prime Minister should send the King. The first had been drafted a week earlier by a group of senior civil servants led by Warren Fisher, the Permanent Secretary to the Treasury, who had already interfered in the crisis to the extent of trying to get Mrs Simpson to give up her divorce.* The second was the work of Fisher's political boss, Chamberlain himself, who made the message even more drastic. The first letter read:

> Unless steps are promptly taken to allay the widespread and growing misgivings among the people, the feelings of respect, esteem and affection which Your Majesty has evoked among them, will disappear in a revulsion of so grave and perilous a character as possibly to threaten the stability of the nation and of the Empire. The dangers to the people of this country of such a shock, the disunity and loss of confidence which would ensue at a time when so much of the world is looking to the United Kingdom for guidance and leadership, through a sea of troubles, cannot but be obvious to Your Majesty. In Mr Baldwin's opinion there is but one course which he can advise you to take, namely to put an end to Your Majesty's association with Mrs Simpson.

The second letter, by Chamberlain, which was intended to cover the first, read:

> I have before me an official communication in which the advice of Your Majesty's Government is formally tendered, to the effect that in view of the grave dangers to which, in their opinion, this country is being exposed, your association with Mrs Simpson should be terminated forthwith. It is hardly necessary for me to point out that should this advice be tendered and refused by Your Majesty, only one result could follow in accordance with the requirements of constitutional monarchy, that is, resignation of myself and the National Government. If Mrs Simpson left the country forthwith,

---

* Hardinge had been shown this draft by Warren Fisher, and even he claims to have considered its terms excessively hostile (Helen Hardinge, *Loyal to Three Kings*, p. 132).

this distasteful matter could be settled in a less formal manner.[15]

Baldwin's biographers write that he 'had not seen the drafts and was deeply shocked by their tone. He knew he could not send either to the King; if they were made public, they would inevitably rally the country in the cause of a popular monarch, whom the Government were apparently blackmailing'.[16] MacDonald's diary suggests that the group as a whole approved of the draft submissions[17]; but Baldwin himself made no comment on them, merely saying that he would take them to Chequers to think them over.

Meanwhile he was being made aware of opinion in the Dominions. He received a letter dated 9 November from Lord Tweedsmuir, the Governor-General of Canada, to whom Hardinge had written asking for impressions. 'Canada is the most Puritanical part of the Empire and cherishes very much the Victorian standards of private life . . . Canada's pride has been deeply wounded by the tattle in the American press . . . '[18] On Sunday 15 November, Bruce, the Australian High Commissioner in London, lunched with Baldwin at Chequers. He afterwards wrote to the Prime Minister repeating his views, which coincided closely with those of Chamberlain:

There is no denying that there is sufficient evidence before you to show that there is a possibility that the King may be contemplating marrying the woman . . . If his answer was that he had such an intention, then I think you have to advise the King of what the consequences would be, e.g. [sic] that the people of this country and of the Dominions would not accept this woman as Queen . . . and that because of the perils both to the Throne and the Empire the King's conduct had created, there would be a demand for his abdication that you would find impossible to resist . . . You would have to tell him that unless he was prepared to abandon any idea of marriage . . . you would be compelled to advise

101

him to abdicate, and unless he accepted such advice you would be unable to continue as his adviser and would tender the resignation of Government.[19]

Finally, Baldwin heard from Lord Salisbury of a plan that a deputation of elder statesmen no longer closely involved in everyday politics – Lord Derby, Lord Crewe, Lord Fitzalan, Sir Austen Chamberlain and Salisbury himself – should approach the King and threaten to resign from the Privy Council* unless he agreed to choose between Mrs Simpson and his throne. (Winston Churchill had been asked to join this group but had refused.) This plan had been evolving ever since the divorce, and had concerned Ramsay MacDonald in his role as Lord President.[20] Baldwin received the privy councillors for an hour on Tuesday the 17th to hear them express 'their great perturbation at the information which had reached them concerning the King's intentions'.[21]

Meanwhile, on Monday afternoon, he had received his summons to the Palace. Had he not received it, he would have gone to the King that same week: he proposed to move as soon as the King returned from the visit to Wales he was due to make from Tuesday to Thursday. On Friday the 13th Hardinge had called at 10, Downing Street to show him the letter he was sending the King and ask if the Prime Minister might put off any meeting until Hardinge had received some reply. (None, of course, was ever received.) Baldwin replied 'that he could postpone that talk no longer; the pressure on him had become overwhelming . . .'[22]

Of the historic interview at Buckingham Palace between sovereign and premier at 6.30 on the evening of

---

* The *de jure* and ceremonial executive of the realm which consists of all present and former senior politicians, bound to the sovereign by an ancient oath.

Monday 16 November, there are three accounts. The most circumstantial is the one given by Baldwin to his wife Lucy that same night and recorded by her in her diary. The others, more sketchy, are those of Baldwin to the House of Commons during the debate on the Abdication Bill, and of the King in his memoirs, which he began towards the end of 1948. There are also some relevant remarks made by Baldwin to political colleagues shortly after the meeting.

The King began by coming to the point. 'I understand that you and several members of the Cabinet have some fear of a constitutional crisis developing over my friendship with Mrs Simpson.'

'Yes, Sir,' replied Baldwin, 'that is correct.'[23]

There is some dispute as to which of them first raised the subject of the marriage. According to the Duke of Windsor, it was Baldwin who did so: 'Until this moment the word "marriage" had never been mentioned between us.'[24] In the account Baldwin gave his wife, however, the conversation begins with the Prime Minister explaining that he could no longer guarantee the silence of the press, after which the King asks whether a marriage between himself and Mrs Simpson would be approved.[25] Baldwin's biographers are probably correct when they suggest that Lucy Baldwin's account, taken down hours after the event, is more likely to be reliable, and that the Duke of Windsor, trying twelve years later to remember exactly what had been said, may have been misled by Baldwin's account to the House of Commons, which contains the ambiguous statement: 'I began by giving him my view of a possible marriage.' The question, however, is irrelevant, because obviously the whole purpose of the meeting, from the point of view of the King, who had initiated it, was formally to acquaint the Prime Minister with his marriage plans and discuss these with him.

Having been asked, after whatever preliminaries, to comment on the marriage, Baldwin, as he later told

Parliament, held forth on the subject for fifteen or twenty minutes, making it abundantly clear that he did not believe such a union would be acceptable to the country.

> . . .That marriage would have involved the lady becoming Queen. I did tell His Majesty that I might be a remnant of the old Victorians, but that my worst enemy would not say of me that I did not know what the reaction of the English people would be to any particular course of action . . . I pointed out to him that the position of the King's wife was different from the position of the wife of any other citizen of the country. His wife becomes Queen; the Queen becomes the Queen of the country; and, therefore, in the choice of a Queen the voice of the people must be heard. [26]

Baldwin emphasized that it was only marriage to Mrs Simpson that would be unacceptable; there could be no objection to the sovereign's keeping her as a mistress. When the King protested that this was hypocritical, Baldwin replied: 'There has always been a leniency regarding the private relations of Kings just because they are the only people subjected to strict regulation with regard to their marriages and wives.'[27]

When Baldwin had finished his discourse, the King made a dramatic announcement. This is how he described it in his memoirs:

> Then, as dispassionately as I could, I told Mr Baldwin that marriage had become an indispensable condition to my continued existence, whether as a King or a man. 'I intend to marry Mrs Simpson as soon as she is free to marry', I said. If I could marry her as King, well and good; I would be happy and in consequence a better King. But if, on the other hand, the Government opposed the marriage, then I was prepared to go.[28]

This is how Baldwin described it to the House of Commons:

Then His Majesty said to me . . . that he wanted to tell me something that he had long wanted to tell me. He said, 'I am going to marry Mrs Simpson, and I am prepared to go'.[29]

And this is what Lucy Baldwin noted:

> And then the King said to him these words: 'I want you to be the first to know that I have made up my mind and nothing will alter it – I have looked at it from all sides – and I mean to abdicate to marry Mrs Simpson.'[30]

Baldwin was evidently shaken by this announcement, whatever exact form it may have taken: he declared that he found it 'grievous'. According to his wife's account, he stayed on for some time, attempting to reason with the King and dissuade him from marriage. He mentioned that, in the view of some people, there was an element of irregularity about the divorce: this angered the King. He spoke of the Dominions, of how Bruce of Australia and Mackenzie King of Canada had both agreed that the marriage would 'break up the Empire', respect for the throne being the link that held everything together. But the King refused to be moved by any appeal or argument; and when the Prime Minister had finished, he repeated: 'I have made up my mind and I shall abdicate in favour of my brother, the Duke of York, and I mean to go and acquaint my mother this evening, and my family. Please don't mention my decision except to two or three trusted Privy Councillors until I give you permission.'[31]

The King asked Baldwin to try to secure the continued silence of the press; he also asked if he might see his friends in the Cabinet, Hoare and Cooper. Baldwin agreed to both requests.

Throughout the interview, Baldwin told his wife, the King, though impervious to reason, had been 'most charming'. He escorted the Prime Minister to his car; and as they parted, 'the King held Stanley's hand for a long time and there were almost tears in his eyes as he said goodbye'.[32]

But what exactly had the King proposed? According to Lucy Baldwin's account, he had been quite definite about leaving the throne: 'I mean to abdicate to marry Mrs Simpson'; whereas, according to the Duke of Windsor's distant recollection, he was merely 'prepared to go' if 'the Government opposed the marriage'. A consideration of this question is surely essential to any proper analysis of the reign of Edward VIII. Did he, on 16 November, speak of abdication in absolute or conditional terms? Was it something upon which he was now determined, whatever happened; or was it merely a threat of something he might do if he did not get his way?

Remarks made by Baldwin to some of his cabinet colleagues at Westminster that evening are equally ambiguous. To Ramsay MacDonald, he said that the King was 'determined to marry Mrs S. and prepared to abdicate'[33]; while he told Duff Cooper that the King 'intended to marry Mrs Simpson and to abdicate', adding that he was 'not at all sure that the Yorks would not prove the best solution'.[34] However, the message which filtered through to the courtiers appears to have been less equivocal. Hardinge's wife wrote in her diary that night, lapsing into French lest such secret information fall into the wrong hands: 'Le Premier Ministre a vu le roi ce soir – le souverain va partir.'[35]

In this writer's view, Baldwin's account to his wife is the true one; and by this time the King had definitely decided to abdicate, a decision from which, in spite of appearances to the contrary, he never wavered.

In the opinion of some observers, he had never really intended to remain on the throne at all: such views have been considered in the first chapter of this book. While he was certainly unhappy about many aspects of a sovereign's life, and had always realized that abdication might be the price for marriage, it is unfair to suppose that he had come to his office filled with the intention of giving it up. He had meant to give the thing a try. As Baldwin afterwards told Lord Ponsonby: 'Once he became King he liked it but gradually found he was caged and his arcane infatuation gave him the spur to break through.'[36] And there is one piece of evidence that cannot be overlooked: he had gone to great lengths to try to ensure that Mrs Simpson would receive her decree absolute before the Coronation. Hence the Ipswich affair. He wanted to be King; and he wanted Mrs Simpson to be Queen.

There are, to be sure, a number of curious indications which suggest that he believed – or had a premonition – that he would not be on the throne for long. One may cite his dislike of discussing his own coronation; his amazing appointment of such men as Hardinge and Lascelles as his private secretaries; and his reluctance to establish himself in Buckingham Palace. On the other hand, there is the evidence of his gardening in preparation for the following spring.

One must conclude that, at some point between the beginning of October and middle of November, he came to realize, after painful reflection, that he would have to choose after all between Mrs Simpson and kingship. And for him there was no real choice; she had become, as he was to tell Baldwin, an 'indispensable condition' to his 'continued existence'.

What, then, was the moment of decision? Was it after Baldwin's visit to the Fort on 20 October? That meeting had certainly affected him far more than Baldwin realized at the time. Was it four days later, when he told Monckton that 'one doesn't know how things are going to turn out', and that his brother might make a better king? Was it after the divorce itself, when the tide of criticism in high circles, and of speculation in the foreign press, reached such uncomfortable proportions? Was it during the week-end of 7 November, when Mrs Simpson appears to have had some kind of reckoning with him? It was after that week-end that he had told Monckton of his determination to marry. Was it on receiving Hardinge's letter on the 13th? The speed and firmness with which he acted – in spite of the restraining efforts of both Monckton and Mrs Simpson – suggest that, by the time this unwelcome epistle arrived, he had already made up his mind.

The excellent work that the King performed during the first half of November may indicate that he knew his time to be short, and wished to use it to make the best impression. His excellent spirits throughout that time may be interpreted, in psychiatric terms, as a kind of manic-depressive reaction to an inner struggle, as he felt himself ineluctably driven to do something which he did not want to do.

Between the interview of Monday 16 November and the King's formal notice to the Government of his intention to abdicate on Tuesday 8 December, there was an interval of three weeks. During that time, he considered, and asked the Government to consider, two possible solutions to his problem other than abdication: the idea of a morganatic marriage, and the idea that he might broadcast, go abroad, and allow the people in some way to reach a 'verdict' about his marriage. He toyed with these notions because they were dear to the heart of Mrs Simpson, who was desperate to stop him abdicating; but all the events of those days suggest that he did not take them very seriously. He advanced them in a lukewarm fashion, without any of the skill he could demonstrate on occasion; and he accepted the Government's refusal of them as final. During those three weeks, he also consulted a number of political friends and supporters, notably Cooper, Beaverbrook and Churchill. But he did so only for a kind of moral reassurance: all the advice they gave with a view to saving his throne he rejected. The consultation with supporters, the consideration of alternative solutions, did not represent any true change of heart on the King's part: at most they delayed the outcome for a week or so.

At the time, many observers regarded what was happening in terms of struggle, the King wishing to remain on the throne on his own terms, what one would now call the Establishment (the word was not yet in use) resolved that he should either conform or go. There was in fact no struggle, merely an interval. Even in his own memoirs, the Duke of Windsor sought to give the impression that he had fought, valiantly but against hopeless odds, to find some means of retaining his throne. He wrote of Baldwin as a cunning adversary, out to make political capital from the issue of the royal marriage. But a dozen years had passed, during which his recollection of those painful events had become clouded and confused; he wished to do justice to himself before history; he did not want to disappoint those who had tried to help him at the time, including Beaverbrook and Churchill who had been Baldwin's political enemies; above all he did not want to upset his wife, who had tried so hard at the time to make him change his mind. Also he wrote, in the first place, for a magazine serial; and it would have been a poor serial that admitted that the drama of the Abdication Crisis was no true drama at all, merely the working out of the inevitable, an inevitable to which the King had resigned himself from the start.

The truth, however, was that the 16th of November marked not the beginning but the end. Ten months after coming to the throne, the King had reached his decision; he was not to alter it. What happened after is in a sense merely postscript.

Chapter Six

After the Decision

16 November–20 November

Following his dramatic interview with Baldwin on the evening of 16 November, the King went to dine with his mother at Marlborough House. He wanted her 'to hear from my own lips what had passed between the Prime Minister and me, before anybody had padded off to her with a distorted version of this momentous conversation'. Also dining that evening, he discovered on arrival, were his sister Princess Mary and sister-in-law the Duchess of Gloucester. The latter had married into the Royal Family less than a year before and was 'almost a stranger'; and Queen Mary, who knew perfectly well why her son had 'proposed' himself, meaningfully remarked 'that Alice was tired and would go to bed directly after dinner'.[1]

Nothing did more to arouse hostility against Edward VIII, either at the time or afterwards, than the attitude of martyrdom taken up by Queen Mary in the face of his relationship with Mrs Simpson. As one of her ladies in waiting has testified, she simply refused to accept that, as King, he had any right to conduct a private life of his own choosing.[2] George V had been indignant over the affair, and had made the Queen promise never to receive Mrs Simpson.[3] During the early months of the reign, she had twice seen Baldwin – in February and again in July – to ask him to do something to put a stop to the relationship: the Prime Minister declared himself helpless to intervene. To the King himself, who

110

saw her frequently and behaved punctiliously towards her in her widowhood, she said nothing. As the Duke of Kent told Chips Channon, 'she was shy, nervous and ineffectual. All her life she had been reserved with her eldest son, and the habit of a lifetime was too strong for her to break.'[4] But she discussed the matter freely with the rest of the family and with the Archbishop of Canterbury, making her views plainly felt; and she regularly summoned Hardinge and other courtiers to report on the progress of the royal infatuation. When the King moved into Buckingham Palace in October, Hardinge and his wife conferred with a member of the Queen's household on how to avert any possibility of the Queen coming to the Palace while Mrs Simpson was present.[5] As the autumn wore on, the Queen received cuttings from the American papers sent by worried subjects across the Atlantic; and her reactions of suffering and outrage soon became the common talk of London. 'Poor Queen Mary is in anguish', wrote Marie Belloc Lowndes that November. 'She can neither sleep nor eat.'[6] It was to this bitter and inflexible parent that the King came on the evening of 16 November, to explain his decision and seek her understanding.

'The meal, for which I had little appetite, seemed endless', he recalled. 'I was preoccupied with what I was going to say afterwards . . . I tried to ease the tension by keeping the conversation on a light plane.' Finally dinner came to an end, Princess Alice fled upstairs, and the King retired to a private room with his mother and sister. His memoirs continue:

Settling down in a chair, I told them of my love for Wallis and my determination to marry her; and of the opposition of the Prime Minister and Government to the marriage. The telling was all the harder because until that evening the subject had never been discussed between us. Neither my mother nor Mary reproved me; in fact, they sympathised with me. But as I went on and they comprehended that even the alternative of abdication would not deter me from my course, I became conscious

111

of their growing consternation that I could even contemplate giving up the Throne of my forbears. My mother had been schooled to put duty, in the stoic Victorian sense, before everything else in life. From her invincible virtue and correctness she looked out as from a fortress at the rest of humanity, with all its tremulous uncertainties and distractions . . .

All the while I was waiting for the right moment to make a request I did not believe would be refused. 'Please won't you let me bring Wallis Simpson to see you?' I asked. 'If you were to meet her you would understand what she means to me, and why I cannot give her up. I have waited a long time to find the person whom I wished to marry. For me the question is not whether she is acceptable to me but whether I am worthy of her.' But they could not bring themselves to unbend even this much. It was not, I was sure, because they were wanting in understanding: it was rather because the iron grip of Royal convention would not release them.

For all her self-control, my mother was obviously distressed. Yet she made no effort to dissuade me from the action I contemplated . . . [7]

When the Duke of Windsor published these words in 1951, he had to pay some regard to the sensibilities of his mother, who was then still alive. But in fact he never forgave her for her lifelong refusal to meet the woman who became his wife: and he held her responsible for the fact that he was treated as an outcast after the Abdication. After her death in March 1953, he wrote to his wife from London: 'My sadness was mixed with incredulity that any mother could have been so hard and cruel towards her eldest son for so many years and yet so demanding at the end without relenting a scrap. I'm afraid the fluids in her veins have always been as icy cold as they now are in death.'[8]

Things might have been different had Queen Mary agreed to receive Mrs Simpson. For Mrs Simpson herself now clearly wanted the King to give up their affair and any thought of marriage and remain on the throne. Individually, these two women who played the dominant part in his emotional life were incapable of inducing the King to change his mind; together, they might have succeeded. This, at all events, was the view of Monckton, who is reported as saying that, had the meeting materialized, the whole crisis might have been avoided.[9]

The following day, the King explained his decision to the man who would succeed him upon abdication – his brother Prince Albert, Duke of York. As he wrote: 'Bertie was so taken aback by my news that in his shy way he could not bring himself to express his innermost feelings at the time' – meaning presumably that he broke down and was unable to make any coherent comment. 'This, after all, was not surprising, for next to myself Bertie had most at stake: it was he who would have to wear the crown if I left, and his genuine concern for me was mixed with the dread of having to assume the responsibilities of kingship.'[10]

Dread the Duke of York may have felt at the destiny which threatened shortly to descend upon him: but the news cannot have come to him as anything of a surprise. Even during the 1920s, there had been much talk in the Royal Family that the Prince of Wales, with his impetuous personality, might not reach the throne or stay there very long, and that sovereignty would descend upon the Yorks.[11] There is some evidence, indeed, that this was an outcome for which George V himself hoped: a few weeks before his death he remarked to a friend, Lady Algernon Gordon-Lennox: 'I pray to God that my eldest son will never marry and have children, and that nothing will come between Bertie and Lilibet* and the throne.'[12] Throughout the reign of Edward VIII, a stream of discontented

---

* The future Queen Elizabeth II.

Palace courtiers made their way to the Yorks' London residence, 145, Piccadilly, carrying tales of the King's unsatisfactory conduct and predicting that he would have to go. As early as 10 October, before anyone knew of the divorce, Hardinge had told the Duke, who had just returned from Scotland, that abdication was on the cards; and he had repeated this warning on 28 October.[13]

The King had no doubts of Prince Albert's fitness to succeed him. 'I believe they would prefer someone more like [George V]', he had remarked to Walter Monckton on 24 October. 'Well, there is my brother Bertie.'[14] It remained to be seen to what extent his brother, who was too distressed to say anything on 17 November, would accept the situation.*

At his meeting with Baldwin, the King had asked if he might consult the two cabinet ministers he knew best, Sir Samuel Hoare, First Lord of the Admiralty, and Duff Cooper, Secretary of State for War. Baldwin having agreed, the King saw the Ministers at separate interviews at the Palace on Tuesday the 17th, Hoare in the morning, Cooper in the afternoon.

Hoare owed a personal debt to the King, who had given him much-needed private moral support the previous December when Hoare had been forced to resign as Foreign Secretary over a secret plan made with the French (to which historians now give more approval than British public opinion did at the time) which would have accorded international recognition to most of Mussolini's conquests in Abyssinia. Their friendship dated back to the twenties, when Hoare was Secretary of State for Air and the Prince of Wales had an interest in aviation. After his reappointment to the Admiralty, Hoare had been invited to the King's dinner

---

* See below, pp. 133–4.

party at York House on 9 July 1936, where he had met Mrs Simpson*; he had attended the King's shooting party at Sandringham in October; and only the previous week he had accompanied the King on his visit to the Home Fleet. Hoare was also close both to Monckton and to Beaverbrook: he is said to have drawn a secret annual subsidy from Beaverbrook, who consulted him on political matters. But he was not now the man to help the King. He was austere and conventional and a devout Anglo-Catholic; above all, he was obsessed with his career and advancement, which had already been sufficiently compromised by recent events.

And in fact the King himself held little hope, that Tuesday morning, that Hoare would be his man. As he wrote in his memoirs:

> The First Lord of the Admiralty's temperament was not such as to encourage the belief that I might convert him into a champion of my cause. The most that I hoped from our meeting was that, after hearing my story, he would understand the compulsions working upon me . . . But I failed to win him as an advocate. He was sympathetic, but he was also acutely conscious of political realities. Mr Baldwin, he warned me, was in command of the situation; the senior ministers were solidly with him on the issue. If I were to press my marriage project on the Cabinet, I should meet a stone wall of opposition.[15]

In his own memoirs, Hoare accepted this account of the interview; and in private notes made at the time, he had only two other comments to make about the King's discourse. The first was: 'Decision irrevocable'; the second: 'No single middle-aged man willingly stays in a tomb.'[16]

---

* Hoare had already encountered Mrs Simpson socially through Sir Robert Vansittart, Permanent Secretary for Foreign Affairs: both men sought, through Mrs Simpson, to influence the King in favour of the pro-Italian policy which they favoured in order to keep Mussolini out of the arms of Hitler.

Cooper was forty-six, a man of the King's and the Great War generation; he was also a man of the world, who enjoyed a convivial social life, was admired for his conversation and intellect, and combined a happy and successful marriage to one of the most brilliant and beautiful women of the time with a wide-ranging romantic activity. He and his wife Diana had long been in the King's social circle and frequent visitors at Fort Belvedere; they had been included in the *Nahlin* party. Cooper had not seen the King to speak to since he had left the yacht at Athens in August.

He has left a full account of the meeting.[17] He had already been briefed by Baldwin and knew of the King's decision; and the King, having greeted him, broached the subject at once. He could not reign unless married to Mrs Simpson. His father's success as King had been based on a happy marriage, and since he himself had become King 'he had realized that it was a task which could not be properly carried out except by a married man'. The life was 'impossibly lonely' for a bachelor.

Cooper tried to point out some of the personal consequences to him of abdication. He warned that all blame for the event would fall on Mrs Simpson, who would find herself excoriated before history. This seemed to shake the King, who remarked that such an outcome would be very unjust. Cooper then asked if the King had considered what sort of existence he would have as an ex-monarch: it was the 'most miserable' a man could lead. He pointed to the example of Alfonso XIII of Spain, deposed in 1931; but the King merely remarked: 'Oh, I shan't be like Alfonso. He was kicked out. I shall go of my own accord.' But what, asked Cooper, would he do with his time? 'Oh, you know me, Duff,' said the King. 'I shall find plenty to do.'*

The King insisted that nothing would dissuade him

---

* Cooper was to remember this reply when, as Ambassador to Paris nine years later, he was to witness the pathetic lack of occupation of the Duke of Windsor.

from his plan. The previous day, Baldwin had told him that while the country would never accept marriage, they would not object to her being his mistress. That was surely 'the height of hypocrisy'. Society and its values were organized not on principles of right and wrong, but of keeping up appearances. If she were to be his helpmeet, it was only right that he should marry her; and if he married her as King, she would have to be 'Queen or nothing'.

Cooper then said that, while the project of marriage on the throne was certainly 'very difficult', it might, 'given time', prove 'not impossible'. This remark aroused the King's interest: Hoare, he said, had told him quite definitely that if he married he would have to go; and his mother the previous evening, though she had been 'very nice about it', had expressed the same view. Cooper continued that it was 'a question of time': and he then put forward the same plan which Monckton had advanced eight days earlier, that the King should not think of marrying before the Coronation. He should wait for a year; Mrs Simpson should go away; meanwhile he should be crowned and attend a Durbar in India. After a year his position would be 'immensely strengthened'.

Cooper (as he later explained in his autobiography) secretly hoped that, if the King waited, he would change his mind, as his passion for the distant Mrs Simpson cooled and his taste for kingship increased.[18] But the King rejected Cooper's formula in the same terms as he had rejected Monckton's the previous week. His desire to marry Mrs Simpson, he insisted, could be kept secret no longer. As he wrote in his memoirs:

For me to have gone through the Coronation ceremony while harbouring in my heart a secret intention to marry contrary to the Church's tenets would have meant being crowned with a lie on my lips . . . My soul contained enough religion for me to comprehend to the full the deep meaning attached to the Coronation service. Whatever the cost to me personally, I was determined, before I would think of being crowned, to settle once and for all the question of my right to marry.[19]

The meeting had lasted an hour. Throughout, noted Cooper, the King had been calm, reasonable and friendly. He spoke bitterly only of Hardinge; and, having a word with Cooper before the audience, the Private Secretary, indeed, had spoken bitterly of the King.*

In these interviews, the King had explained himself to two friends in high political positions; he had satisfied his conscience, reaffirming to himself that what he had decided to do was indeed the only thing to be done; and he had recruited, it seemed, at least one confidant and well-wisher in the Cabinet who might help when it came to discussing the details of abdication. It is hard to believe that he had expected much more from the meetings.

That Tuesday night, following the busy day during which he had seen his brother and the two ministers, the King departed by train for his two-day tour of the South Wales mining valleys. This had been organized months before, and Baldwin at their latest meeting had agreed to the King going ahead with it. Accompanying him were two members of the Cabinet – Ernest Brown, Minister of Labour, and Sir Kingsley Wood, Minister of Health – and two courtiers – Charles Lambe and Hardinge. Hardinge had made the arrangements for the tour; he noted with surprise that the King, who continued to say nothing whatever to him about the letter and the crisis, treated him with 'particular friendliness'.[20]

This, the King knew, was likely to be his last official

_____

* Hardinge later argued that the King had borne him no ill-will before the Abdication, and that his animosity developed subsequently; but Cooper's notes would seem to belie this.

trip; and it filled him with some emotion. It occurred to him 'that Wales was a truly prophetic place to wind up the many years of my public life', for it had been his titular principality since 1911, when amid great pomp and ceremony he had been invested as Prince of Wales at Caernarvon. But Wales was now in the grip of appalling unemployment and depression. 'In place of brilliant flags and princely paraphernalia, I was now met by humble arches made of leeks from Government-sponsored co-operative farms, and of unlighted Davy lamps strung together by jobless miners.'21

Throughout Wednesday and Thursday they toured the villages of the Rhondda and Monmouth valleys, witnessing scenes of desolation. He knew this country well, having returned to it year after year since the Great War; and he was deeply moved by the sight of idle pits and unemployed workers. They counted on him to give them hope: a flag stretched over the railway approach to Brynmawr read *We Need Your Help*. The King moved among the crowds of men and spoke to them individually, showing the utmost concern for their plight. 'Everywhere the people looked delighted and hopeful at his visit', wrote Charles Lambe. 'They obviously loved and trusted him.'22

He asked to visit the Bessemer Steel Works at Dowlais, which had not been on his original schedule. Here, where nine thousand men had once been employed, dereliction now reigned. Hundreds of men gathered to meet him, sitting on heaps of twisted metal; and as he came among them, they rose and sang the Welsh hymn *Crugybar*. The national press were present in force to report such scenes. At Blaenavon, he went up to talk to an unemployed miner. Afterwards Hannen Swaffer, the star reporter of the Labour *Daily Herald*, asked the man to repeat what he had heard. The King's words had been: 'Something must be done to meet the situation in South Wales, and I will do all I can to assist you.'23

On Wednesday evening, the King asked a number of officials involved in the affairs of the region to dine with his party in his private railway coach at Usk: these included not only Sir George Gillett, Chief Commissioner for Special Areas, but also Gillett's predecessor Percy Stewart, who had resigned the previous year over the inadequacy of the Government's relief efforts. They discussed the measures which were being taken to revive the derelict pits; the King was observed through a window of the train, talking heatedly and banging his fist on the table.[24]

That night he began suffering from a heavy cold.[25] On Thursday the weather turned grey and wet; but he continued in the same form. At a housing estate at Pontypool he said: 'You may be sure that all I can do for you I will; we certainly want better times brought to your valley.'

Hardinge wrote to Baldwin that the visit had gone off 'extremely well' and would be 'a shock for the Communists'.[26] The King had gone to South Wales without any notion of interfering in politics, merely with the desire to do his best on what promised to be the last of his official tours.[27] But a section of the press, knowing but as yet silent about the crisis over Mrs Simpson, chose to interpret his expressions of concern, his casual statements to individual workers, his invitation to a disgruntled ex-official, as a deliberate criticism of the Government's failure to tackle the problems of the depression – and a conscious effort to improve his public position prior to a struggle with the powers that be. The News Chronicle commented on the tour: 'The man in the street feels that Whitehall stands condemned.'[28] And, the following Monday, the Daily Mail wrote an article of which we shall hear more:

The King was openly disturbed and afflicted by his survey. The lot of the humblest people has always been his nearest anxiety and continual preoccupation – and the people of South Wales realised that here was a man who cares supremely for their well-being . . . The King has called for action. He will want to review the Government's plans and to be kept posted of their progress . . .

The King had not in fact called for anything. At the end of the tour, he embodied his sentiments in a telegram to the Lords Lieutenant of Glamorganshire and Monmouthshire, the only official message to emerge from the tour. His feeling was one of

> admiration for the spirit in which the people of the Special Areas of South Wales are facing the ordeal of prolonged unemployment. I have been encouraged by seeing the fine efforts . . . to help them until, as I sincerely hope, some revival of industrial activity may bring them back to the prosperity which is their due. In the meantime I urge them not to lose heart and to rest assured that their troubles are not forgotten.[29]

'All England is convinced that there was nothing electioneering, so to speak, about the King's journey to South Wales', wrote James Agate in his diary. 'It was not a move in a game of political chess; it was the outcome of something the King has been feeling and showing he felt for many years. It made an enormous appeal to the country, which recognised that here was somebody . . . who was not content to see whole sections of the community starve.'[30]

In political circles, however, anxious men saw danger. On Saturday 21 November Ramsay MacDonald, having lunched with Gillett, the Government Commissioner who had dined with the King in Wales three days before, remarked in his diary that the visit had

> aroused expectations . . . [which] will embarrass the Government. These escapades should be limited. They are an invasion into the field of politics & should be watched constitutionally. Besides he might easily use this method for cloaking the other troubles in which he plunges at present.[31]

The King arrived back in London on the evening of

Thursday 19 November. His first act was to telephone his brother the Duke of Kent to tell him of his decision to marry Mrs Simpson. They had not seen much of each other since Balmoral in September, but were due to meet later that evening at a dinner party given by the Chips Channons. The Duke was abreast of the King's interview with Queen Mary and intensely distressed about the whole affair; he hardly knew whether to offer his congratulations or not.[32]

The Channon party, which the King attended with Mrs Simpson and Lord Brownlow, was a glittering occasion: apart from the Kents, the other guests included the Duchess of Kent's sister Princess Olga and her husband the Regent Paul of Yugoslavia, Victor Cazalet and the Duff Coopers. This was the last large social gathering in which the King participated; and we have three interesting accounts of it – those of Cazalet, Duff Cooper, and Channon himself.

On one fact all accounts agree: in spite of the strain of the lightning tour of Wales from which he had returned that same evening,* of having slept for two nights in a train, of suffering from a bad cold, of having just disclosed his intentions to his favourite brother who sat irritably at the same table, and of the political reckoning which lay before him, the King's mood was buoyant. He was, recorded Cooper, 'in the highest spirits'. 'I saw at once', wrote Channon, 'that he was in a gay mood . . . nothing could mar his excellent temper as we marched in to dinner . . . [He] ate a lot, drank claret and laughed much . . . The King was jolly, gay and full of cracks.' Cazalet was seated next to Mrs Simpson at the table, and noted: 'Every few minutes he gazes at her and a happiness and radiance fills his countenance such as makes you have a lump in your throat . . . '

---

* The King arrived at Paddington station at seven and at the Channons' at nine-thirty.

Of his conversation, Cazalet noted: 'The King talked a lot about politics and about his trip to S. Wales. He was very pleased with his visit. He talked on and on, much as his father did, I suppose, disconnected and without any real sequence or understanding. He thinks Nat. Govt. has given way too much to the Socialists.' To Cooper, he talked

about recruiting, about the artillery mess, and about the BBC. He asked why the Government didn't exercise more control of the BBC. I explained to him the measure of its independence. 'I'll change that', he said, 'it will be the last thing I do before I go.' He said this quite loud with a laugh, as though he were looking forward to going.

Both Cazalet and Cooper independently took Mrs Simpson aside and asked her – as so many others had done that month – why she did not leave England. Cazalet recorded: 'She believes that if she left he would deteriorate and drink. I think she's right . . .' Cooper 'tried to impress upon her the importance of leaving the country. She said he wouldn't hear of it, and that if she went he would follow . . . I tried to convince her that separation now was the only alternative to abdication, which would be disastrous . . .'33

This too was the view of Walter Monckton, who warned that Mrs Simpson's divorce suit might be imperilled if she remained in England close to the King. In a letter dated 18 November, received by the King on his return from Wales, he wrote that he had devoted himself since the week-end to sounding out opinion 'in the House of Commons, Bar, Stock Exchange and Press and other places where this problem is the one topic of discussion'. He reported 'widespread and vehement criticism' of the King in these circles, disapproval of his continued association with Mrs Simpson, and a belief that 'the [divorce] suit was for Your Majesty's convenience and that you are getting advantages that an ordinary person would not have . . . I cannot help thinking it is worth considering whether you could not both bear a purely temporary separation for the immediate future in order to secure our real objects [i.e. the divorce] . . . '[34]

The following day – Friday 20 November – the King saw Monckton, but was evidently unmoved by the latter's skilful plea for separation and reconsideration. Monckton wrote to Baldwin after the meeting:

> He was very glad that we have both met and discussed the problem; he trusts us both, I'm sure. You will find his decision unchanged on the main question. And he is facing the rest, considering all that is involved, with a real appreciation of the interests which you would wish him to have in mind. I think he will want to see you about Tuesday or Wednesday . . . At present his ideas are a little fluid . . . He will not do anything precipitate or selfish, saving *il gran refiuto*.[35]

On the day after his return from Wales, therefore, the King's mind was still fixed on abdication.

We have an interesting account of the King and Mrs Simpson that Friday afternoon – probably the last picture of them together in a relaxed mood in London. Cecil Beaton, who had taken some photographs of her during the King's recent absence,* called on her at Cumberland Terrace to deliver the proofs and make a drawing of her. He found his hostess 'immaculate, soignée and fresh as a young girl . . . She spoke

---

* Of their photographic session while the King was in Wales, Beaton wrote: 'Whatever fantastic changes have taken place in Mrs Simpson's life, she has obviously suffered. There is a sad look to be seen in her eyes. The camera is not blind to this . . . ' Beaton tried to photograph her against a background of ermine, but she refused to accept 'anything connected with the Coronation'.

amusingly, in staccato sentences punctuated by explosive bursts of laughter that lit up her face with great gaiety . . . ' They discussed the Coronation, and Mrs Simpson remarked (as she was remarking to everyone) that the talk of marriage was 'absolute nonsense'. Beaton was asking whether he might photograph the King, when the sovereign himself came in, wearing a silk jersey and still suffering from the heavy cold he had contracted in Wales.

> The King, in bright spirits and not nervous at all, laughed and examined my photographic proofs laid out on the sofa. Quickly he gave his definite opinion as to which were good and which were not. Jokes and laughter ensued. 'I like this', the King commented; 'that one, too. In fact, all these are good. I want the lot.'
> 'Oh, Sir, wouldn't that be too much of a Wallis collection?' And we all laughed.

The King allowed Beaton to do a sketch of him in profile. While he was being drawn, he drank a whisky and soda and, glancing at a newspaper, talked easily about the Spanish Civil War and unemployment in South Wales.

> The King has an enormous store of general knowledge. He never forgets names, remembers statistics. He knows, too, the average man's tastes and inclinations, is himself a kind of average man *par excellence*. He will be a very popular King, as one instinctively respects him.

They looked at snapshots of the *Nahlin* cruise; Aunt Bessie joined them and 'sat back quipping'; a tray of exquisite hors d'oeuvres was served; the King darted about the room, talking merrily and untying parcels. 'At last the King – like a child whose before-dinner play hour had come to an end – was told that we must all go.'[36] The King and Mrs Simpson departed to dine with Lady Cunard, before leaving to spend the week-end at Fort Belvedere.

It was during that week-end that Mrs Simpson suggested to him that, if he remained intent on marrying her, and the Government remained intent that she should not become Queen, a possible solution might be found in the idea of a morganatic marriage.

Chapter Seven

Morganatic Marriage

20 November–25 November

A morganatic marriage is defined by the *Shorter Oxford Dictionary* as one

> between a man of exalted rank and a woman of lower station in which it is provided that neither the wife nor her children shall share the dignities . . . of the husband.

It belongs to the world of the old German monarchies, where membership of ruling families was confined to those already possessing a required number of royal quarterings. If a prince sought to marry a woman who was not of equal birth – *Ebengeburtig* – the marriage might be legally valid, but would not have the legal effect of conferring princely status on either wife or children, who would be known by lesser titles and unable to inherit royal property. The best-known twentieth-century example of such a union is that of the Archduke Franz Ferdinand, heir to the Austrian throne, and his consort Sophie, a mere countess by birth, who were killed together at Sarajevo in June 1914 during a tour which had been conceived as a treat for a wife who was generally unable to share in any of her husband's royal and public functions.

Morganatic marriage is said to have been unknown to English law; but it was certainly far from unknown to the English Royal Family, which during the later years of Queen Victoria (who was notably liberal in questions of marriage) had become closely allied to two German families of morganatic origin. First there were the Tecks, descended from Prince Alexander of Wuerttemberg who acquired a Hungarian morganatic wife in 1835; their son, Francis of Teck, married Queen Victoria's first cousin, Princess Mary Adelaide of Cambridge, in 1866, and the daughter of that union, Mary of Teck, married the future King George V in 1893. Secondly there were the Battenbergs, descended from Prince Alexander of Hesse who had married a Polish commoner in 1851; two of their four sons, Louis and Henry, had taken British nationality and married respectively a granddaughter and a daughter of Queen Victoria in the 1870s, Louis of Battenberg becoming the senior serving officer of the Royal Navy and father of the future Lord Louis Mountbatten.

Thus morganatic controversies were nothing new to Edward VIII: his own mother, as well as one of the closest friends of his youth, had been born as the grandchildren of morganatic marriages, and he knew of the intense feelings of humiliation and embarrassment which both had experienced during their early lives as a result of their uncertain, semi-royal status. For him, both the word and the thing represented everything that was insulting and distasteful. The possibility of a morganatic marriage for himself had evidently crossed his mind long before Mrs Simpson broached the subject in the days after Wales: and it was not something he wished to envisage. On 17 November, he had told Duff Cooper that, if he remained King and married Mrs Simpson, she would have to be 'Queen or nothing'. If he now examined it as a political proposal which offered him a faint chance of saving his throne, he did so as a matter of duty and without enthusiasm.

The matter developed in the following way. One day, Mrs Simpson was invited to lunch at Claridge's

Edward VIII by
Ernest Fosbery, RCA

With Mrs Simpson,
June 1935

Walking behind the coffin of George V, 24 January 1936, with the Dukes of York and Gloucester

With the Life Guards at Windsor, 7 July 1936

Meeting tenants on the Duchy of Cornwall estate, 3 June 1936

Watching an RAF display at Northolt Aerodrome, 8 July 1936

At Royal Lodge, Windsor, with the Duke of York and the Princesses Elizabeth and Margaret Rose

Early morning constitutional in the Mall

With veterans (Alexander Hardinge is second from the right)

Chatting to station officials at Saraniovo, Bulgaria, 7 September 1936

Snapshots of the *Nahlin* Cruise, August 1936

On the Balmoral estate

Before the State Opening of Parliament, 3 November 1936, when the King was described as looking 'like a boy of eighteen'

With Queen Mary on Remembrance Day, 11 November 1936

With the unemployed
of South Wales,
18 November 1936

In the uniform of the
Seaforth Highlanders

by Esmond Harmsworth, Lord Rothermere's son and chief executive of his Associated Newspapers press empire centred on the *Daily Mail*. Still in his thirties, Harmsworth had for some time been on easy social terms with both the King and Mrs Simpson; he had been a guest at Balmoral in September and played a large role in the efforts to restrain the press over the divorce in October. There is some conflict about the precise date of this meeting; but a careful examination of the sources suggests that it took place on Thursday 19 November, the last day of the King's Welsh absence.* After some talk of the American publicity she had been receiving, Harmsworth told her that he knew the King wanted to marry her 'and of the difficulties involved', and asked her if she had given any thought to the idea of morganatic marriage. He himself had evidently looked closely into the subject, for he went on to explain the morganatic convention at some length, giving numerous examples. He concluded: 'I realize, Wallis, that all this is not very flattering to you. But I am sure you are one with us in desiring to keep the King on the throne.' Mrs Simpson found the idea 'astonishing' and said that

---

* According to the Duchess of Windsor's memoirs, the lunch took place while the King was still away, which would mean either Wednesday or Thursday. In his own memoirs, the King says that Mrs Simpson spoke to him about a morganatic marriage on the same afternoon as the Harmsworth lunch, which would mean that it took place at the earliest on Friday 20 November, since the King had not yet returned from Wales the previous afternoon. Lord Beaverbrook, in his memoir of the Abdication, says that the King told him the lunch occurred on Saturday 21 November. This however seems odd, for the King and Mrs Simpson were, as a rule, together at the Fort for Saturday lunch. On Monday, Channon recalled having seen Harmsworth and Mrs Simpson lunching at Claridge's 'a few days ago', which would seem to rule out Saturday and rather suggests Thursday, since Channon, again according to his diary, was recovering from an all-night sitting of the House of Commons on Wednesday, and in bed with a hangover on Friday.

she could not possibly express an opinion on it; but she accepted Harmsworth's suggestion that she put it to the King.[1]

In her memoirs, the Duchess of Windsor writes of Harmsworth's proposal as a bolt from the blue, a completely novel element in the situation. In fact, it was something which had been hotly discussed in London society ever since the divorce hearing at the end of October, which had led to the widespread belief in those circles that the King meant to marry her. In the week following Ipswich, Harold Nicolson, Victor Cazalet and Tom Jones had all mentioned it in their diaries as something which was being generally talked about.* Historians have speculated as to who first had the notion of suggesting it to Mrs Simpson. Harmsworth was apparently acting at the behest of his father[2]; who, then, had planted the idea in the head of Rothermere? Some ascribe the initiative to Rothermere's friend Collin Brooks (1893–1956), a writer and broadcaster who was at this time running a Rothermere-backed campaign in favour of rearmament.[3] Others attribute it to another friend of Rothermere, Winston Churchill. Leo Amery noted in his diary early in December: 'As for the suggestion of a [morganatic] compromise, Sam [Hoare] told me that this was really Winston's and confided to the King *via* Esmond Harmsworth. From all I hear then and since it is clear Winston has thought this a wonderful opportunity of scuppering B[aldwin] by the help of Harmsworth and Beaverbrook.'[4] It is difficult to say quite how closely Churchill was involved in putting the proposal up to the King; for political reasons, he did not afterwards wish to be known as a proponent of the morganatic marriage. But it is certain that Churchill, with his profound knowledge of history, had been giving active consideration to a

---

* See above, pp. 79–80.

morganatic solution*; and it is equally certain that Harmsworth made great play of Churchill's name as that of a political heavyweight who might be willing to champion the proposal, or even form an alternative government should Baldwin be driven to resign over the marriage issue.

Mrs Simpson (as she tells us) kept the Harmsworth meeting to herself until she was alone with the King at the Fort on the evening of Friday 20 November;† she then broached the subject 'with many misgivings'. Both their memoirs agree that the King's first reactions on hearing of the proposal were of extreme distaste. He winced at the very mention of the word, which 'repelled me as one of the least graceful that might be applied to the relations between men and women'. He told her that the result of the last such marriage in the British royal house, some ninety years earlier, had been 'lamentable'. This was probably a reference to the marriage in 1847 of his great-uncle, the 2nd Duke of Cambridge, to Miss Fairbrother, an actress who had already borne him two children and became known as Mrs FitzGeorge. It was not in fact morganatic but invalid under the Royal Marriages Act of 1772; but it was indeed an ominous portent of the sort of situation a morganatic marriage might create.

---

* The English historical model which Churchill especially had in mind was that of Caroline of Brunswick, consort of King George IV, who was considered unsuitable to fulfil the role of Queen when that sovereign (from whom she had long been estranged) came to the throne in 1820. Her name was omitted from the liturgy; she was not allowed to attend her husband's coronation; she continued to be known officially as Princess of Wales and Duchess of Cornwall. This was scarcely a very happy precedent; but what is interesting is that 'Queen' Caroline was effectively deprived of her regal rights and privileges without any reference to Parliament. (See Martin Gilbert, *Winston S. Churchill*, Companion Volume V, Part III, pp. 475–6.)

† They were joined there on the Saturday by two guests, George and Kitty Hunter.

The Duke – who became Commander-in-Chief of the British Army – enjoyed many years of tender happiness with his illicit consort, at whose death in 1890 he was broken-hearted; but he was compelled to lead a miserable double life in which the woman he adored received no social recognition and was unable to give him any support in his official role (in which he could have done with some, for he performed it clumsily). Recalling this unsatisfactory episode of family history, the King concluded: 'Whatever the outcome of our situation, I can't see a morganatic marriage as right for you.'[5]

Nevertheless, Mrs Simpson persisted with the idea in the course of the week-end, telling him 'that if there was the slightest possibility that Esmond Harmsworth's proposal might . . . keep him on the throne, it was our duty to consider it'. Finally the King agreed, 'wearily', to examine the matter, and arranged to see Harmsworth on Monday morning at Buckingham Palace.* There is no record of their interview, though Harmsworth almost certainly mentioned Churchill as one who believed in and might champion a morganatic solution.† In spite of continuing 'misgivings', the King consented to Harmsworth doing what he wished to do, which was to consult Baldwin about the morganatic scheme, and generally sound out opinion concerning it in senior political circles.[6] In this passive way, the King gave the scheme his approval. Harmsworth went to see Baldwin that same evening.

---

* Baldwin is reported as saying that Harmsworth had gone to see the King at the Fort; but Mrs Simpson says the meeting took place in London, and presumably she would have remembered if Harmsworth had come to the Fort.

† In his memoirs, the King does not mention Churchill at all in connection with the morganatic marriage. These memoirs, however, were published in 1951, when Churchill was about to return to power; and the Duke of Windsor was concerned to do nothing which might cause political embarrassment to his former supporter.

*

On Monday 23 and Tuesday 24 November, while he was awaiting the outcome of Harmsworth's consultations, the King himself had important communications in two quarters. First, he asked for advice on the morganatic question from Monckton, who was now his principal adviser in all constitutional matters. Monckton was discouraging, warning that 'even in the unlikely event of the Cabinet's approving a morganatic marriage, special legislation would be required and the prospects of such a Bill's ever passing Parliament were dubious'.[7] The King also asked Monckton two significant questions. Was there any means of getting the courts to make Mrs Simpson's divorce absolute immediately? And was it possible for him, without involving the Government and using his personal prerogative, to create Mrs Simpson a Duchess in her own right? In a handwritten letter dated 24 November, Monckton replied that, while some element of technical possibility existed in both instances, he did not believe that success could be achieved 'in the case we were discussing'.[8]* That the King asked these questions at all might seem to suggest that he was thinking of 'springing' a morganatic marriage on the Government. All one can say is that if he had wished to resort to subterfuge there were numerous other possibilities of which he never availed himself.

Secondly, it will be remembered that, at a private

---

* In his letter, Monckton wrote that there were exceptional precedents in which the court had granted an 'early' decree absolute – where a soldier husband awaiting divorce had to return to the front, for example – but that the proceeding took place in open court and was one in which the judge had complete discretion. And although the King was the 'fountain of honour' and theoretically conferred all titles, as a matter of constitutional practice peerages were now created by Letters Patent countersigned by a Secretary of State.

meeting on Tuesday 17 November, the King had told his brother the Duke of York of his decision to abdicate, but that the Duke had been too overcome with emotion to express himself on that occasion. On Monday 23 November, however, both the Duke and Duchess of York – who had probably heard by this time of the morganatic marriage proposal from the stream of Palace courtiers who kept them abreast of developments – wrote reassuring letters to the King from their residence at 145, Piccadilly, the general sense of which was that, if he wanted to leave in order to pursue his happiness, then they were ready to take over.

The Duke wrote that he had not meant to be unsympathetic when the King had told him of his decision to marry Mrs Simpson. It was true that the news had come to him as 'a great surprise', and he had not been able to express himself very well at the time. But he had been reflecting deeply, and absolutely wanted the King to find happiness 'with the one person you adore'. He was sure that whatever the King decided to do would be in the best interests of Country and Empire; and he would like to see the King to tell him all this personally.[9]

The Duchess wrote that 'Bertie' had been going through a difficult time, but that they both felt nothing except love and loyalty towards the King and concern for his happiness and welfare. She urged the King to be patient with the Duke during their forthcoming meeting, for there were important things the Duke wished to say, but he was too shy to express himself easily.[10]

On Tuesday 24 November the King and the Duke of York had their second meeting, which left the King with the reassurance that, upon his abdication, his brother would be prepared to undertake the succession.

In the view of the present writer, the King never expected or even hoped for much from the morganatic proposal; it was something he went along with half-heartedly and mainly for the reason that it had become dear to the heart of Mrs Simpson. Yet there were many in influential social, intellectual and political circles who favoured it, whether to prevent the King from abdicating or Mrs Simpson from becoming Queen of England. This is clear from the writings of diarists; and it is also clear from the attitude of the press when it started to discuss the crisis two weeks later: the morganatic marriage was supported by the main Catholic daily, the main Nonconformist daily, and such serious periodicals as the *New Statesman*. And Harmsworth, in his general conversations, discovered important potential supporters of all political shades: among those who 'saw possibilities' in the morganatic solution were the Conservative Duff Cooper, the Liberal Lord Lothian, and Julius Elias, the self-made printing tycoon who published the Labour *Daily Herald*.[11]*

But any chance that the proposal would find official favour was prejudiced at the outset by an extraordinarily inept action of Harmsworth himself. On Monday 23 November, undoubtedly with Harmsworth's full knowledge and approval if not at his instigation, a leading article about the King appeared in the *Daily Mail* – an article which Dawson of *The Times* considered 'outrageous', and even the King's unconditional partisan Chips Channon thought 'so fulsome and exaggerated as to be almost dangerous'.[12] Entitled *The King Edward Touch*, it began by giving a glowing account of the sovereign's visit to South Wales the previous week, and went on to contrast his solicitude and energy with the indifference and lethargy of the Government.

The royal technique repays study. In the first place he approached the difficulties of South Wales resolute to find

* When the storm broke, however, Elias fell in with the position of the Labour leaders and supported the Government. For this turn-around he was rewarded with a peerage in the Coronation honours of 1937. (See R. J. Minney, *Viscount Southwood* (1954), pp. 287–93.)

a remedy however novel the methods of treatment might be. He went to see for himself, personal investigation being the basis of every job of work the King touches . . . The contrast . . . can escape nobody. There is consultation, committees are appointed and conferences take place in the solemn apartments of Whitehall, but how often does a Minister . . . go boldly forth to see for himself and measure the problem with independent judgment, following this with action? . . . Even such deadweight lethargy as surrounds Britain's most vital need — rearmament — would yield to the King Edward touch.

Surely those who have recently confessed that they dared not tell the people the truth three years ago and have accomplished so little towards defence will realise the gulf between their conduct and the King's methods in Wales.

This last paragraph was a dig at Baldwin, who in a painful performance in the House of Commons only eleven days previously had admitted with 'appalling frankness' that the Government had misled the public in matters of defence and rearmament in order to win the 1935 General Election.

It was on the Monday that this leader appeared that Harmsworth saw the King at the Palace in the morning and Baldwin at Downing Street in the evening. Possibly the purpose of the piece had been to 'soften' the King towards Harmsworth's proposal. It may or may not have had this effect; but what is certain is that it scuppered any possibility that the morganatic plan might receive a sympathetic hearing from the Prime Minister, who now saw Harmsworth as one of the moving figures in a 'King's Party' determined to exploit the marriage question in order to embarrass the Government politically. As Baldwin complained to Tom Jones: 'There is a "set" which is backing the marriage. I don't know but I suspect that the Beaverbrook–Rothermere press will take that line . . . The *Daily Mail* is flying kites over the South Wales visit but really with the marriage business in mind . . . You can see what they are up to . . . ' He added that Churchill had refused to join the deputation of privy councillors who had seen him the previous week to express their anxiety; 'and you may be sure he is in . . . on this and does not feel about it as we do . . . '[13]

Thus it was a wary and hostile Baldwin who received Harmsworth on the evening of Monday 23 November. He had received advance warning of the subject of the visit from his friend John Davidson, Chancellor of the Duchy of Lancaster, who noted afterwards with sarcasm: 'We discussed the matter, and tried to picture the scene in the House of Commons when SB had to explain why Mrs Simpson was good enough to be the King's wife but not good enough to be Queen . . . '[14] In a conversation with his niece, Baldwin later had the following to say about his interview with Harmsworth:

> . . . I told him that he and his filthy paper did not really *know* the mind of the English people: whereas I *did*. And I explained to him that a morganatic marriage would mean a special Bill being passed in Parliament; and that Parliament would *never* pass it. Harmsworth said: 'Oh, I'm sure they would. The whole standard of morals is so much more broadminded since the War.' I replied: 'Yes, you are right: the ideal of morality . . . certainly *has* gone down since the War: but the ideal of Kingship has gone up . . . '[15]

When Harmsworth had gone, Davidson reappeared and Baldwin said to him: 'He wants Mrs Simpson to be a Duchess – not to be royal, but less than royal, but rather better than an ordinary Duchess.'[16] In private conversations with Duff Cooper and Tom Jones during the next two days, Baldwin made clear his 'strong opposition' to the proposal and his 'great hostility' to Harmsworth. He declared he would be unable to carry the Commons on the proposal and would resign rather than attempt to do so. 'Is this the sort of thing I've stood for in public life?' he remarked bitterly to Jones. 'If I have to go out, as go I must, then I'd be quite ready to go out on this.'[17]

While waiting for the King to make a formal move on the new proposal, Baldwin addressed himself to the political challenge to the Government implied by the salvo in the *Daily Mail*. On the night of the 23rd, after seeing Harmsworth, he received Geoffrey Dawson, and approved a strongly worded leader which Dawson had written as a direct reply to the *Mail* leader. This appeared in *The Times* the following day:

> It is right that the King's contribution . . . should be applauded. But it is a wholly mischievous suggestion . . . which would set his well-known sympathy with the distressed areas against the measures taken by the Government . . . The King's Ministers are His Majesty's advisers, and to contrast his personal and representative concern with the well-being of a section of his people with the administrative steps of his advisers is a constitutionally dangerous proceeding which would threaten, if continued, to entangle the throne in politics.

Baldwin then turned to the parliamentary opposition to discover what their attitude would be in the event of a clash with the King over the marriage question. On the morning of Wednesday 25 November, amid great secrecy, he invited Attlee, the Liberal leader Sinclair, and Churchill to Downing Street to discuss the crisis. At this meeting, the Labour and Liberal leaders (though there were many in their ranks who would shortly emerge as 'King's men') both affirmed that, if Baldwin were driven to resign over the royal marriage, they would support him and decline to form an alternative administration. Churchill replied more cautiously that 'though his attitude was a little different, he would certainly support the Government'.[18] In this way, Baldwin safeguarded his political rear before his next meeting with the King.

Meanwhile, the King had been awaiting Harmsworth's

report. According to his memoirs, Harmsworth eventually returned with the news that Baldwin's reaction to the morganatic proposal had been 'surprised, interested and non-committal'; that he had promised to refer the plan to the Cabinet; and that he had said nothing more.[19] In writing his memoirs, the King was relying on a fallible memory; and if this was all Harmsworth reported he had not been entirely frank, for though Baldwin may have guarded himself from expressing outright hostility to the morganatic plan when he saw Harmsworth on 23 November, he had certainly expressed a measure of doubt. Nevertheless, the King took the step of summoning Baldwin to an audience at the Palace on Wednesday evening.

A couple of hours before he was due to present himself at this audience, Baldwin convened another meeting of the inner 'group of five' – Chamberlain, Halifax, MacDonald, Runciman and Simon – to tell them of the Harmsworth initiative and also of his secret talks that morning with opposition leaders. He confided to the group his unease about Churchill, whom he suspected of being 'mysteriously in the background' of the Harmsworth plan. The ministers agreed that 'we must act cautiously, and find out the attitude of . . . Dominions before committing ourselves. S.B. should point out various difficulties but not turn anything down'.[20]

The third meeting that autumn between the King and the Prime Minister took place at six-thirty on the evening of Wednesday 25 November. Of their eight meetings, it is the least documented and also appears to have been the shortest. Baldwin gave a brief account of it to the House of Commons in the debate on the Abdication Bill, to which the King had not much to add in his memoirs.

I asked him at once what he thought of the Harmsworth proposal. Slowly and with careful attention to his words, Mr Baldwin replied that he had not yet considered it.

I must have registered surprise: for after an uncomfortable pause, Mr Baldwin added that he had not meant to give the impression that the proposition had been ignored, but only that he was not yet ready to render a considered judgment. If, however, I desired a 'horseback opinion', he would have to tell me that Parliament would never pass the necessary legislation.

'Are you sure that it wouldn't, Mr Baldwin?' I asked.

'Sir, would you like me to examine the proposition formally?' he asked.

'Yes, please do so,' I answered.

The Prime Minister then reminded me that this meant submitting the morganatic proposal not only to the British Cabinet but to all the Dominion Cabinets as well. 'Do you really wish that, Sir?'

My answer was that I did. Thereupon the Prime Minister hurried off . . . [21]

At the cabinet which took place two days later, Baldwin is reported to have described the meeting in somewhat more colourful language. The King had declared 'that he would have the sympathy and support of a very large part of the people, and that while he realised that they might be unwilling to accept her as Queen, they would accept a morganatic marriage if the Government were willing to introduce legislation authorising it'. To which Baldwin had replied bluntly 'that if he thought he was going to get away with it in that way he was making a huge mistake'.[22]

A curious point is that the King agreed Baldwin should consult the Dominion premiers. As the Statute of Westminster had recognized in 1932, the Dominion Governments were no longer responsible to the British Government, to which they were now linked only by sentiment and the Crown; and the natural constitutional course would have been for the King to consult them himself through his personal representatives, the governors-general. But the King writes in his memoirs that he was 'loath to employ this channel. The matter was much too personal, too delicate to be handled by the King himself.' He thus passed over, whether deliberately or carelessly, a golden opportunity to put his own case. But it was clearly Baldwin in the first place who asked to undertake the Dominion enquiries: that he should do so had (according to Chamberlain's diary) been envisaged at the 'group of five' meeting earlier that day.

Only one other remark is recorded. According to Baldwin's official biographer, G.M. Young, the Prime Minister warned the King that 'his popularity could not protect Mrs Simpson if the fury of the people was once aroused'. This, Baldwin told a friend, 'was the only time that something like anger' showed itself in their talks.[23] Baldwin, however, was well-informed: within forty-eight hours, the hostility of those Londoners who knew of her existence had driven Mrs Simpson to leave the capital for good.*

The morganatic proposal is important in the history of the reign for two reasons. First, it significantly altered the attitude of Baldwin. Partisans of the King who afterwards wrote about the crisis, and indeed the King himself in his memoirs (which were deeply influenced by Beaverbrook), tend to portray Baldwin as out from the start to get rid of Edward VIII in order to advance his own political interests.[24] With what we now know, it is difficult to sustain this view. It is true that one cannot read too much into Baldwin's initial reluctance to confront the King about the marriage, for it was his method to ignore any crisis until it had become acute and then tackle it vigorously. But up to 16 November, there is ample evidence that he hoped the King would give up Mrs Simpson and remain. Even after the fateful meeting that day, at which the King had declared his intention of marrying and leaving, he probably still hoped the sovereign would change his mind. But now that his bitterest enemies, Rothermere and Churchill,

---

* See below, pp. 155–8.

appeared to have sponsored a solution which would enable the King to marry and to stay, Baldwin changed his position and henceforth appears to have been concerned that abdication should take place as quickly and with as little debate as possible.

And the morganatic marriage itself gave him his opportunity. For the second point is that the proposal finally turned the marriage question into an official matter, to be formally considered by the British and Dominion Cabinets whose advice the King was bound to follow. Up to that point, the King's contacts with the Prime Minister had been of a private and informal nature; and his remarks on 16 November that he was prepared to abdicate amounted to no more than an informal declaration of intention. It was not easy to see how the question could be officially brought before the Cabinet until the King made some other move. Now he had made such a move, by asking that the morganatic proposal be placed before his Governments at home and overseas. Thus the proposal, far from delaying or impeding the process of abdication, hastened it along by starting the constitutional machinery moving. The King himself seems to have been aware of this. He wrote of the interview with Baldwin:

> . . . As the door closed behind him I realised that with that simple request I had gone a long way towards sealing my own fate. For in asking the Prime Minister to find out the sentiments of the British and Dominion Governments, I had automatically bound myself to submit unquestioningly to their 'advice'.[25]

Some authorities question whether he understood quite so clearly the position into which he had now put himself. But he certainly understood it the following day, for Beaverbrook then put these aspects to him very forcefully, but without, as we shall see, moving the sovereign to alter the stand he had taken.

The question remains. Did the King seriously believe in morganatic marriage as a desirable and realistic project which offered some means of his retaining his throne? Or did he go along with it merely to appease Mrs Simpson, or possibly even as a means to abdication?

Baldwin, rattled as he was by the element of political controversy introduced by Harmsworth, certainly thought that the proposal represented a change of heart on the King's part, that he was in effect reconsidering his decision. This is what he was to tell the Cabinet. To Tom Jones he said, early on 25 November before he had seen the King:

> . . . The King agreed to go quietly, and he afterwards told his mother and brother. But he has clearly now gone back on that. Mrs S. was down at Fort Belvedere over the week-end and has talked him out of it, because on Friday he was where I left him. Walter Monckton wrote telling me that, with the King's knowledge . . . *

And the King, in his memoirs, does indeed imply that he had come to believe in the morganatic solution. In spite of his 'earlier misgivings', he was 'at this stage . . . ready to welcome any reasonable suggestion that offered hope of allowing me to marry on the throne without precipitating a political struggle'. He reflected that it was 'not the form but the content of things that matters'; he was sure that, 'even without the formal symbolism of the two gilt thrones side by side', Mrs Simpson could play a proper role as his consort. He admits he was pessimistic about the chances of securing the necessary legislation, a point confirmed by Monckton.[26] Yet according to Beaverbrook, the ex-sovereign is said to have remarked to one of the aides who accompanied him into exile that he had always thought he could 'get away with the morganatic marriage'.[27]

But Beaverbrook wrote with the passionate and

---

* See above, p. 124.

indeed reproachful conviction of one who believed that the King should have fought for his throne, and that by the morganatic proposal he had ruined his chances. And the King himself, writing after a dozen years, may have taken a distorted view of a past which he did not fully remember. For all the circumstances, if one examines them closely, point to the conclusion that his heart was not in the plan at all. The sheer carelessness (one can find no other word) with which he invited Harmsworth to carry out his informal consultations, and then Baldwin to proceed with his formal political enquiries; his invitation to the Prime Minister to consult the Dominion premiers, when one of his few trump cards was his right to communicate with these men himself; his insistence on going ahead after being warned by Beaverbrook that the proposal would make abdication more and not less imminent; his refusal to allow his press allies to make any public appeal in favour of the proposal – all suggest that he did not really desire a morganatic marriage, and just wanted to be done with the whole thing.

One thing above all confirms this view. Ironically, the marriage which the Duke of Windsor did contract the following June was in nature morganatic. By Letters Patent issued in the name of George VI on 27 May 1937 (the legality of which has been much disputed), it was provided that he should remain royal, but that his future wife and children should be unable to share his royal attributes. The Duchess of Windsor thus became the only wife of an Englishman in recent centuries not to share her husband's rank. For the ex-King, this was a festering wound which blighted the rest of his life. That the wife he adored should not be permitted to share his status he found humiliating and at times insupportable. He strove constantly but in vain to have the edict reversed: the consequence was a bitter and permanent estrangement from his family. During one of his revisionary efforts, in April 1949, he personally visited the Lord Chancellor, Lord Jowitt (who had in fact, as a barrister in private practice in 1937, advised him that the Letters Patent were legally invalid), in order to plead his cause. In his note of the conversation, Jowitt wrote:

> He [the Duke] said that the position which had arisen was exactly what would have happened had there been a morganatic marriage; and this was exactly the position which Mr Baldwin had said was impossible in this country; *and was a position to which the Duke of Windsor, when King, would never have assented.*[28]

Chapter Eight

An Official Matter

26 November–2 December

On the morning following the King's third meeting
with Baldwin, the morning of Thursday 26 November,
Beaverbrook arrived back in England. At the urgent
behest of the King, who had wished to consult him on
receiving Hardinge's letter on the 13th, he had confined
his stay in New York to the daylight hours and returned
by the same boat. He drove directly to the Fort, where
the King had ordered a lunch to conform with his latest
diet. 'You have done a fine thing by me', said the King
on greeting him, 'and I shall always remember it.'[1]

Beaverbrook's motives in rallying to the King have
been much debated. Randolph Churchill later claimed
he was out 'to bugger Baldwin' (whom he certainly
hated), and Beaverbrook himself said afterwards in
casual chat that he had regarded the whole affair as
'just a bit of fun'. Yet men who knew him also detected
a romantic motive. 'I do not think his pro-King attitude
was inspired entirely by his anti-Baldwinism', wrote
Bruce-Lockhart on 9 December. 'I think the King "got"
him, and the little man, taken up for the first time by
royalty, saw himself as a crusader defending his monarch when men of much better blood had "ratted".'[2]
Whatever the force that drove him, Beaverbrook's intervention is historically important for two reasons. His
very appearance on the scene was calculated to rattle
Baldwin and his colleagues and increase their desire
to see the King go quickly; and there is the significant

fact that the King, having obtained the services of this energetic and resourceful ally, proceeded to ignore his advice.

While Beaverbrook ate his lunch at the Fort that Thursday, the King gave a detailed account of events. Beaverbrook listened intently; but when the King came to his interview with Baldwin the previous evening, and request that the morganatic marriage proposal be placed before the Cabinet, his 'face darkened'.[3] He urged the King to withdraw the proposal at once. As he later wrote:

> The request for permission to make a morganatic marriage would place the King in the hands of Baldwin and the politicians. The politicians had no status at all in the main issue of the marriage. The King was free to marry whom he chose and the Government had no power to forbid it.*
>
> But he was not free to make a morganatic marriage, because such a marriage was unknown to English law, and could only be made possible by Act of Parliament . . . and only the Prime Minister could grant or refuse parliamentary time for the necessary bill.

While recommending that the King withdraw the morganatic marriage proposal, Beaverbrook made two other suggestions: that the King find 'some friend in

---

* This proposition has been debated. The Attorney-General, Sir Donald Somervell, advised Baldwin that it would be unconstitutional for the sovereign to marry contrary to the advice of his ministers: he based himself on the fact that Queen Victoria, at the time of her marriage, had sought the approval of Lord Melbourne. However, the Government would certainly have found it extremely difficult to offer advice, or threaten resignation, merely on the basis of the King having informally intimated to the Prime Minister that he hoped at some time to marry a woman who was not yet free to marry him. In this sense, the King's formal request for 'morganatic' legislation was certainly, as Beaverbrook argued, playing into the hands of those who sought his departure.

the Cabinet who would represent his case', and that he 'measure the strength on either side' before allowing the Cabinet 'to reach any decision'. Beaverbrook offered to undertake the necessary consultations himself in conjunction with Monckton. The King appeared to be convinced by Beaverbrook's arguments, and invited him to go ahead.[4]

Beaverbrook hurried back to London. That afternoon he went to see Monckton, who appeared to agree that the morganatic marriage idea would not improve the King's chances. He also spoke on the telephone with Churchill, who was shooting with the Duke of Westminster near Chester; Churchill supported the morganatic plan ('I don't see any other way') and indeed admitted to having been involved in putting it up to the King, but was nevertheless eager to join forces with Beaverbrook in an effort to save the sovereign.[5] Beaverbrook then talked to Sir Samuel Hoare, who was the man he had in mind to put forward the King's point of view in the Cabinet. This might seem strange, since Hoare had seen the King nine days previously and given him no comfort or support. But Hoare, as some historians believe, had for years been secretly in Beaverbrook's pay and quietly passing him inside information on the doings of the Government; he may therefore have been a man upon whom Beaverbrook felt he could put pressure. How Hoare reacted to what was proposed is not entirely clear from the available sources.[6] * It is certain, however, that he promised to keep Beaverbrook closely informed of developments in the Government quarter.

---

* Beaverbrook writes that Hoare simply refused, at this meeting, to take the King's side. But Beaverbrook's memoir of the Abdication, written some years later, is extremely muddled as to dates and the sequence of events; and the picture given by Hoare in some contemporary (but perhaps deliberately not very comprehensible) notes is that he seriously considered what he calls Beaverbrook's 'offer', but changed his mind during the cabinet meeting the following day.

Beaverbrook prepared to continue his efforts to rally support for the King. But in the early hours of Friday morning, the King telephoned Beaverbrook at his London residence, Stornoway House in Green Park, to say that, on reflection, he had decided not to withdraw the morganatic marriage proposal, which remained the solution most favoured by Mrs Simpson. As the King wrote, he had come to the conclusion that Beaverbrook's strategy 'would involve me in a long course of seeming dissimulation for which I had neither the talent nor the appetite'.[7]

When he received the King's nocturnal call, Beaverbrook 'knew my warnings were in vain'.[8] The King had consulted Beaverbrook, as he had consulted Cooper, because he possessed a deep psychological urge to explain himself to his friends and hear their salutary advice. But he did not mean to accept such advice, for the evident reason that he did not wish to be saved.

Beaverbrook's meeting with the King on Thursday and subsequent conversations that day did have one result, however. They startled Baldwin into bringing forward and giving a new urgency to the cabinet meeting which, at the King's request, he had agreed to call to discuss the morganatic marriage proposal. On Thursday evening an emergency Cabinet was summoned for the following morning. Several ministers were out of town and were ordered to return immediately from their provincial engagements.

The Cabinet met in the Prime Minister's room at the House of Commons at half past eleven on the morning of Friday 27 November, and remained in session for an hour and a quarter. Baldwin began by emphasizing the great secrecy of the proceedings: no agenda had been circulated, and the lobby correspondents had been told that the subject of the meeting was the Spanish Civil War. He then outlined the whole story of his dealings with the King that autumn, describing their meetings

of 20 October and 16 November in much the same
terms as he was later to use explaining the affair to the
House of Commons.[9] This, of course, was not news to
the inner 'group of five' whom Baldwin had taken into
his confidence over the previous three weeks, or to
Hoare and Cooper who had been consulted by the King
himself; but other ministers were stunned. 'I have seldom heard a more dramatic narrative', wrote Zetland,
Secretary of State for India, to the Viceroy Linlithgow.
' . . . I ask myself if these things are really happening,
or if they are of the stuff that dreams are made of, the
insubstantial phantasmagoria of some incredible form
of mass hallucination . . . '[10]

Baldwin continued that up to the previous Sunday
the King had seemed determined to go quietly and
make things as easy as possible for his successor; 'but
that day he changed his mind apparently under advice
given by her or someone behind her, and he wished the
Cabinet to be consulted as to whether legislation allowing a morganatic marriage could be introduced and
carried'.[11] He described their meeting of the 25th and
said he would shortly be seeing the King again, whose
'present intention seemed to be to refuse to withdraw
from his position'. Baldwin did not himself condemn
the morganatic marriage proposal in so many words,
and stressed that the Cabinet were not yet being asked
for a decision. But he clearly expressed his worries
about the political controversy that was developing.
He spoke 'with great contempt' of Harmsworth. He
mentioned the criticism of the King's visit to Wales,
reporting the remark of a Labour member: 'Are we to
have a fascist monarchy?'[12] He pointed out that the
King's latest request

might involve the resignation of the Government and that
in this case it would give rise to a Constitutional Crisis
of the first magnitude, viz the King v. the Government.
It seems that the King has been encouraged to believe
that Winston Churchill would in these circumstances
be prepared to form an alternative Government. If this

were true there would be a grave risk of the country being divided into two camps – for and against the King. This clearly would be fraught with danger of the most formidable kind.[13]

Baldwin confirmed, however, that Attlee had promised his support in the event of such a crisis.

There was 'very little discussion' after the Prime Minister had spoken. Almost everyone seemed to agree that a morganatic marriage was 'unthinkable'.[14] MacDonald thought it 'degrading to women' and 'offensive to the country'.[15] Chamberlain felt sure that 'if it were possible to arrange the morganatic marriage this would only be the prelude to the further step of making Mrs S. Queen with full rights'.[16] Hoare remained silent: in his contemporary notes, he infers that he had now changed his mind about putting forward the King's view.[17] Only Duff Cooper spoke up for the sovereign. He did not in fact support the proposal, but pleaded that they should give the King time. He said that, when 'the wrong people' wanted to marry in ordinary private life, it was usual to allow them a year to change their minds. The King had already abandoned his position that Mrs Simpson should be Queen; perhaps, given time, he would change his mind about marrying her too.[18] It would be dangerous to put him under pressure: it was not impossible that he might commit suicide if 'by her action or ours he could not marry her'.[19] Baldwin, however, said frankly that 'he thought the situation had gone too far to admit of any postponement'; and most of the Cabinet seemed to agree.[20]

The matter of sending consultative telegrams to the Dominion prime ministers was also discussed by the Cabinet, and the drafting of these documents was entrusted to a committee of ministers and civil servants which met twice over the next twenty-four hours, the telegrams being approved and signed by Baldwin and despatched from the Dominions Office on Saturday the 28th. It is questionable whether this was a strictly constitutional proceeding, since these consultations theoretically involved Baldwin as the personal agent of the King and not in his role as head of the British Government.[21] There has been much debate as to whether Baldwin actively connived at getting the responses the Government wanted and therefore hostile to the King's wishes. Anthony Eden wrote that the telegrams were 'worded with a scrupulous impartiality, which would have defied the reader to guess the judgment of the Government at home'. According to Hoare's notes, the first draft produced by the committee spoke of Mrs Simpson's dubious moral character and merely asked whether she ought to be allowed to marry the King morganatically.[22] In the final version, however, these 'moral' comments were omitted. After describing the essence of his three interviews with the King, Baldwin concluded that in his opinion

> there is not any possibility of dissuading the King from this marriage if decree is made absolute and such a course does not therefore appear to form one of the practicable alternatives in front of us . . . In my consideration of the question it would be very helpful to me if as soon as possible I could have your personal view and what in your opinion would be view of the public opinion in your Dominion regarding three following possibilities: (i) marriage of His Majesty to Mrs Simpson, she to become Queen; (ii) King's marriage to Mrs Simpson without his abdication but on basis that she should not become Queen and accompanied by necessary legislation; (iii) a voluntary abdication in favour of Duke of York . . . [23]

It will be noted that these enquiries were represented as being not at the behest of the King but for the political information of the British Government. And in the days that followed, intense behind-the-scenes efforts were made to ensure that the Dominion replies harmonized with the position of the British Government. We know that Baldwin himself made personal representations in certain quarters which affected at least the Canadian and New Zealand replies. In the case of Ireland, the Permanent Secretary at the Dominions Office personally visited De Valera (who originally saw no objection to the King's marriage) to plead with him for the reply desired. The Attorney-General, Sir Donald Somervell, wrote in his memoir that 'in the crisis I spent most of my time with Malcolm MacDonald [Dominions Secretary] over the intricate problem of getting the Dominion to agree a course of action'[24]; and Malcolm MacDonald himself has written that 'it was vital that [the Dominion prime ministers] should reach quickly, spontaneously [sic] and unanimously the same conclusion about the constitutional solution'.[25]

It was therefore the case that the Dominion enquiries were not in the least impartial, but a political canvassing operation in favour of abdication. This was doubtless a course of political wisdom for those, including the Prime Minister, who were concerned with imperial unity and a smooth outcome of the crisis. But if the King realized in time what was happening, would he try to stop Baldwin's telegrams and send his own?

As soon as the cabinet of 27 November was over, Hoare lunched with Beaverbrook at Stornoway House and gave a full report of the proceedings, making it clear that he could not now act for the King. This report confirmed Beaverbrook's fears that the King had destroyed his chances by placing his future at the mercy of a cabinet decision. And he was particularly shocked to learn that Baldwin had been entrusted with the reference to the Dominions: this was something which the King had apparently omitted to mention at lunch the previous day.[26]

Beaverbrook asked for an immediate audience with the King, and arrived at Buckingham Palace that afternoon in a state of 'unusual agitation'. 'Sir, you have put your head on the execution block', he exclaimed.

153

'All Baldwin has to do now is to swing the axe.'[27] He asserted that the King had made a potentially fatal error in asking Baldwin to consult Dominion opinion: his only hope lay in 'sending out his own question, framed in his own terms, in the manner most favourable to himself'. He begged the King to stop Baldwin's telegrams to the Dominion premiers, which were at that moment being drafted, and insist upon his rights. As a Canadian, Beaverbrook knew that the replies, under the circumstances of the moment, could only be unfavourable.[28]

The King's reaction, however, was to Beaverbrook 'profoundly unsatisfactory'. To be sure, he admitted the justice of Beaverbrook's arguments. He agreed that Baldwin's telegrams 'were hardly likely to be compassionate pleas on behalf of my proposal'. Nevertheless, he refused to stop them. He felt that

> matters had already progressed much too far for me to wish [sic] to reverse the Government machinery. The die was cast; I was impatient for the answer from the Dominions.[29]

But one can only conclude that the King was impatient, not so much to see the Dominion replies, but to abdicate. For not only did he refuse to stop the telegrams: he did not even ask to see them. Yet he had an absolute right to be shown them and approve them, for in this matter the Prime Minister was acting on behalf of the sovereign personally. Nor was the King shown the minutes of the cabinet of 27 November – though here again it was his constitutional right to be kept informed.* Here is further evidence that, by

---

* 'The following [Saturday] morning I waited anxiously for the arrival of the red box containing the secret minutes of the Cabinet Meeting. I opened it myself with the gold key that had been my father's. But the solitary paper that I found inside, purporting to describe the momentous discussions of the day, was blank except for a perfunctory paragraph relating to the carriage of arms to Spain' (A King's Story, p. 346).

the last days of November, the Government wished to get rid of the King, and the King (*pace* the morganatic marriage proposal) did not wish to stay.

'All classes now know about the affair', wrote Marie Belloc Lowndes to a friend on Thursday 26 November, 'and Mrs Simpson receives by every post frightful letters from religious lunatics threatening to kill her. She is closely guarded, and goes practically nowhere.'[30] There was a permanent knot of curious and sometimes hostile gapers outside the house in Cumberland Terrace where she continued to live with her aunt, and even shopping had become difficult for her.

On the evening of Thursday the 26th, Mrs Simpson made what was to be her last appearance in London society, when she dined without the King at the house in Belgrave Square of Lord Stanley, a junior member of the Government.* Chips Channon found her 'charming, sweet and gay, and we had a semi-confidential talk about dictators, communism, and how much we both disliked Americans'. But there was an element of sadness: she confessed 'that she had not dared to be funny for three years'; and when it was suggested that she move to Belgravia for the Coronation, she became mysteriously silent. Did she believe she would be installed at the Palace at the time? wondered Channon. Or was it that she would not be in England at all? [31]

The following morning – the Friday morning on which the Cabinet discussed the crisis – Mrs Simpson received by hand a note from the King (the original of which has not been found among her papers in Paris) saying (as she recalled in her memoirs) 'that

---

* Under Secretary for the Dominions and a Member of Parliament.

he thought it would be wiser if Aunt Bessie and I got out of London for a bit and stayed at the Fort, where we should not be bothered. He added that he would pick us up in his car in the late afternoon and in a PS advised that I instruct the servants not to disclose our whereabouts.'[32] Mrs Simpson duly cancelled a dinner party she had planned to give at Cumberland Terrace that evening, telling her friends that she was feeling ill owing to the strain of recent events and had been ordered to take a week's complete rest.[33] (This was surely not far from the truth.) At six o'clock, accompanied by Mrs Merryman and enough luggage for a week, she drove off with the King to the Fort, never to see pre-war London again.

Undoubtedly the King's main reason for removing Mrs Simpson from the capital was his concern about her safety and health and the strain under which she had been living: the latest anonymous letters spoke of a plot to blow up her house. But he may have had another reason. His partisans were about to make a concerted effort to get her to leave him or otherwise force him to change his plans. Possibly he feared or suspected this, and therefore wanted her under his protection and supervision during the coming days.

But her removal to the Fort had another effect. Her isolation there (for there were now no guests other than her aunt) gave her an opportunity for calm self-examination; and she finally decided that she must do what she had wished to do ever since mid-September, and disappear abroad and from the King's life as soon as possible. This decision she expressed in confidential letters which she sent on the last day of November to some of her best friends in London. To Sibyl Colefax she wrote on Monday the 30th:

> I am very tired with and of it all – and my heart resents the strain – so I am to lie quiet . . . I am planning quite by myself to go away for a while. I think everyone here would like that – except one person perhaps – but I am planning a clever means of escape. After a while my name

will be forgotten by the people and only two people will suffer instead of the mass of people who aren't interested anyway in individual feelings but only the workings of a system. I have decided to risk the result of leaving because it is an uncomfortable feeling to be stopping in a house where the hostess has tired of you as a guest . . .

The mention of 'the result of leaving' refers to what Mrs Simpson had told Lady Colefax on 8 November – that if she abandoned the King he might go to pieces or try to follow her.* To an old American friend, 'Foxy' Gwynne,† she wrote on the same day: 'Everything is wrong and going more wrong – and I am so tired of it all . . . I think I shall remove myself when I am well enough for a small trip and give it all time to die down – perhaps returning when that d–d crown has been firmly placed.'[34]

Mrs Simpson had been considering flight for ten weeks. In September she had written to the King from Paris pleading for separation, saying they could 'only create disaster' together; in October she had written from Ipswich of abandoning her divorce and 'stealing quietly away'; in mid-November she had wanted to follow Hardinge's advice to leave the country. Now at last she was determined to go.

On Monday 30 November, while Mrs Simpson was screwing her courage to the sticking point of leaving, Beaverbrook had his third and, as it turned out, final personal interview with the sovereign he was trying to

---

* See above, pp. 87–8.
† Mrs Erskine Gwynne, known as 'Foxy' because of her red hair, whom Mrs Simpson had befriended in Washington after the First World War. She married the Earl of Sefton, a friend of the Duke of Windsor, in 1940.

save. He reported that he had seen Hoare the previous evening, who had confirmed that the Cabinet was united behind Baldwin: ' . . . no breach exists: there is no light or leaning in the King's direction'. Hoare had also warned that the newspapers were likely to break the news before long, and that Baldwin was anxious that the press should stand unanimously behind the Government. Beaverbrook, however, had made it clear that he stood behind the King. 'I have taken the King's shilling', he said. 'I am a King's man.'[35]

The King was touched by this demonstration of loyalty; and Beaverbrook made yet another effort to get him to give up his intention to abdicate. But the King merely repeated over and over again: 'Mrs Simpson will not be abandoned.' Beaverbrook continued to argue at great length, urging the King to send a message to Baldwin (whom Monckton was seeing that evening) to the effect that he no longer wished to receive any advice from the Government on the subject of his marriage. In his memoirs, Beaverbrook states that the King finally agreed to send such a message; but this sounds most improbable – he had, after all, most definitely refused to call off either the morganatic marriage proposal or Baldwin's 'Dominion' enquiries – and it is certain in any event that the King continued to make quite clear to the Prime Minister that there was no question of his giving up the idea of marriage with Mrs Simpson.[36] The King did, however, agree to Beaverbrook seeing Churchill and reporting his royal conversations, which Beaverbrook did later that day.

Now Beaverbrook resolved on a new plan of campaign – and this plan was henceforth to set the tone for all efforts to 'save' the King. Since the King had proved unamenable to the persuasion of his friends, it seemed evident that only Mrs Simpson herself could talk him out of marriage. That Monday night, following his third meeting with the King and his talk (of which there is no known record) with Churchill, Beaverbrook gave a dinner at Stornoway House for some of the men who at that moment were closest to the sovereign.* Among those present were Monckton, Allen, Harmsworth and Brownlow. Brownlow reported the substance of the meeting to Lady Honor Channon, who in turn repeated it to her husband Chips, who noted in his diary the following day:

They were all in agreement that the marriage cannot be allowed to take place, and that the only avenue of approach to the demented lovesick sovereign was Wallis Simpson herself. And they bullied Perry Brownlow into promising to see Wallis today, and warn her confidentially that the country will not accept the marriage, and that she must go away for a few weeks, and allow the talk to simmer down, and put all thoughts of marriage out of the King's mind. Perry reluctantly but very patriotically agreed . . .

These men could hardly have realized that Mrs Simpson herself had that same day come to an identical conclusion. But when, on the morning of Tuesday 1 December, Brownlow tried to get in touch with Mrs Simpson, he was unable to do so. She was at the Fort; she was not well; the King was with her; he refused to allow her to take any telephone calls.[37]

Though the silence of the press continued, it had by now become extremely fragile. Rumours of marriage and abdication, of grave meetings between sovereign and Prime Minister, ministers and civil servants, were

---

* In their memoirs, written many years afterwards, Beaverbrook and the King both describe this gathering as having taken place on the night of Wednesday 2 December. However, Channon writes of it on 1 December as having occurred the night before; and if his journal is authentic this must be correct.

now so abundant that 'the King's matter' (as the Archbishop of Canterbury termed it) was certain to become public property within a very short time. Restraint now rested mainly on the fact that no newspaper wished to incur the odium of the Establishment, and the hatred of jealous rivals, by 'jumping the gun' with the news. But clearly, it only required some public remark from an official person for the news to break everywhere with the force of a pent-up explosion.

At *The Times*, Dawson was very restive. He was determined that his newspaper should be first to speak, and restrained himself from open comment in the last days of November only on the urgent advice of Monckton and Hardinge.[38] Even so, a leader published on Monday 30 November contained a strong hint of the impending crisis. It congratulated Parliament on the 'steadiness and balance' it had shown in recent months, and continued:

> Given the continuance of this spirit – and it shows no signs of weakening – the House of Commons may well prove itself what the country has required in similar times during its long history, but has seldom been given – namely a Council of State which is able to demonstrate its solid strength in any crisis that may arise, whether foreign or domestic.

We know that, during these last days of November, the King heard, through private channels, from the editors of at least two opinion-forming weekly journals, who offered to create publicity in a sense strongly favourable to his cause. These were the *New Statesman*, at this time the outstanding literary organ of the liberal intelligentsia, edited by Kingsley Martin; and *The Week* edited by Claud Cockburn, a news-sheet noted for its well-informed political gossip and which, though small in circulation, was read avidly by many influential people including the King himself. Both men had lines leading to the King:

Cockburn's friend John Strachey was a friend of Lord Louis Mountbatten; Martin's friend, the barrister and radical politician D. N. Pritt, was a colleague and friend of Walter Monckton. In both cases (as we learn from the memoirs of Cockburn and Pritt) the King expressed pleasure and satisfaction at the offers of the editors; he showed initial interest, and went so far as to invite Martin to submit a copy of the article he proposed to publish; but in the end, he begged them not to make any move in his support.[39]

The event which finally lit the fuse occurred on the morning of Tuesday 1 December, coming from a most improbable quarter. Addressing his annual diocesan conference, the Bishop of Bradford, the aptly named Dr A. W. F. Blunt − a man of whom the King had never heard and who was virtually unknown outside his diocese − talked about the religious significance of the Coronation and of the King's need of God's grace 'if he is to do his duty faithfully'. He continued: 'We hope that he is aware of this need. Some of us wish that he gave more positive signs of his awareness.'

The rest of Blunt's life* was to be blighted by the consequences of these words; and he was afterwards at pains to explain what he had meant by them.[40] They had been intended to refer, he said, not to Mrs Simpson, of whom he had not heard at the time he wrote them, but only to the King's lax churchgoing. And the speech as a whole had been intended as an attack, not on the King, but against Blunt's theological enemy, the maverick Bishop Barnes of Birmingham, who in a controversial sermon delivered on 1 November had argued that the Coronation should cease to take the form of an Anglican communion service and become

* He remained Bishop of Bradford until 1955 and died in 1957.

161

an essentially secular ceremony.* Blunt, a fervent Anglo-Catholic, sought to rubbish Barnes' unconventional views by pointing out that the Coronation was, above all things, the moment of the sovereign's religious 'self-dedication'; and in so doing he could not resist a fleeting moment of regret that the King, since coming to the throne, had not shown himself to be much of a churchman.

But though Blunt may not have had Mrs Simpson in mind when he wrote his speech, he certainly knew of her when he delivered it. For on the afternoon of 17 November – the day after the King had seen Baldwin and offered to abdicate – the Archbishop of Canterbury, Dr C. G. Lang, had summoned a secret meeting at Lambeth Palace of all the bishops (who were then in London attending the annual Church Assembly) to tell them 'that his [the Archbishop's] plan for a religious preparation of the Coronation was now out of place, that the King was much in the company of a twice-divorced American lady whom the American press openly called the Queen-designate of England' and that 'the British newspapers were responsible but could not be silent for ever'.[41] At this meeting, a fellow-bishop, Furse of St Albans, actually showed Blunt a file of cuttings about Mrs Simpson from the American papers.[42] Having been enlightened in this dramatic manner precisely two weeks before he was due to make his address, Blunt must certainly have been staggeringly naive if he failed to realize the furore his remarks (which he now saw no reason to revise) were bound to cause. It was unheard-of in recent times for a bishop to utter any criticism of the monarch. That

---

* As Barnes' son points out in his biography of his father, a flaw in Blunt's 'explanation' is that he claims to have written his address six weeks previously; whereas Barnes' sermon which it attacks was delivered only thirty days previously (John Barnes, *Ahead of his Age: Bishop Barnes of Birmingham* (1979), pp. 332–5).

Tuesday, Duff Cooper was visiting Leeds to encourage the local army recruiting drive and give a talk to students at the University. At five o'clock, he bought two local evening newspapers to read on the train back to London, and reacted with amazement to the Bishop's words published therein. 'I suppose', he wrote, 'it was the first time in the century that the Sovereign of Great Britain had been openly rebuked.'[43]

That same afternoon, Arthur Mann, editor of the Conservative *Yorkshire Post*, was in the London office of his newspaper when the text of Blunt's speech arrived by telegraph from the main Yorkshire office in Leeds.* During his stay in London, Mann – a traditionalist who took a staunchly pro-Government view – had been much preoccupied by 'the King's matter', which he had discussed with Dawson during the week-end.[44] He knew of Lang's secret meeting with the bishops on 17 November. 'On reading the Bishop's words', he wrote many years later to Blunt's biographer, 'I rather naturally assumed that he had been inspired by higher authority to speak as he had done . . . and I thought the time had come for the silence to be broken and the issue squarely faced.'[45] Mann thereupon wrote a leader for the next morning's issue, which contained the words:

> Dr Blunt must have good reason for so pointed a remark. Most people [sic], by this time, are aware that a great deal of rumour regarding the King has been published of late in the more sensational American newspapers . . . But certain statements which have appeared in reputable United States journals, and even, we believe, in some Dominion newspapers, cannot be treated with quite so much indifference: they are too circumstantial and have plainly a foundation in fact.

---

* Blunt had in fact obligingly sent an advance copy of his speech to the Bradford office of the *Yorkshire Post* (John Peart-Binns, *Blunt*, p. 155).

For this reason, an increasing number of responsible people is led to fear lest the King may not yet have perceived how complete in our day must be that self-dedication of which Dr Blunt spoke if the Coronation is to bring a blessing to all the peoples of the Empire, and is not, on the contrary, to prove a stumbling block.

Having written these fateful lines, Mann communicated them, along with the relevant extract from Blunt's speech, to the Press Association wire service, for transmission to every newspaper office in the country.

That Tuesday night Beaverbrook telephoned the King to inform him of these sudden developments. The Wednesday editions of the so-called 'quality' London newspapers, he said, would be reporting Blunt's speech without comment: the news had come too late in the evening for them to decide how to react. But this last act of restraint could only be a twenty-four-hour reprieve: and on Thursday morning the King could expect bitter attacks, especially from *The Times*. Meanwhile all the great provincial dailies – the *Manchester Guardian*, the *Birmingham Post* – would be reproducing the *Yorkshire Post* leader, with their own commentaries. The silence was over. But, continued Beaverbrook, the popular dailies (mostly controlled by himself and Rothermere) were on the King's side: would the King allow them to begin a great campaign in his support? [46]

The King refused. As he wrote in his memoirs:

Max . . . urged me forcefully to allow his newspapers to strike back vigorously. 'Many others hold with me that there is nothing wrong in the King's marrying a woman who has divorced her husband. A strong case can be made.'

But I could not see it that way. While it pleased me to hear that many shared this view, 'many' was not enough. My whole life – the ordered, sheltered existence that I had known since birth – had blown up and was disintegrating. And in the chaos around me I had three instinctive desires: to dampen the uproar if I could; to avoid the responsibility of splitting the nation and jeopardising the Monarchy on the issue of my personal happiness; and to protect Wallis from the full blast of sensationalism about to overwhelm us both. These were the keys to my actions in the days that remained to me as King . . . When we rang off, Max's natural belligerence seemed confounded and frustrated by my attitude.[47] *

Meanwhile, most of the replies from the Dominions had come in. That they gave little comfort to the King was, as we have seen, an outcome the Government had gone to considerable secret efforts to ensure. Yet only one of them showed outright hostility to the sovereign. This was from the Australian socialist premier Lyons, an ardent Roman Catholic who was undoubtedly horrified that the King should consider marrying a divorcée, and whose High Commissioner in London, Bruce, had taken a stern view in his conversations with Baldwin.† Lyons' reply was to the effect that the King's behaviour had so undermined the prestige of the monarchy that he would have to abdicate whether he married Mrs Simpson or not: 'the situation has now passed the possibility of compromise'. The other Dominion premiers replied more soberly to the general effect that their Governments would support the attitude of the British Government, concerning which they evidently had been or were being enlightened. In the case of Canada, this reply was given only hesitantly

---

* There is some dispute as to precisely when this conversation – in which the King refused to allow Beaverbrook to launch a press campaign in his favour – took place. Beaverbrook suggests it was part of the talk on Tuesday evening when he rang up to inform the King of Blunt's words and their press consequences; the King suggests it was a separate telephone conversation which occurred on Wednesday afternoon, just before he saw Baldwin. Which of them is correct is not of great importance.

† See above, p. 101.

and nervously. Mackenzie King, the Canadian premier, was most unwilling to be seen to take any action against the sovereign; during his visit to London in October he had refused various appeals to approach the King about the harm he was causing to the Empire; he himself was a lonely man with a tortured private life who may well have had much sympathy with the personal crisis of Edward VIII. But the Governor-General of Canada, Baldwin's friend and appointee John Buchan, put pressure on him to support Baldwin, and with reluctance he agreed. The New Zealand reply was complicated by the fact that the Prime Minister there, Savage, had never heard of Mrs Simpson; but Baldwin saw Walter Nash, the New Zealand Finance Minister, who was then in London, and finally obtained the tactful but adequate reply that the Government in Auckland would support anything the King might do or anything the Government might do to restrain him. The position in South Africa and Ireland was complicated by the fact that both premiers wished to exploit the crisis to assert their countries' independence: Herzog by introducing separate legislation to make the Abdication law in South Africa (no such legislation being thought necessary in Canada and Australia), De Valera by amending the Irish constitution so as virtually to eliminate the position of the crown altogether. But both premiers (after an original response from De Valera that Ireland did not care one way or the other) came out against the marriage. Ireland and New Zealand were the last to give their replies, which had not yet been received on Wednesday 2 December, the day the news broke in the British provinces.[48]

Although the file was not yet quite complete, Baldwin was due to see the King that evening to report on his enquiries, exactly one week to the hour since their last meeting. There was a cabinet that morning. It discussed a normal agenda of current political issues, notably a proposal of Duff Cooper concerning army recruitment; but when the general business was over, Baldwin announced that 'he was to see the King again and proposed to tell him that the Cabinet were not prepared to introduce the necessary bill to legalise the morganatic marriage'. Everyone agreed with this, except for Cooper. He made a final plea for delay. Kingsley Wood, the Health Minister, thereupon asked: 'But if he agreed to separation and delay of a year, would you promise to introduce the legislation at the end of that period if he wanted it?' Cooper replied that the whole question would then have to be reconsidered, but none of the other ministers was prepared to accept this and he bowed to their unanimous verdict.[49]

Ramsay MacDonald commented in his account of this meeting:

> I share the PM's view that the country when the issue has been fairly put before it will uphold the Cabinet, but not his optimism that it will be practically unanimous. To underestimate the resources of the King (the PM believes his word that he will abdicate without trouble, but I doubt it), Beaverbrook & very likely Churchill would be a mistake.[50]

The fourth meeting between the King and the Prime Minister took place at Buckingham Palace at six o'clock that evening, Wednesday 2 December. Baldwin came in looking extremely grave.* He reported that 'the enquiries among the Dominions . . . were still incomplete, but it was already clear . . . that the necessary legislation would not be forthcoming'. He showed the King the most uncompromising of the replies, that from Lyons of Australia. He was sure the House of Commons' reaction would be equally unfavourable. When the King pointed out that they had not yet been consulted, Baldwin

---

* Dawson had seen him that afternoon at his room in the House of Commons, and found him 'nearly at the end of his tether', sitting 'with his head on his hands on the table' (Evelyn Wrench, *Geoffrey Dawson and our Times*, p. 349).

replied that he had 'caused enquiries to be set afoot in the usual manner', and was convinced that the King's marriage, whether morganatic or otherwise, would not be supported on either the Government or Opposition benches.

The King's account of the meeting continues:

> Almost pedantically, he summed up for me the three choices that had faced me from the outset:
>
> (1) I could give up the idea of marriage.
> (2) I could marry contrary to the advice of my Ministers.
> (3) I could abdicate.
>
> The Prime Minister prayed that I would take the first course. The second course, he continued, watching me closely, was manifestly impossible; if I married in the face of the advice of my Ministers [who would thereupon resign], I could not hope to remain on the throne. Never taking his eyes off me, he went on to say that if I would not abandon the project there was really no choice for me but to go.
>
> 'So, Mr Baldwin', I said, 'you really leave me with only one choice.'[51]

In his account, the King seems to be suggesting that Baldwin's news that the morganatic solution was off came to him as a great disappointment. All other evidence, however, suggests that this was not the case at all. It has been seen that he had put forward the solution with the greatest pessimism and half-heartedness, and that he had refused to take any of the steps (such as consulting the Dominions personally about it, or allowing his press allies to support it) which might have given it a chance. Certainly all accounts which Baldwin gave of the meeting show the King accepting the political verdict without the slightest hesitation. 'I gave the reply that I was afraid [the morganatic marriage] was impracticable', the Prime Minister told the House of Commons eight days later. 'His Majesty said he was not surprised at that answer. He took my answer with no question and he never recurred to it again.' According to Baldwin's intimate and biographer G. M. Young, the King's remark when told that marriage would inevitably entail abdication was not the petulant *you really leave me with only one choice*', but the resigned '*I have known that all along*'.[52] And according to an account given by Baldwin to his niece, the King kept on repeating again and again throughout the interview: 'I can't do my job without her. I am going to marry her, and I will go.'[53]

In other words, the King's position had not changed at all since he had first spoken to Baldwin of abdication on 16 November. But for the first time he gave way to a pang of self-pity. Picking up the *Birmingham Post* – which of all the provincial newspapers to have broken the news that morning had been most critical of him* – he said: 'They don't want me.'[54]

This, it appears, was the signal for Baldwin to make (as on 16 November) another impassioned and lengthy plea to the King to give up Mrs Simpson and stay. As before, the King seemed to pay no attention to this. 'To all arguments based on responsibility towards his people', Mrs Baldwin wrote in her diary that evening, 'the King did not react . . . ' Baldwin later told his niece: 'I appealed to one thing after another. Nothing made the least impression. It was almost uncanny . . . He seemed *bewitched* . . . '[55] At all events, he had not changed and had no intention of changing his mind.

The King had only one request to make of Baldwin. He had been told (probably by Beaverbrook) that *The*

---

* The *Post*'s leader commented: 'The Bishop of Bradford's words are words of reproof – such reproof as no-one, whether cleric or layman, has thought proper to address to the King for many a long day.' And it supported Blunt's right 'to speak the truth when he gives warning – as in effect he does – that in the eyes of the people . . . the private and public life of the King-Emperor are inseparable'.

169

Times was preparing a personal attack on Mrs Simpson, and wanted this stopped if possible. While stressing that the press was free, Baldwin agreed to see what he could do, and later that evening rang up Dawson apologetically to ask to see the leader proposed for the next day's issue: it did not in fact mention Mrs Simpson at all.[56]

The audience concluded with the King reiterating: 'Wallis is the most wonderful woman in the world.' To which Baldwin made the weary but kindly reply: 'Well, sir, I hope that you may find her so. Whatever happens, I hope that you may be happy.' Their parting was friendly.[57]

Thus the position was exactly what it had been sixteen days previously, and the morganatic marriage proposal had served no other purpose than to get the machinery of abdication moving. But something had now happened which could not have been foreseen. By sheer coincidence, three vital developments had occurred at almost the same moment. Mrs Simpson had decided to leave England; the press had begun to speak out; and Baldwin had formally advised the sovereign that marriage would mean departure. (Previous accounts of the crisis have represented the first of these developments as merely a consequence of the second and third: but it is now seen that this was not the case. Mrs Simpson had written of her decision on 30 November, the day before Blunt spoke at Bradford and two days before Baldwin saw the King.)

The circumstances of the Abdication might well have been different had Mrs Simpson made her decision a week earlier, or the press broken silence a week later. As it was, the sudden convergence of these three critical events submitted the King to an intense personal strain, and this was to be apparent in the days which followed.

Chapter Nine

The Broadcast Proposal

2 December–4 December

Following his fourth interview with Baldwin on the night of Wednesday 2 December, the King returned to the Fort to dine with Mrs Simpson. After dinner, he took her for a walk on the terrace; and there, in uncomfortably cold and foggy atmospheric conditions which struck him as appropriate to the occasion, he told her that he had formally been advised by the Prime Minister that 'I must give you up or abdicate', the former of which courses was unthinkable to him.[1] Mrs Simpson naturally reacted with horror, protesting that under no circumstances should he abdicate. And she now made two urgent proposals.

First, she declared her intention of leaving him and going abroad – an intention which, as we have seen, she had formed at least two days earlier, for she had written about it to some of her best friends on the Monday. Standing with him in the darkness, she declared: 'I'm going to leave. I've already stayed too long. I should have gone when you showed me Hardinge's letter. But now nothing you can say can hold me here any longer.' This was not the first time she had tried to escape that autumn, and on the previous occasions the King had made terrible scenes and refused to accept her departure; but this time, to her relief and doubtless her surprise, he did not argue with her, merely replying: 'It will be hard for me to have you go. But it would be

171

harder still to have you stay.' By way of explanation, he then revealed to her his other dramatic news: that the London press were about to break silence and would be 'ablaze' the following morning with stories of their friendship and his desire to marry her. As her situation in England was therefore about to become 'harrowing beyond belief', her rapid disappearance from the scene was indeed desirable. Nor did he wish her to be with him when the moment came for final decision: he would have to 'handle this in my own way, alone'.

Mrs Simpson's second proposal to avert the looming catastrophe was for the King 'to make a radio broadcast to the nation and the Empire, telling his story and letting them hear his voice'. As she wrote in her memoirs: 'I was not unmindful of the extraordinary impact on public opinion of President Roosevelt's "fireside chats" and, indeed, of the famous Christmas broadcasts of David's father.'[2]

The King's apparently serious acceptance of the idea that, while still on the throne, he might deliver a broadcast concerning his proposed marriage is one of the most curious facts surrounding the end of his reign. Lord Birkenhead, Monckton's biographer, has described it as 'indicative of a strange blockage of vision in certain directions, understandable in youth, but baffling in maturity, which existed in a mind otherwise alert and intelligent'.[3] It was one of the few episodes Baldwin did not wish to mention in his account to Parliament of his dealings with the sovereign. The mystery deepens when one considers exactly what the King was meant to broadcast about. Though neither of them says so in their memoirs, it now seems clear that Mrs Simpson wanted him quite simply to declare that he was giving her up, which by this time undoubtedly represented her fervent wish. Just before leaving England the following day, Mrs Simpson scribbled a final note to the King, which read: 'Be calm with B [Baldwin, whom the King was seeing that evening to discuss his desire to broadcast]

172

but tell the country tomorrow I am lost to you . . . '*
However, the broadcast which the King actually proposed to Baldwin following Mrs Simpson's departure mentioned nothing of the sort, and appeared to be a plea *for the morganatic marriage.*

But by this time the morganatic marriage was a dead duck. As the King had heard from the Prime Minister's own lips, the British Government had firmly vetoed it, as already had most of the Dominion Governments. Furthermore, everything indicates that the King had never really wanted it or believed in it; and finally, he had expressly forbidden his press allies to launch an appeal in favour of it, lest this stimulate controversy and exacerbate the crisis. Yet now he was proposing to launch such an appeal himself in his own voice – the one thing, one might have thought, calculated to provoke something in the nature of civil war.

Finally and paramountly there was the fact that, constitutionally, the King could only make such a broadcast under the advice of his Ministers; and it was hardly probable that a ministry which had already advised him that he could not marry Mrs Simpson, morganatically or otherwise, and remain on the throne, would now advise him to make what was in effect an appeal to the country against their verdict.

Evidently the King was under tremendous strain at this time, and not thinking clearly. But it is also evident that he was concerned above all to keep Mrs Simpson happy. She was about to leave him; she was begging him not to abdicate; he did however mean to abdicate and marry her abroad; and it was essential to appease her by giving her the impression that he was working to save his throne. She wanted him to broadcast; therefore

* As part of her escape plan, Mrs Simpson was due to change cars at Newhaven before sailing for the Continent; and the note was given to the driver of the first car who would be returning to the Fort. It is reproduced in facsimile on p. 216 of *Wallis & Edward: Letters 1931–1937.*

he would try to broadcast – not indeed to say that he had renounced her but to explain to the world his love for her and desire to marry her (a desire which, he would have to say, was not accompanied by an insistence that she should become Queen of England).

In so far as he took the idea of broadcasting seriously, he seems to have regarded it as a preliminary to, rather than a means of avoiding, abdication – an apology to his people, as it were, before he performed the fatal act. As he is alleged to have said to Baldwin at their coming interview: ' . . . before I go, I think it right, for her sake and mine, that I should speak'. For on the night of 2 December the King does not seem to have doubted he would have to go. After his talk with Mrs Simpson on the terrace he telephoned Beaverbrook, to whom he reported the latest meeting with Baldwin, reiterated his determination to marry Mrs Simpson as soon as she was free, and declared that, barring some unforeseen miracle, he intended 'to retire into private life'.[4]

The following morning, Thursday 3 December, the news broke in the London press – but not quite in the manner that the King had been dreading. Surveying the various leading articles half a century later, one feels that the vast majority of contemporary readers, who had never heard of Mrs Simpson and still knew nothing of any crisis, must have reacted with total bafflement; for, even that morning, few papers openly discussed her relationship with the King or so much as mentioned her name, editors hardly knowing how to broach the subject after bottling it up for so long and tending to confine themselves to vague generalities. The Times, in what Harold Nicolson called 'an amalgam of tortuous and pompous nothings',[5] wrote of Blunt's address, the previous day's comment in the Yorkshire Post, the superiority of the Crown to its wearer, and the damaging gossip in the American press which had 'gone to the length of predicting a marriage incompatible with the throne'. The *Morning Post* wrote in similar vein, but 'shrank from believing that there is solid foundation for the current gossip, because if it were true the gravest injury to every national and imperial interest must result'. The *Daily Telegraph* (whose owner, Lord Camrose, was informed by Baldwin's close colleague J. C. C. Davidson[6]) most accurately reported the constitutional position, inferring that the King was about to make a choice between private desire and public duty. The Labour *Daily Herald* (whose owner, Elias, had changed his mind about supporting the King) did not mention the marriage at all, but carried an article by Professor Harold Laski arguing that, as the King could act constitutionally only under the advice of his Ministers, opposition to such advice must result either in royal dictatorship or abdication.

Much to the surprise of those who knew of the King's meetings with Harmsworth and Beaverbrook,[7] the *Daily Mail* and *Daily Express* – restrained by the King himself – did no more than refer without comment to a constitutional crisis which had arisen because of the King's wish to make a marriage of which the Cabinet disapproved. The only London daily to give comfort to the sovereign that Thursday was the Liberal and Nonconformist *News Chronicle*,* which in a long leader argued that, while it might be for Parliament to decide who should or should not be Queen, it was for the King himself to decide who should be his partner for life.† The only morning paper to deal sensationally

---

* Controlled by the Quaker Cadbury family and 'directed' by Sir Walter Layton, a distinguished Liberal economist, the *News Chronicle* had been formed in 1930 through the amalgamation of the *Daily News* and the *Daily Chronicle* and remained the great organ of Liberal opinion until its disappearance in 1960.

† This view was reiterated on Friday in the daily *Catholic Times* and weekly *New Statesman*. After that, little more was heard about the morganatic marriage, following Baldwin's statement to the House of Commons on Friday afternoon. (See below, p. 192.)

with Mrs Simpson herself was the *Daily Mirror*, then one of the titles of the Harmsworth group: in its later editions, it carried a studio portrait of her by Dorothy Wilding over its entire front page, and various stories about her history and royal affair on its inside pages. Once the ice had been broken in this fashion, all the evening papers carried pictures of and stories about Mrs Simpson, so helping to enlighten a still largely dazed and mystified public.

Thus the Thursday morning papers still showed considerable restraint, and cannot have provided much of a surprise for the King: he had after all muzzled his own journalistic allies, and the 'Establishment' press naturally supported the Government. Such bitterness as he felt was caused by philosophical reflections on the fickle ways of the fourth estate: 'The Press creates; the Press destroys. All my life I had been the passive clay which it had enthusiastically worked into the hackneyed image of Prince Charming. Now it had whirled around, and was bent upon demolishing the man who had been there all the time.' Mrs Simpson's main feeling as she read the headlines was one of self-reproach; she kept repeating to herself: 'Why didn't you follow your first instinct? Why didn't you go when you first knew it was the only thing to do?'[8]

At the Fort, the day was spent in hectic preparations for Mrs Simpson's departure abroad that evening. She had decided to go to stay with Herman and Kitty Rogers at their villa at Cannes. The Rogers were a charming American couple whom she counted among her oldest and closest friends: she had first lived with them in China in 1924. They had been frequent guests at the Fort and had accompanied the King and Mrs Simpson on almost all the holidays they had taken together, participating during the summer of 1936 in both the *Nahlin* cruise and the Balmoral party. At the end of October, learning of the divorce case and the misery Mrs Simpson had undergone in the course of it, they had written to her begging her to come to them if ever she needed a refuge.[9] She now took advantage of this invitation, telephoning them in guarded language to invoke their hospitality.

As her companion and protector on the potentially adventurous journey ahead, the King selected his Lord-in-Waiting and most trusted courtier Lord ('Perry') Brownlow, a fellow-Grenadier from the First World War, whom Mrs Simpson knew and liked and who was also incidentally a friend of Beaverbrook. As the King wrote in his memoirs, Brownlow was 'by temperament, instinct and association . . . uniquely and eminently qualified for this delicate mission – almost too well, I was presently to discover . . . ' For what neither the King nor Mrs Simpson yet knew was that, at Beaverbrook's secret meeting of 'King's friends' on the night of 30 November, Brownlow had been chosen as the man to persuade Mrs Simpson to make a final and effective break with the King. Since then, he had been unable to communicate with her; now he was presented with a heaven-sent opportunity to influence her (though such influence would prove futile, not because Mrs Simpson was disinclined to accept it – quite the contrary – but because, on the marriage issue, the King was to prove no more amenable to her entreaties than anyone else's).

Her other escorts were to be the King's head chauffeur, George Ladbrook, and one of his Scotland Yard detectives, Inspector Evans. Aunt Bessie would have to be left behind, as would the symbolic cairn terrier which the King had presented to Mrs Simpson at the outset of their romance. The plan was that she, Brownlow and Evans should drive to Newhaven in Brownlow's Rolls, which would attract no press attention; there, under the aliases of 'Mr and Mrs Harris', they would board the night ferry, on which Ladbrook would already have stowed the King's Buick. The King left Ulick Alexander to work out the details of this journey, and devoted most of that afternoon to drafting his proposed broadcast. Mrs Simpson busied herself with ordering a few possessions from the house in London she would never see again, packing such few cases as she would be able to take with her, and drawing up a will in which she made legacies to her aunt and servants, appointed the King her residual legatee, and asked that her ashes be scattered at the Fort.[10]

Brownlow arrived at dusk, and the company partook of a gloomy tea. The King's last hours with Mrs Simpson were 'infinitely sad and forlorn'. For her, it had the poignancy of a final parting: she did not imagine she would ever see him again. But his last words to her, before she drove off at seven in the evening, were: 'I don't know how it's all going to end. It will be some time before we can be together again. You must wait for me no matter how long it takes. I shall never give you up.'[11]

By this time, all had learned of Mrs Simpson's existence from the evening papers. 'The Country and the Empire now know', wrote Channon, 'that their Monarch, their young King-Emperor, their adored Apollo, is in love with an American twice divorced, whom they believe to be an adventuress. The whole world recoils from the shock; but very few know that she is a woman of infinite charm, gentleness, courage and loyalty, whose influence upon the King, until now, has been highly salutary.'[12]

That afternoon, at Question Time in the House of Commons, Attlee had by arrangement put a private notice question to the Prime Minister asking him whether he had any statement to make concerning possible constitutional difficulties. Baldwin, looking 'ill and sad',[13] replied that no constitutional difficulty existed and that the nature of the situation made it inexpedient for him to be questioned for the moment, though he had it 'very much in mind' to make some announcement at a suitable opportunity. Churchill, in his first public intervention, then rose to ask by way of a supplementary question: 'Would Mr Baldwin give the House an assurance that no irrevocable step would be taken before a formal statement had been made to Parliament?' Baldwin replied coldly that he had nothing to add to what he had already said.

Meanwhile, back at the Fort, the King, in a state of some wretchedness following the departure of Mrs Simpson, was devoting his troubled mind to the question of the broadcast, concerning which he had arranged to see Baldwin at the Palace later that evening. The proposal he now wished to make was that he speak to his subjects and then immediately go abroad to await the nation's 'verdict' on the matter of his marriage, delegating his authority to a Council of State. How exactly the public will was to be tested he does not appear to have considered, nor does he seem to have reflected on the public controversy which would be engendered; in fact the whole project testifies to his overwrought state at that moment. It is uncertain where he intended to go if he left England as King; in his memoirs he mentions Belgium, though he told Brownlow and Churchill that he wanted to make for Switzerland. Indeed, such was the strain under which he was labouring that, broadcast or no broadcast, he seems to have been toying with the notion of flying off to Switzerland with a couple of equerries merely in order to escape for a few days from the claustrophobic pressures of the British atmosphere; as he told Churchill, 'a complete change in the Alps' was what he required.[14]

The draft broadcast he had written that afternoon – in circumstances which can hardly have been conducive to literary composition but with some assistance from his solicitor George Allen – has never before been published in its entirety. Though crude, it spoke from the heart: the fifth and sixth paragraphs were a particularly frank expression of his feelings. Aside from the mention of the morganatic marriage, it is in some respects reminiscent of the speech he was in fact to deliver eight days later upon ceasing to reign. This tends to confirm the view that (contrary to what is said in the King's memoirs) it was not in reality a bid to save his throne, but rather a means of explaining his motives to the country in the light of a decision which he knew he would have to make.

By ancient custom, the King addresses his public utterances to his people. Tonight I am going to talk to you as my friends — British men and women* wherever you may reside, within or without the Empire.

The last time I broadcast to you all, on Saint David's Day, I told you that you had known me better as Prince of Wales. I am still that same man whose motto was 'Ich Dien', 'I serve'; and I have tried to serve this country and the Empire for the last twenty years. And tonight I am not forgetting the great Dominions and Dependencies beyond the seas, who have always shown me such open-hearted kindness.

Now I realize that the newspapers of other countries have given you full cause for speculation as to what I am going to do — as to what is going to happen. And I want here to express my gratitude to the newspapers of Great Britain for the courtesy and consideration they have shown.

It was never my intention to hide anything from you. Hitherto it has not been possible for me to speak, but now I must.

I could not go on bearing the heavy burdens that constantly rest on me as King, unless I could be strengthened in the task by a happy married life; and so I am firmly resolved to marry the woman I love, when she is free to marry me.

You know me well enough to understand that I could never have contemplated a marriage of convenience. It

* The King originally wrote 'Britishers', but changed this on the advice of Beaverbrook and Churchill, who studied the draft that evening (Beaverbrook, *The Abdication of Edward VIII*, p. 71).

has taken me a long time to find the woman I want to take as my wife. Without her I have been a very lonely man. With her I shall have a home and all the companionship and mutual sympathy and understanding which married life can bring. I know that many of you have had the good fortune to be blessed with such a life, and I am sure that in your hearts you would wish the same for me.

Neither Mrs Simpson nor I have ever sought to insist that she should be Queen. All we desired was that our married happiness should carry with it a proper title and dignity for her, befitting my wife.

Now that I have at last been able to take you fully into my confidence, I feel it is best to go away for a while, so that you may reflect calmly and quietly, but without undue delay, on what I have said. Nothing is nearer to my heart than that I should return; but whatever may befall, I shall always have a deep affection for my Country, for the Empire, and for you all.[15]

As soon as this draft (such as it was) had been completed, the King asked Sir Godfrey Thomas – the most trusted of his private secretaries who had served him throughout his post-1918 career as Prince of Wales – to visit Sir John Reith, the head of the BBC, with a view to making provisional arrangements for a possible broadcast. Interestingly enough, when he had seen the newspapers that morning it had immediately occurred to Reith that the King might wish to explain himself 'over the air'; and he had already taken the precaution of consulting the heads of the civil service as to what he should do in the event of an approach by the sovereign. Sir Horace Wilson, Baldwin's senior adviser, told him that it was 'quite likely' the King would try to broadcast and that Reith 'must consult the PM before agreeing'. When Godfrey Thomas arrived at Broadcasting House that evening, he asked, according to Reith's diary,

if in the event of the King's wishing to broadcast we could arrange it at short notice and from Windsor Castle. I said we probably could do it very quickly – even tomorrow night. I asked if the PM would know of it, and he said yes, the King was going to talk to him tonight and would only do it if the PM agreed.

Thomas was 'in a dreadful state' and spoke frankly to Reith about the crisis. The King was 'insane' about Mrs Simpson and 'wouldn't listen to anyone' – though he seemed to have good relations with Baldwin and confided (alone among his staff) in Monckton. 'He [Thomas] said he had done his best to "keep the flag flying" all these years and now it had gone for nothing. He was sure that even if the King now did everything he was advised, he could never recover the lost ground.' Thomas had never met Mrs Simpson until the *Nahlin* cruise, when he had been surprised by her modesty and good manners; 'in fact if she hadn't had a husband . . . he wouldn't have seen anything wrong . . . He didn't think the King ever really thought he could make the woman Queen.'[16]

That night and for the last time, the King motored from Fort Belvedere to Buckingham Palace. On his arrival there he had a short meeting with the Duke of York, who had returned from Scotland that morning and been 'surprised and horrified' to see the newspaper placards announcing the crisis. The Duke found the King 'in a great state of excitement', saying 'that he would leave the country as King after making a broadcast to his subjects & leave it to them to decide what should be done'.[17] The King also saw Walter Monckton and George Allen and asked them to show a copy of the draft broadcast to Beaverbrook and Churchill, who were due to meet at Stornoway House later that evening. It seems that this was the first time the King had actively sought Churchill's advice during the crisis.[18]

The King's fifth meeting with the Prime Minister took place at the Palace at nine o'clock that evening, Thursday 3 December. By this time both men were under immense strain – on top of everything, Baldwin had been involved in a car crash a couple of hours earlier

– and some of the studied courtesy which had marked their previous meetings seems to have been missing. The King came to the point and explained his latest proposal. According to Baldwin's official biographer, G. M. Young, whose work was published in 1952, the King read his draft broadcast aloud to Baldwin and asked for his views. Baldwin replied that he would consult his colleagues in the morning, but believed they would take the view that the proposed broadcast was 'thoroughly unconstitutional'. The King thereupon said: 'You want me to go, don't you? And before I go, I think it is right, for her sake and mine, that I should speak.' The Prime Minister then (still according to Young) delivered the following homily:

> What I want, Sir, is what you told me you wanted: to go with dignity, not dividing the country, and making things as smooth as possible for your successor. To broadcast would go over the heads of your Ministers and speak to the people. You will be telling millions throughout the world – among them a vast number of women – that you are determined to marry one who has a husband living. They will want to know all about her, and the press will ring with gossip, the very thing you want to avoid . . . [19]

As the British press had finally broken loose that day on the subject of Mrs Simpson, and 'millions throughout the world' were already reading and talking about very little else, it does seem strange that Baldwin should have used these particular words in speaking to the King that evening, and one wonders where G. M. Young got his story from. All that the King remembered of the meeting was that it was brief; that Baldwin promised to summon the Cabinet the next morning to discuss the broadcast; and that, while he did not condemn the proposal, he listened to it with an air of exasperation as if to say: 'Damn it, what will this young man be thinking up next?' The King did not recall reading out his draft; and he could not remember whether he had put it into the Prime Minister's hands or not (though this hardly mattered since Monckton, fixing up the interview earlier in the day, appears to have presented the Prime Minister with a copy).[20]

At all events, the Prime Minister cannot have been too discouraging, for the King continued to believe for the moment in the possibility that he might be making his broadcast the following evening. Just before midnight, Godfrey Thomas telephoned Reith of the BBC to say that 'the King probably would broadcast tomorrow night – [in the event of] the PM agreeing. Anyhow it was advisable to get Windsor Castle fixed up on chance.'[21] And the King also ordered his private aeroplane to be got ready for a possible journey 'at a moment's notice'.[22]

Following his meeting with Baldwin, the King went to Marlborough House to see his mother, who had written him a note that morning complaining that the newspapers were 'somewhat upsetting' and that he had not visited her for ten days. He apologized for his 'apparent aloofness', explaining that he had not wished 'to bring the family into all this' and felt he had to handle the crisis on his own. The Duke of York and their sister Princess Mary were also there; and before the three of them he reiterated that he could not live without Mrs Simpson and was determined to marry her – 'a dreadful announcement' as the Duke of York described it in his diary, though hardly one which by this time can have surprised any of them. Indeed the King tells us in his memoirs that his mother gave no sign that she wished him to change his mind. (According to the diary of Princess Paul of Yugoslavia, who at this time was staying with her sister the Duchess of Kent and much involved in family discussions, the prevailing mood in the Royal Family was 'that he had better go as he can't be trusted to play the game'.[23]) As the King left, he asked his brother to meet him at the Fort the next morning – though he subsequently postponed the meeting (much to the Duke's irritation) and they did not see each other again until Monday evening.[24]

The King then returned to the Palace, where he saw Monckton and Allen on their return from the conference at Stornoway House. Beaverbrook and Churchill had made various suggestions about redrafting the text 'if the broadcast was still to be delivered', but both believed the King would not be allowed to deliver it and that it would be vetoed by the Cabinet as unconstitutional. Moreover, Churchill thought the King's idea of leaving the country tactically unsound as it would 'leave Baldwin in undisputed command of the situation'. The King was too exhausted to consider these judgements, and contented himself with the reflection that 'the Cabinet would supply the last word in the morning'.[25]

It was now well after midnight, and the King was indeed shattered after an endless day which had seen the explosion in the press, Mrs Simpson's flight, the writing of the broadcast, another interview with the Prime Minister and a further strained meeting with his family. He prepared to return to the Fort; but Monckton was alarmed at the prospect of his returning alone in his depressed and unpredictable state and insisted on accompanying him. As they drove out of the Palace gates at one o'clock in the morning, a sizeable crowd which, learning of his presence, had gathered in the course of the evening gave a loud cheer. 'Ah, that's better!' said Monckton, rubbing his hands. The King's spirits rose at this 'simple, spontaneous demonstration' and, as he frankly tells us in his memoirs, he suddenly had a bizarre thought: what was to stop him from descending from his motor and addressing the crowd there and then in the sense of his proposed broadcast? 'My parents' practice of "showing" themselves on the balcony . . . provided a precedent. The spotlights playing on the facade, the lonely figure of the King pleading his cause – the scene could have been extremely effective. But no sooner had the image formed in my mind than it vanished. For one thing, it smacked too much of balcony politics, of which there was already too much in the Europe of that era. What was more important, it would have meant driving a wedge into the nation.'

What the King now decided to do, in fact, was to remove himself from his cheering supporters completely, 'to withdraw altogether to The Fort, away from the warring pulls and the emotionalism of London in the throes of controversy'. As he wrote:

> . . . I was determined to keep my negotiations with the Government at a highly impersonal level. London is a metropolis, subject to the emotions of the hour. I did not want to be accused of seeking to rally support for myself against the Government by encouraging popular movements to which my continued presence at Buckingham Palace might well have given rise; nor did I wish, having been so often in my life the object of friendly demonstrations, to expose myself to the temptations which proximity to such manifestations might have excited. But beyond all that I also wished to be alone with my thoughts at this time of decision, unhampered and undisturbed by the associations of the past.

The King's resolve not to return to London (he was not to see the city again until September 1939) was the clearest indication that he did not mean to lend himself to a political movement in his support. It came as a great relief to Baldwin, who praised his decision before the Cabinet on 6 December[26] and the House of Commons on 10 December.

At the Fort, the King now deliberately isolated himself from his family and Court and surrounded himself with a tiny unofficial circle of his own choosing – Monckton, his solicitor George Allen, the recently appointed (and therefore untainted) Keeper of the Privy Purse Ulick Alexander and his financial adviser Sir

Edward Peacock. On Friday morning the King surveyed his property – 'its row of cannon, its vine-covered ramparts, its tall tower' – and found it 'a most appropriate place for a King making his last stand'. And in one sense it was literally under siege, surrounded as it now was by journalists and photographers. For the remainder of his reign, the King was to be 'virtually a prisoner inside my own house'.[27]

On Friday 4 December it was not yet known that the King had patriotically decided to put himself beyond the reach of his partisans. That day, there were significant public demonstrations in his favour all over the capital, groups singing God Save the King and For He's A Jolly Good Fellow and carrying placards with such legends as God Save the King from Baldwin. A whole section of the press now came out in his support: the Express and Mail showed themselves to be on his side, as did almost the whole of the rest of the popular press with the exception of the Daily Herald; and a morganatic marriage was advocated not only in the News Chronicle but in the Catholic Times, the weekly New Statesman and Tablet, and important provincial papers such as the Western Morning News.

In this atmosphere, the news that broadcasting equipment was being installed at Windsor Castle, and that the King had put his private aircraft on standby, caused a flurry of panic in official circles. It was thought not impossible that he might try to 'crash' into a broadcast without permission and simply fly out of his kingdom without having renounced the crown, leaving the Government to handle the appalling situation he would leave behind.[28] Reith spoke to Horace Wilson at 10 Downing Street and assured him that it would be impossible for the King to broadcast without a go-ahead from his own office, which would not be given without official consent.[29] As a precaution, Wilson made certain arrangements to ensure that the King's plane remained grounded.

Hastily summoned, the Cabinet met in the Prime Minister's room at the House of Commons at half past ten that morning. Baldwin explained the King's broadcast proposal and read aloud the text of the proposed broadcast, which ministers were unanimous in rejecting. Nobody could imagine what the King meant when he proposed to 'go away for a little and leave the country to think it over'. Even Cooper fully agreed with the general argument of the meeting, which he summarized as follows: 'So long as the King is King, every utterance that he makes must be on the advice of his ministers, who take full responsibility for every word. If, therefore, we could not advise him to make this speech, we could not allow him to.'[30] Some thought the whole idea sinister; MacDonald considered it 'a plausible & blatant attempt to get the country & Empire to throw over his ministers. As it was read, I felt convinced that Churchill's hand was plain in it. Of course on constitutional grounds we refused. But what next? We are well within the danger zone.'[31]

The cabinet was twice interrupted. First, an alarming message was brought in that the King was busily engaged in secret consultations with Churchill and Beaverbrook and might be preparing flight or some other surprise move. This message came from Alan Lascelles, the King's hostile Assistant Private Secretary, and proved to be quite untrue.[32] Secondly, Baldwin received word from Attlee that he was under pressure to put a further question in the House of Commons; Baldwin therefore went to the chamber to announce that he had nothing to add to what he had said the previous day. This was followed by another interjection from Churchill, demanding an assurance that no irrevocable step be taken before Parliament had been consulted. This time, Churchill's remarks were greeted by cheers in the House. (Margesson, the Government Chief Whip, wrote to Baldwin later in the day that support for the King was growing and there were already at least forty MPs favourable to his cause.[33])

When Baldwin returned to the meeting there was a long discussion as to what if any statement the Prime Minister might make to the House before it rose for the week-end. Although there was nothing definite he could say until he had seen the King again that evening, the view emerged 'that we might now inform the House that the Cabinet had definitely turned down the possibility of a morganatic marriage. It was strongly felt that it would be of great value to get this proposal out of the way so that during the week-end the situation would present itself as one of two alternatives – renunciation or abdication.'[34] The Cabinet was undoubtedly alarmed that the morganatic solution had been supported by so much of the press that morning; and Simon as Home Secretary was asked to draft a message which Baldwin might deliver during the afternoon.

Finally, the Cabinet urged Baldwin to get the King to make up his own mind over the week-end. Neville Chamberlain warned that the crisis was 'holding up business and employment' and 'paralysing our foreign policy'.[35] Some ministers wanted an outright ultimatum – a decision within twenty-four hours or the Government would resign; but Baldwin saw the public danger of putting the King under obvious pressure, and eventually it was agreed that he should 'lay before the King the desirability of his being placed in a position to make a definite statement to Parliament not later than Monday.'[36]

After the meeting, a group of younger members of the Cabinet – Duff Cooper, Ernest Brown,* Leslie Hore-Belisha,† Oliver Stanley,‡ 'Shakespeare' Morrison§ – had a private talk about the crisis. All were men of the

* The (National Liberal) Labour Minister, who had recently accompanied the King to South Wales.
† The (National Liberal) Transport Minister, who had been appointed to the Cabinet only five weeks earlier.
‡ Education Minister.
§ Agriculture Minister.

King's generation and basically sympathetic to him; but the situation alarmed them even more than it seemed to alarm the Prime Minister. They thought 'a *coup d'état* was not impossible'. The Government might be forced to resign; Churchill might take over, and go to the country on a populist platform which would cause great divisions; parliamentary government might disappear altogether.[37] The nervousness of these men, none of whom was hostile to the King and some of whom regarded themselves as his friends, illustrates the great uncertainty in London that Friday, before it had become clear that the King had no intention either of challenging the advice of the Government or giving the least encouragement to his own supporters.

At the Fort, the King received a telephone call from Monckton telling him of the Cabinet's verdict concerning the broadcast. This was not his main worry that day, however; for he had also learned – from Bernard Rickatson-Hatt, the editor-in-chief of Reuters who was Ernest Simpson's best friend – that Mrs Simpson's presence in France had been discovered by the press, and that she and Brownlow appeared to be engaged in an uncomfortable race across the country attempting to evade the news-hounds on their trail.

Mrs Simpson's journey had been adventurous from the first. Soon after leaving the Fort, they were stopped by the police for speeding and allowed to continue only after Inspector Evans' intervention. Meanwhile Brownlow had been talking with Mrs Simpson in whispers in the back of the car. Having satisfied himself that she was serious in her desire to break off relations with the King in order to put an end to the crisis, he ordered his driver to pull up at the side of the road and made a proposal to her: would she not call off the French plan and retreat with him to Belton, his great house in Lincolnshire? As he explained:

You are the only person who can influence the King. Has it not occurred to you that by leaving him to make up his mind alone you will almost certainly bring to pass the conclusion that you and all of us are so anxious to avert? . . . With you gone the King will not stay in England.

Here Brownlow was trying to put into effect the secret plan which had been worked out the previous Monday night at the Beaverbrook–Harmsworth–Monckton–Allen meeting. After much turbulent discussion, Mrs Simpson insisted she had no choice but to leave the country: anything else would be deeply resented by the King as an underhand manoeuvre, destroy such influence as she might have, and put in him a condition where he might do anything. 'You know what David is like when crossed. Any change in his plan, in the state he's in, will drive him wild.' Besides, her only wish was to put England behind her and disappear. 'I am sure there is only one solution: that is for me to remove myself from the King's life. That is what I am doing now.'[38]

After this unscheduled interlude they arrived late at Newhaven and almost missed their boat. The crossing proceeded without mishap; but at Dieppe Mrs Simpson was quickly recognized by French customs officials – the plan had overlooked that the papers for the Buick remained in the King's name. They put up for the night at a hotel at Rouen, but had to bolt from there early in the morning when the building was surrounded by a crowd of curious spectators. To avoid pursuit by the press, Brownlow decided to make for the south by a roundabout route. They stopped for lunch at Evreux in the Eure, from where Mrs Simpson – seriously rattled by Brownlow's warning that her departure might not avert the King's – attempted to telephone him, begging him not to abdicate. But the line was so bad that the King understood nothing except that she was at Evreux – a fact which deeply worried him, since it was not on her planned itinerary. The party continued on their way, took a wrong turning back to the coast, and by nightfall had got no further than Orléans to the south-west of Paris, from where Mrs Simpson tried again and unsuccessfully to telephone the King.

That afternoon, just before the House of Commons rose at four thirty, Baldwin made the announcement which had been agreed on by the Cabinet and drafted by Simon on 'certain possibilities in the event of the King's marriage'. He declared that there was 'no such thing as what is called a morganatic marriage known to our law'. The woman the King married automatically became Queen; she would be entitled to the same dignities as Queen Mary and Queen Alexandra; and her children would be in line of succession to the throne. This situation could only be altered by leg-islation, both in Britain and the other self-governing territories under the Crown. The Cabinet in London were not prepared to introduce such legislation, and the Prime Minister was satisfied from enquiries that this was also the case in the Dominions. Baldwin's demeanour, wrote Channon, was 'unsmiling and ungra-cious'; and the Cabinet, 'looking like a picture by Franz Hals, a lot of grim Elders of the Kirk, squirmed uneasily'. When the statement was over, there was some cheering; 'but this was more for the man who has been through an appalling few days than for the pronouncement, which slams the door to any possible compromise'.[39]

Baldwin left the House and, accompanied by his PPS Dugdale, drove directly to the Fort for his sixth audience with the King. As soon as they met, he handed the King a formal note – drafted by Simon, who had evidently had a busy afternoon – which embodied the Cabinet's refusal to countenance the King's proposed broadcast. This note stressed the point that there was nothing to stop the King broadcasting once he had abdicated.

In the case of broadcasting (as in the case of any other form of public address) there is a fundamental difference between the position of the King and the position of a private person. As long as the King is King he can only speak in public in that capacity. If a Sovereign takes the formal action which is necessary to renounce the Throne, and if he becomes a subject of the reigning Sovereign, his claim to broadcast stands on quite a different basis. But the suggestion that the King should broadcast in the terms proposed is a suggestion that he should broadcast as King and while occupying the Throne. Such a broadcast could only be given on the advice of his Ministers, who would be responsible for every sentence of it. In these circumstances Mr Baldwin cannot advise that the King should broadcast as proposed.[40]

The King read the note carefully, and seemed impressed by the fact that he would be able to make his broadcast after all once he had renounced kingship. Accepting the position, he asked somewhat naively whether it would be possible to announce in the House of Commons that he had wished to speak to the people but had been advised against doing so; Baldwin promised to put this to the Cabinet. (When the Cabinet briefly met the following morning, it rejected the proposal on constitutional grounds, making the point that 'when the time came, the whole story could be told [to Parliament]'.[41] However, when Baldwin eventually told 'the whole story' on 10 December, he said nothing about the broadcast proposal, which remained unknown to the public until the King's memoirs were published in 1951.)

Baldwin then came to the other point which the Cabinet had wished him to put forward. He declared (as the King recalled) that the

continued uncertainty . . . if allowed to persist, was certain to create a dangerous constitutional situation not only in this country but throughout the Empire. Could I give the Government my decision without further delay, if

193

possible during the week-end? Better still, could I supply it before he started back for London?

I answered, steadily, that he knew my views and that I had not altered them. 'You will not have to wait much longer, Mr Baldwin.'

Moving to the edge of his chair, he looked at me fixedly. 'There is still time for you to change your mind, Sir. That is indeed the prayer of Your Majesty's servants.'

I studied the Prime Minister some time before answering . . . For me to do what he asked would have meant my abandoning, in the full view of the watching world, the woman whom I had asked to marry me. If it were indeed Mr Baldwin's prayer that I should save my crown by so base a surrender, that noble ornament would have been laid upon a head forever bent in shame.

'Mr Baldwin', I finally said, 'I will let you know as soon as possible.'[42]

The King's refusal to give Baldwin an immediate decision on the late afternoon of Friday 4 December did not mean that he had not yet made up his mind (which in the view of the present writer had been firmly made up three weeks previously), still less that he was thinking of changing it. Two events which occurred earlier that day indicate that he fully intended to abdicate. First, he suddenly broke off relations with Beaverbrook, to whom he sent a message to say that he 'was engaging on negotiations with the government on the terms of the abdication and must dissociate himself from those who were in the other camp'.[43] (Possibly the King knew by now of Beaverbrook's 'conspiracy' to get Mrs Simpson to renounce him, and this was the true motive for his dissociation; but he would hardly have told Beaverbrook he was abdicating unless he meant it.) Secondly, he summoned Sir Edward Peacock, the Receiver-General of the Duchy of Cornwall, to discuss how the Duchy's revenues and pensions would be affected by his abdication.[44]

The probable reason for the King's prevarication was that he wished to indulge in one final luxury before giving his decision. He asked Baldwin if he might be allowed to see Winston Churchill as a personal friend whom he had known all his life.* When Baldwin hesitated, the King continued: 'You can see anyone you like. You can send for anyone you like. You can consult with any number of people . . . But I cannot see anyone except those you send me . . . I want to see Mr Churchill.'[45]

When the Cabinet met the following morning, Baldwin began by announcing: 'I have made my first blunder.'[46] He explained that he had agreed to the King's seeing Churchill and then immediately regretted it. There was an anxious pause as ministers took in this news, which seemed to portend that the King was about to do battle with the Government. Then Ramsay MacDonald said: 'May I be allowed, as your predecessor, to say that I very much doubt whether you were wrong in giving your consent.'[47]

---

* According to the King's memoirs, his request to see Churchill had taken place at the audience with Baldwin the previous evening, 3 December; but accounts of the cabinet meeting of 5 December prove this to be clearly incorrect.

Chapter Ten

The Final Week

4 December–11 December

Immediately following Baldwin's accession to the King's request at their sixth meeting on the evening of Friday 4 December, Winston Churchill was invited to dine at the Fort. The Prime Minister departed at seven o'clock and Churchill arrived an hour later, this being the first time he had seen the King during the whole of the autumn. They were five to dinner, the King and his principal guest being joined by the diminutive court of Monckton, Allen and Alexander. 'His Majesty was gay and debonair for the first quarter of an hour', wrote Churchill, 'and no-one would have thought him in a serious crisis. But after this effort it was obvious that the personal strain he had so long been under and was now at its climax had exhausted him to a painful degree.'[1]

Even now that most of his own papers for the period have been published, it is not easy to establish Churchill's exact role in the closing weeks of Edward VIII's reign. The evidence is distorted by two factors. First, the crisis proved such a personal disaster for Churchill that he afterwards sought to minimize his part in it. Secondly, among the active politicians Churchill was so obviously both the King's oldest friend and the Government's leading Conservative critic that many people (including Baldwin and both his predecessor and successor as premier) assumed at the time that he was consistently working with and for the sovereign and urging him to challenge the Prime

Minister. This was not the truth. During the summer Churchill had offended the King by obliquely warning him about the dangers of his relations with Mrs Simpson, as a result of which the King had nothing to do with him for the next four months.[2] On 16 November, he had been invited to join the deputation of senior privy councillors who were visiting the Prime Minister to recommend that the King be presented with an ultimatum*; and although he had refused to participate, this was because (as he told Salisbury, the deputation's leader) he did not wish to prejudice his possible influence with the King, which might yet be used to dissuade him from marriage.[3] The following day, Duff Cooper, who had just had his meeting with the sovereign, saw Churchill in the House of Commons and confided that the King meant to abdicate to marry Mrs Simpson. Churchill reacted with anger and horror, saying that 'the country was now in great danger, and just as men had given arms and legs and indeed their lives for the sake of the country, so the King must be prepared to give up a woman'.[4] And as late as 25 November he assured Baldwin (albeit with apparent reluctance) that he would support the Government in the event of a conflict with the King over the marriage issue.†

All the while, however, Churchill was gradually shifting his position, under the influence of his own inherent romanticism undoubtedly reinforced by a strong desire to humiliate the Government and make a political comeback. We have seen that he played a shadowy role in the morganatic marriage proposal, a role of which he did not afterwards wish to tell the world. Beaverbrook's return to England on 24 November seems to have stirred him to action; and though Churchill was still not allowed access to the King, Beaverbrook kept him abreast of events and the

---

* See above, p. 102.
† See above, p. 138.

two men vigorously exchanged views on how to save Edward VIII. By the end of the month, Churchill was itching to do battle as the King's champion. When he saw Cooper again on 30 November, he indicated the new direction in which his mind was working. What crime had the King committed? Had they not sworn allegiance to him? Was he to be condemned unheard? Was he seeking to do anything that was not permitted to the meanest of his subjects?[5] On 3 December and again on the morning of Friday the 4th he put his famous supplementary to Baldwin in the House of Commons, asking that Parliament be consulted before any irrevocable step was taken. On Friday afternoon, Leo Amery found him 'completely on the rampage, saying that he was for the King and was not going to have him strangled in the dark by ministers and bumped off without a chance of saying a word to Parliament or the country in his own defence . . . '[6] Then, at five o'clock, Churchill heard from Monckton, who asked if he might hold himself in readiness for a possible summons to the Fort; and two hours later, the King having seen Baldwin and obtained his consent, the summons was duly issued.

At dinner that evening, the King (after his bright opening effort) seemed to be labouring under great pressure, and his conversation wandered. He insisted that he had not yet abdicated; he had not mentioned the word abdication at his latest meeting with the Prime Minister. He wanted to broadcast and had been told that this would be possible once he had abdicated. He had asked the Prime Minister if a statement on his behalf could be made to the House of Commons, and feared that the Government would insert into any such statement a reference to abdication. He felt a prisoner at the Fort; he longed to go to Switzerland with a couple of equerries to think out matters calmly. What would happen if he made this request when he saw Baldwin the following afternoon? Did Churchill think the Government would resign unless he immediately agreed to abdication?[7]

Churchill's advice, delivered with great force and eloquence, was that the King should ask for time.

> If you require time there is no force in this country which would or should deny it to you. Mr Baldwin would certainly not resist you. If he did you could remind him that he himself took nearly three months rest in order to recover from the strain of the [previous parliamentary] session. Your strain is far more intense and prolonged. Mr Baldwin is a fatherly man and nothing would induce him to treat you harshly in such a matter. Ministers could not possibly resign on such an issue as your request for time.[8]

Under no circumstances, Churchill continued, should the King go abroad. This would produce the worst possible impression: everyone would say he had gone to visit Mrs Simpson. If he wished to leave the Fort, he 'should retire to Windsor Castle and close the gates', stationing at each of them one of the great royal physicians, Lord Dawson and Sir Thomas Horder.[9] For Churchill was convinced that the King was urgently in need of medical care and advice. 'I was sure he was in no condition to take so grave a decision as that which lay upon him. He twice in my presence completely lost the thread of what he was saying, and appeared to me to be driven to the last extremity of his endurance . . . '[10]

In Churchill's memoir of the Abdication, there is nothing to suggest that, during this dinner, he encouraged the King to fight the Government; he says that, 'never having been consulted at all for so many months', he only wanted to advise the King to ask for time to make up his mind. Both the King and Monckton, however, recalled that Churchill was nothing if not combative. 'He said that he could not say the King would win if he stood and fought', wrote Monckton, 'but that he ought to take time to see what measure of support he received.'[11] The King remembered, indeed, that Churchill urged him (as others had done) to drop the whole question of marriage until Mrs Simpson had received her decree absolute and the Coronation had taken place; and then, if the Government still would not agree, to accept their resignation rather than offer his own.[12]

Whatever the King may have thought of such advice, he clearly found Churchill's dramatic and supportive presence a moral tonic at this moment of depression and strain. 'Although I had long admired Mr Churchill', he wrote in his memoirs, 'I saw him that evening in his true stature.* When Mr Baldwin talked about the Monarchy, it had seemed a dull and lifeless thing. But when Mr Churchill spoke it lived, it grew, it became suffused with light.' Churchill proposed a plan of campaign: he himself would write to the Prime Minister to obtain time for the King, and would also issue a manifesto on the King's behalf for publication in the Sunday press. Meanwhile he was off that very night to join forces with Lord Beaverbrook. His last words as he took leave of the sovereign were: 'We must have time for the big battalions to march. We may win. We may lose. Who can tell?' Returning to the house with his advisers, the King, much improved in spirits and 'without the slightest malice', mimicked Churchill's delivery of these stirring phrases.[13]

Although the King had broken off relations with Beaverbrook, he telephoned the press lord to announce that Churchill was on his way; this, and the tale Churchill told on arrival at Stornoway House at two o'clock in the morning, filled Beaverbrook with renewed optimism about the outcome of the crisis. This was especially so as Beaverbrook had by now received a telegram in code from Brownlow in France making it clear that Mrs Simpson wished to give up the

---

* It should be remembered that the Duke of Windsor wrote these laudatory lines in the late 1940s, at a time when Churchill was Leader of the Opposition and the ex-King looked forward to his returning to power.

King. Churchill's 'vigour, eloquence and enthusiasm appeared to have put fresh heart into the King . . . Winston Churchill's enthusiasm was infectious and I felt I had good reason to believe that the King had reversed his fatal decision.'[14] Churchill then departed to spend the rest of the night drafting two letters – one to the King, the other to Baldwin – and a long statement which he proposed to issue to the press on the morrow.

But what had Churchill suggested to the King? He had advocated a policy of delay – delay until Mrs Simpson was free and he was crowned as King, delay to allow a party of supporters to form itself and make its influence felt. But for the whole of the preceding month this same policy of delay had been advocated by all who wished to save the King; and on every occasion it had been put to him he had rejected it unhesitatingly and unconditionally. Monckton on 9 November and Duff Cooper on 17 November had pleaded with him to drop the marriage proposal until after the Coronation: he had objected that this would amount to being 'crowned with a lie on my lips'. Beaverbrook on 24 November, in almost exactly the same terms as Churchill was using now, had urged him to 'measure the strength on either side' and 'adopt a Fabian strategy of delay'. As the King wrote in his memoirs: 'Many brilliant men besides Max Beaverbrook . . . were in the next few days to advocate this same Fabian policy . . . [but] I was troubled inwardly by the realisation that . . . it would involve me in a long course of seeming dissimulation for which I had neither the talent nor the appetite.'[15]

It is therefore reasonable to assume that the King had summoned Churchill because he felt that an evening with this great orator, actor and *homme de cœur* would cheer him up (which indeed it had), but without the slightest intention of following his advice, advice which was not new to him and which ran counter to his inmost feelings and principles. As Sir Edward Peacock noted in his diary on Sunday the 6th: 'At dinner the

201

King referred to his talk with Winston, and said that Winston had been very amusing but was quite wrong in what he suggested, and that such a course would be inexcusable.'[16]

In his memoirs, the King writes that, following Churchill's departure, he spent a sleepless night trying to reach a final decision. This may be regarded as a rhetorical device to give a climax to his story: the evidence suggests that his mind had in fact already been made up for three weeks, and at most all he can have experienced now was a momentary qualm about what he had long resolved to do. Nevertheless, this page of the memoirs, perhaps their most eloquent and moving, is worth quoting as a general illustration of the thoughts which had undoubtedly been running through the King's mind and guiding him throughout that autumn.

> It was a night of soul-searching. While I paced my bedroom floor my mind retraced the myriad paths of my life. In the end, the decision I reached was the one which had been implicit throughout the course of my action – to put out of my mind all thought of challenging the Prime Minister . . . Even though I might have been able to recruit a commanding majority, I could not have persuaded the entire nation and all the Dominions . . . By making a stand for myself, I should have left the scars of a civil war . . . True, I should still be King. But I would no longer be King by the free and common consent of all . . . The cherished conception of a Monarchy above politics would have been shattered . . . I felt I had come to the limit of a man's power to shape events and fend off catastrophe. Were I to wait longer I might indeed reap the whirlwind. And so, in faith and calmness, not unmixed with sorrow, I resolved to end the constitutional crisis forthwith. I would close my reign with dignity, clear the succession for my brother with the least possible embarrassment and avoid all appearance of faction . . .
>
> I reject the notion . . . that, faced with a choice between love and duty, I chose love. I certainly married because I

chose the path of love. But I abdicated because I chose the path of duty. I did not value the Crown so lightly that I gave it away. I valued it so deeply that I surrendered it, rather than risk any impairment of its prestige.[17]

The Duke of Windsor went on to quote with pride from a letter he had received at the time from one of his best friends.*

... When the history of this episode comes to be written it will be realized that your nobility in refusing even to test your popularity was a sign of true greatness, and probably saved the very existence of the Empire ... I must humbly express my intense admiration for your obvious and inflexible determination not to encourage a 'King's Party'. It was within your power to create Civil War and chaos. You had only to lift a finger or even come to London and show yourself, to arouse millions in your support.

Finally (as we read in the memoirs) morning came; and after breakfast the King summoned Monckton to his room to tell him of his decision in the following terms: 'I want you to go to London and warn the Prime Minister that, when he comes to the Fort this afternoon I shall notify him formally that I have decided to abdicate.'[18]

Monckton (who merely recalls in his notes that the King declared that morning that he wished the crisis to be 'quickly resolved') felt that now was the moment to raise a painful but pressing subject. The King seemed to assume that, upon abdication, he would simply join Mrs Simpson abroad and that eventually she would receive her decree absolute and they would marry; but it was far from clear that this would be allowed

---

* The friend was Colin Davidson (1895–1943), the son of a courtier of George V and a clerk to the House of Lords. He was later killed in North Africa.

to happen, owing to the cruel and barbaric divorce laws which existed in England at that time. These provided that a woman petitioning for divorce on the grounds of her husband's adultery (and there were few other grounds) must fail if it could be proved that she herself was engaging in an adulterous relationship. In the six-month interval between decree nisi and decree absolute, it was open to any member of the public to 'intervene' in the divorce by coming forward with alleged evidence of adultery, these claims being examined by a court official known as the King's Proctor who had power to conduct a full investigation into the past life of the petitioner. Now Monckton was fully aware that there was much gossip in London's professional world that Mrs Simpson had been engaging in an adulterous relationship with the King; he had written as much to the King on 18 November.* This was violently denied by the King at the time and ever afterwards; but once he abdicated he would be in the wretched position of any ordinary citizen wishing to marry a woman awaiting divorce, and it was highly probable that some 'muddle-headed busybody'[19] would 'intervene' claiming evidence of such adultery and that the case would then be investigated by the King's Proctor.[2] At best this would mean that the ex-King, in order to calm suspicions, would have to remain apart from Mrs Simpson until she received her final decree the following spring; at worst, it might mean the divorce would be delayed or never go through at all. As Monckton writes: 'I was desperately afraid that the King might give up the throne and yet be deprived of his chance to marry Mrs Simpson.'[20]

---

* See above, pp. 123—4.
† It was constitutionally impossible for the King's Proctor to investigate the private life of the King himself while he was on the throne: this, at any rate, was what Baldwin was advised by the Attorney-General, Sir Donald Somervell (Somervell's Memoir, quoted in H. Montgomery Hyde, *Baldwin*, pp. 566—7).

Monckton's proposed solution to this problem, which he propounded to the King that Saturday morning, was that the Government, at the same time as presenting the Abdication Bill to the House of Commons, should present a second Bill which would have the effect of making Mrs Simpson's divorce absolute immediately. The King accepted this proposal gratefully – 'it was a lifeline thrown across a crevasse' – and authorized Monckton to discuss it immediately with Baldwin's senior advisers. Meanwhile (he tells us) he had not forgotten Switzerland, and he asked Allen to send an agent to inquire into hotel accommodation near Zurich. 'If nothing came of Walter Monckton's proposed two Bills, I would repair there to wait.'[21]

There was a short cabinet meeting early that morning, during which, as we have seen, Baldwin told his alarmed colleagues that, against his better judgement, he had allowed the King to see Churchill. Afterwards Zetland wrote to Linlithgow in New Delhi: 'The King is being advised by two different sets of people – first by his constitutional advisers, the Prime Minister and the Cabinet, and secondly by a body of unofficial advisers whose advice is having the effect of stiffening him against the advice of the Prime Minister and the Cabinet. He is being encouraged to believe that the Cabinet do not by any means reflect the united view of the people in their refusal to introduce legislation to legalise a morganatic marriage . . .'[22] Very shortly, however, Monckton's message was delivered to the effect that the King had no such intention of prolonging the crisis; for later that same morning this news was brought to Beaverbrook by the Home Secretary in person, Sir John Simon. The reason for sending such a senior figure, Beaverbrook conjectured, was to discourage him once and for all from giving active support to the King.[23]

Beaverbrook at once called on Churchill at his Westminster flat. Churchill had not heard the news and was busy putting the finishing touches to his letters to Baldwin and the King and the elaborate press statement which he planned to issue, all of which he proudly showed Beaverbrook. They were stirring stuff. To the Prime Minister he wrote that he had found the King

> under the very greatest strain and very near breaking point. He had two marked and prolonged 'blackouts' in which he completely lost the thread of the conversation . . . I told the King that if he appealed to you to allow him time to recover himself . . . you would I am sure not fail in kindness and compassion. It would be most cruel and wrong to extort a decision from him in his present state.[24]

To the King he wrote: 'News from all fronts! No pistol to be held at the King's head! No doubt that this request for time will be granted. Therefore no final decision or bill till after Xmas – probably February or March.' Churchill advised the King on no account to leave the country; to summon the Prime Minister of Northern Ireland, who was visiting London and agreed with Churchill's stand; and to trust in Beaverbrook. 'The King brought him back across the world. He is a tiger to fight . . . A *devoted* tiger. A very rare breed.'[25] The proposed press statement was a long and rousing manifesto:

> I plead for time and patience. The nation must realise the character of the constitutional issue. There is no question of any conflict between the King and Parliament. Parliament has not been consulted . . . If an abdication were to be hastily extorted, the outrage so committed would cast its shadow forward across many chapters of the history of the British Empire.[26]

Beaverbrook read these belligerent documents but assured Churchill that all would be in vain, explaining: 'Our cock won't fight.' (The following day he said to Channon: 'Our cock would be all right if only he would fight, but at the moment he will not even crow.'[27]) Churchill would not believe this and declared his intention of sending the letters and issuing the statement, but Beaverbrook's parting words were: 'No dice.'[28]

That Saturday, Monckton and Allen lunched at the Windham Club (where Monckton had set up an impromptu headquarters for his royal business) with Dugdale, Baldwin's PPS, who had been at the Fort the previous day, and Sir Horace Wilson, the chief prime ministerial adviser, and put the plan of the Two Bills to them. They all agreed that legislation was the only means whereby the King might join and marry Mrs Simpson upon abdicating, and that such legislation could also usefully deal with the questions of the ex-King's pension and title. But there might be difficulties in the House of Commons. A divorce reform law, sponsored by the great libertarian campaigner A. P. Herbert and extending the grounds of divorce to desertion, was currently before Parliament; a special Bill for the King might lead to demands that this reform include the abolition of the decree *nisi* (which was what Herbert wanted), and this would arouse controversy.* Nevertheless, Wilson, the pragmatic civil servant, strongly supported Monckton's plan; Dugdale, the politician, was more reserved, but agreed that it should be put to the Prime Minister.[29]

Duly apprised of the scheme, Baldwin spent the whole of the afternoon discussing it with the Home Secretary and the Attorney-General. Simon expressed the view that the Monckton plan was quite possible legally and would indeed provide a solution to one problem, but might encounter opposition in a cabinet 'where MacDonald, Wood, Runciman, and Chamberlain represented the nonconformist element, Halifax and Hoare the high churchmen, and Inskip the evangelicals'.[30]

---

* Herbert later wrote that in his Bill he 'sought to abolish the decree *nisi*, but on very high advice the clause had to be withdrawn' (A. P. Herbert, *Wigs at Work* (1966, Penguin paperback), footnote on p. 85).

Early that Saturday evening, Baldwin and Dugdale motored again to the Fort for the Prime Minister's seventh meeting with the King. A problem of protocol was that neither the King nor Baldwin felt constitutionally competent to be the first to raise the subject of the new plan; so Monckton was called in to expound it as his own while his two listeners affected to be hearing it for the first time. Baldwin expressed the view that the plan 'provided the right way out' and said 'he would resign if he could not carry his colleagues. He would see the possibly awkward ones on Sunday.' This was Monckton's recollection.[31] The King remembered that Baldwin described the plan as 'a just accommodation', and that when he made his offer of resignation, Monckton quickly exchanged 'a wondering glance' with the sovereign.[32]

Monckton and Allen followed the Prime Minister back to London to discuss the details of the plan with various Whitehall officials. With Somervell and Simon, they finally saw the text of the proposed legislation and were satisfied.[33] Later that same night, Chamberlain rang Baldwin in a panic to say that two aircraft were waiting at Hendon Airport chartered in the King's name and ready to leave for Zurich. Baldwin gave immediate orders that these planes were to be cancelled.[34]

Meanwhile the King had been intensely preoccupied with the current fate of Mrs Simpson, who had made a distressed telephone call to him from Vienne in southeastern France that afternoon pleading with him not to abdicate. It was evident that her journey through France with Brownlow had developed into a nightmare.

Following Brownlow's circuitous route to the south they had spent Friday night at a hotel at Blois in Touraine, only to discover before they turned in that twenty reporters and cameramen were encamped in the lobby. They bribed the porter to smuggle them out through the staff entrance at three in the morning, thus temporarily evading their pursuers. But the press caught up with them again at Lyons, after an eagle-eyed bystander had pointed at Mrs Simpson and shouted '*voilà la dame*'. They stopped at Vienne to lunch at the famous restaurant run by Madame Point, from where Mrs Simpson telephoned the King.* Madame Point was a kindly soul, and arranged to divert the attention of the pursuing journalists with a tempting lunch while Mrs Simpson and Brownlow, who had themselves been lunching in a private room, escaped through the kitchen. Finally they arrived at the Rogers' villa near Cannes at two thirty on Sunday morning; the villa was surrounded by press, and as they drove through the gates Mrs Simpson was obliged to crouch in the back of the car with a rug over her head. She was now as much besieged as was the King at the Fort; but at least she was 'back among friends'.[35]

Later that Sunday morning, Chips Channon rang the Rogers' villa and spoke to Brownlow, urging him to 'induce Wallis to do something . . . ' Brownlow replied that he was 'doing everything, and that Wallis was in fact very reasonable, and ready to renounce the King, would do anything, in fact, to keep him on his throne, but thought that an independent statement issued by her would only mean that the King would fly to his plane, an undignified exit for the Emperor of India and King of England. Perry said he would go on trying . . . '[36]

When Mrs Simpson herself awoke that morning, she was seized by a 'sense of helplessness' and wished she had taken Brownlow's advice to stay in England. She spoke to the King on the telephone, but found him 'remote and unreachable'. She thereupon wrote him an impassioned letter, fifteen pages long and barely coherent, a testimony to her mood of exhaustion and despair at that moment and aimed above all at getting the King to stay his hand in the obstinate state in which he was. It began: 'I am so anxious for you not

* Madame Point was still running this celebrated hostelry in 1980, when she was willing to talk with pride of her efforts to help the future Duchess of Windsor in December 1936.

to *abdicate* . . .' She pointed out (correctly) that the world would blame her for his abdicating, as all would say she could have prevented it. She begged him to tell Baldwin that he would drop all thought of marriage at least until the following autumn. 'By October Mr B couldn't afford to say no and I think the Dominions could be won over. Think my sweetheart isn't it better in the long run not to be hasty or selfish but back up your people and make an eight-month sacrifice for them? Then they will give you what you want and no one can say that you shirked and ran away when your people were rallying to your aid.' If he insisted on abdicating, she prudently warned him to settle in advance the questions of her divorce, his pension and their titles.[37]

The question of the divorce was to be settled by the Monckton plan; and at half past nine on Sunday morning, Baldwin, as he had promised the King, held a special meeting at 10, Downing Street, to put this to senior or potentially difficult cabinet ministers: Neville Chamberlain, Ramsay MacDonald, Simon, Stanley, Runciman, Inskip, Halifax, Wood and Hoare. The Prime Minister declared his confidence of carrying the measure and 'that he could not be responsible for any other policy'. Hoare supported the plan. It was, he said 'not a moral issue'; the choice was 'between a ramp now or in five months'. When he briefly left the meeting to greet Monckton, who had arrived and was waiting in Horace Wilson's office, Baldwin seemed affable and hoped soon to have a decision. The Prime Minister however was called away to see Queen Mary, who had summoned him for some reason; and when he returned, he found the mood of the meeting had turned strongly against the proposal. Inskip, Halifax and Wood opposed it vehemently, the first two on moral grounds, the latter because it would be electorally unpopular.[38] MacDonald wrote in his diary: 'Astounded on arrival to hear King proposed bargain to Prime Minister last night he would abdicate if the divorce was made absolute . . . He is evidently not responsible. Ministers discussed the proposal and the more they thought of it the more they opposed . . . What a sordid story . . . '[39]

After waiting more than two hours, Monckton was called into the Cabinet Room, where Neville Chamberlain (who had originally supported the proposal in private discussions with Baldwin) gave their reasons for opposing the plan: ' . . . that the two Bills smacked of a bargain where there should be none; that the second Bill would affront the moral sense of the Nation and that it would be resisted and debated, and that in the course of the debate unpleasant suggestions would be made.'[40] When Monckton remained silent, a minister asked how the King would react to their decision. Monckton replied that he would 'undoubtedly ask for more time'. MacDonald asked: 'How much time will the King ask for? How many days?' Monckton said: 'Hardly days. I anticipate that he will require weeks.' Baldwin then declared: 'This matter must be finished before Christmas'; whereupon Chamberlain murmured that the uncertainty was already hurting the Christmas trade.[41] (Monckton noted: 'Baldwin was ready to resign, but I told him the King would not wish that.'[42])

At half past five that afternoon the plan was discussed by the full Cabinet. This time it was supported by Lord Swinton, the Air Minister; and the Scottish Secretary, Walter Elliot, pointed out that there was no period of waiting in divorce under Scots law. The opponents, however, now included even Duff Cooper, who argued that 'it would obviously be said that the Government must want to get rid of him, as they had refused to introduce legislation for a morganatic marriage in order to keep him, but were willing to introduce legislation . . . in order to expedite his departure'. The majority agreed with this view. Accepting the verdict, Baldwin said: 'The King will be very disappointed. He was looking forward to being married on New Year's Day. If it had come off, I should certainly have deputed the Home Secretary to act as our representative on that occasion.' His colleagues appeared somewhat shocked by this levity. When they emerged into Downing Street, there was a large crowd shouting: 'We want King Edward! Down with the politicians!'[43]

What would the King do now? Monckton warned that he might ask for further weeks to consider his decision; Mrs Simpson was pleading with him to drop the whole marriage question until the following autumn; the King himself had proposed, in the event of the Two Bills being rejected, to withdraw to Switzerland to rest and reflect. In the event he did none of these things. At his Friday audience Baldwin had expressed the Cabinet's wish that his final decision should be announced in a parliamentary statement on Monday afternoon. Now it was agreed that this statement should simply say that the King was still making up his mind and that the Government, while sympathizing with him, hoped he would soon reach some conclusion in order to dispel the uncertainty. On Sunday evening the proposed wording of the statement was submitted to the King. It began:

> In considering the whole matter it has always been, and remains, the earnest desire of the Government to afford to His Majesty the fullest opportunity of weighing a decision which involves so directly his own future happiness and the interests of all his subjects.
>
> At the same time they cannot but be aware that any considerable prolongation of the present state of suspense and uncertainty would involve risk of the gravest injury to National and Imperial interests.

At ten o'clock that night, Monckton telephoned Malcolm MacDonald (who as Dominions Secretary had the task of ensuring that advance copies of the statement were received by the Dominion premiers) to confirm that the King approved of this wording.

Four hours later, at two o'clock on Monday morning, Malcolm MacDonald was at home having a late-night bath after a week-end of unremitting work on the constitutional question, when the telephone rang. To

212

his astonishment, it was the King, sounding most friendly and asking if the second paragraph of the statement might now conclude with the words: ' . . . and indeed no one is more insistent upon this aspect of the situation than His Majesty'. MacDonald thanked the sovereign for this amendment, which would make the statement more popular, and said he was sure he could accept it on behalf of his colleagues. As MacDonald recalled, the King then 'thanked me charmingly for my conduct of all the exchanges with the Commonwealth Prime Ministers, saying that these had been most helpful to him'. They chatted genially for some minutes before the King said good night. MacDonald thought this must have been 'the only occasion in Britain's long and glorious history when a King was formally advised on high state affairs by one of his Ministers standing stark naked . . . while his feet splashed in a puddle of bath water'.*

Meanwhile, Churchill's 'manifesto' had appeared in the Sunday press and caused a great furore. He received many letters of support but many more of bitter opposition, some of them from leading supporters of his campaign for rearmament. On Sunday evening he conferred at Chartwell with a group of friends which included his old PPS Robert Boothby and the Liberal leader Sir Archibald Sinclair. After much argument, they persuaded him that it would be politically disastrous for him to continue to urge the King to resist the advice of the Government. Reluctanctly, Churchill agreed to write a message to the King to say that

> the only possibility of Your Majesty remaining on the Throne is if you could subscribe to some such declaration of the following: 'The King will not enter into any contract of marriage contrary to the advice of his Ministers.'[44]

---

* This curious story, related by Malcolm MacDonald in *People and Places* (1969), is confirmed by the diary of his father, Ramsay MacDonald, for 7 December 1936.

Boothby told Chips Channon that 'such a document would give [the King] a way out for the future, as he could still abdicate or, as might easily happen, future ministers might allow the marriage. The problem was, how to get the King to sign it?'[45] The message was confided to Godfrey Thomas, a friend of Boothby, who showed it and explained it to the King on Monday morning. But as Churchill wrote, the King 'turned it aside on the grounds that it would not be honourable to play for time when his fundamental resolve was unchanged and . . . unchangeable. It was certainly this very strict point of honour which cost him his Crown.' Somewhat vainly, Churchill imagined he might have won the King over had he managed to see him again personally; but he had been told the King would not be allowed such a meeting 'as the Ministers were already angry with Baldwin for having given him permission to see me on Friday . . . '[46]

'The world is now divided into Cavaliers and Round-heads', wrote Channon on Monday 7 December. 'People are weary of the crisis, and public opinion is hardening on both sides.' The popular mood in London seemed not much changed from before the week-end. There were still widespread public demonstrations in the King's favour, some spontaneous, others organized by communists or blackshirts. The popular press was more strident than ever in the King's support: the *Daily Mail* carried on its front page an open letter from Lord Rothermere arguing that in no circumstances could the country afford to dispense with a King of 'such superlatively splendid' qualities and that his departure would certainly mean the reintroduction of conscription. The 'King's Party' was still a reality to those who did not yet realize that the King himself wished to have nothing to do with it, as the letters of support which the King received testify.[47]

In the House of Commons, however, the mood was vastly different from three days earlier. Members returning from their provincial constituencies had been made aware of the deep hostility of important sections of the electorate to the King's marriage project. 'There is no doubt that over the week-end opinion has settled down steadily behind the Government', wrote Leo Amery. The marriage might have some support in London, which was 'less puritan and influenced by the Harmsworth and Beaverbrook press'; but 'the country as a whole is getting progressively more shocked at the idea that the King could hesitate between his duty to the Throne and affection for a woman'.[48] A friend later said to Baldwin: 'I believe you were the only man on Friday who knew what the House of Commons would be thinking on Monday.' Baldwin replied: 'I have always believed in the week-end. But how they do it I don't know. I suppose they talk to the stationmaster.'[49] From the moment members reassembled, wrote Ramsay MacDonald, 'it was plain that the House was emphatically behind the Government, strongly resented Churchill's "manifesto" of Sunday, and detested Rothermere and Beaverbrook'.[50] The wisdom of Baldwin's reluctance to pressurize the King into giving a quick decision was now apparent: there was no longer any serious threat from a pro-King group in the Commons.

Baldwin entered the House at Question Time that afternoon to be greeted by cheers. Colonel Josiah Wedgwood, a quixotic Labour supporter of the King's marriage who had himself been divorced, asked if a private member's motion he had put down reaffirming their oath of allegiance to Edward VIII might be heard at the earliest opportunity. Baldwin replied in the negative, and Wedgwood was barracked when he tried to put a further question. In response to an arranged question from Attlee, Baldwin read the statement which the Government had prepared and with which the King had agreed, ending with the words: 'I cannot conclude this statement without expressing what the whole House feels, our deep and respectful sympathy with His Majesty at this time.' Churchill (who was in a dark mood and had not in fact been listening to the statement with its friendly implications for the King) then rose to put, for the third time, his supplementary question demanding parliamentary consultation, only to find himself howled down by a chorus of angry members. 'He was completely staggered by the unanimous hostility of the House', wrote Amery; while Ramsay MacDonald expressed the widespread view that through his ill-timed intervention Churchill had 'ended his career in a ditch'. With a shout of 'You won't be satisfied until you have broken him, will you?' Churchill walked sulkily out of the chamber. George Lambert, a former chairman of the Liberal Party, then asked: 'Does the Prime Minister realise the deep sympathy which is felt for him in all sections of the House?', which evoked cheers and applause.

By Monday afternoon, therefore, it was clear in official circles that the House of Commons was strongly behind the Government in its view that the King if he wished to marry Mrs Simpson would have to abdicate; and it was almost certain that the King accepted this view and intended to abdicate in order to realize his desire to marry Mrs Simpson. The King had not yet formally abdicated, however; and during the next forty-eight hours further efforts were made from various quarters to induce him to remain on the throne. There was something tragically futile about these efforts, because they were all based on the notion that someone should be sent out to Mrs Simpson to encourage her to renounce the King. For hardly anyone as yet realized that renunciation was what Mrs Simpson herself wanted; that she already had an 'encourager' present in the form of Brownlow, who had been entrusted with his mission by those closest to the King; but that the whole project was hopeless in that the King was simply not willing to contemplate her withdrawal and that, whatever line she took, he meant to abdicate in the confidence that, once he had done so, she would consent to marry him.

On Sunday evening, Channon had held a dinner of 'Cavaliers' (by which he simply meant men sympathetic to the King) at his house in Belgrave Square.

Among those present were Duff Cooper and Leslie Hore-Belisha from the Cabinet, David Margesson, the Government Chief Whip, and Esmond Harmsworth. During the meal Channon's wife declared that someone ought to 'get at' Mrs Simpson to make her break with the King. Harmsworth left early; he had not announced his intentions but in fact made arrangements to travel to the South of France on the pretext of visiting his mother. After dinner, Cooper, Hore-Belisha and Margesson held a huddled conference at the end of the table. They agreed that 'every possible effort should be made to prevent abdication and . . . that not sufficient effort had been made hitherto'; and that it was essential that some senior figure go out to Mrs Simpson to 'speak to her in no uncertain terms, impressing upon her the harm she was doing and the hopelessness of the future' in order to convince her 'that her interests lay in giving up the marriage'. They believed that 'if she really decided to give him up, [the King] would accept her decision'. Margesson, who as befitted a Chief Whip possessed a forceful personality, offered to go himself and to discuss this the following morning with leading members of the Cabinet.[51]

On Monday morning Margesson went to Neville Chamberlain to put forward this proposal. Chamberlain announced that he was 'all in favour of it', and that he himself had already been considering much the same idea with senior civil servants, 'but that it had been considered that the best person to send was her own lawyer, Mr Goddard, who is . . . a man of considerable character, who would not be afraid to tell her exactly what he thought'.[52] * It seems odd that Chamberlain,

---

* Goddard had been in touch with senior civil servants at the time of Ipswich, and they had been favourably impressed by his lack of enthusiasm for the divorce case and willingness to tell them of the King's personal involvement in it. He was on friendly terms with several members of the Cabinet, including Ramsay MacDonald, with whom he had lunched on Saturday 5 December.

who in cabinet discussions had shown himself to be one of the ministers most censorious of the King, should have associated himself with these last-minute efforts to save the sovereign; but it appears undeniable that he in fact did so. According to his biographer Iain Macleod, Chamberlain personally wanted Edward VIII to leave, as he had 'felt all through that we should never be safe with this King', but he nevertheless believed that 'the solution the country wanted was the renunciation of the marriage' – and on Monday 7 December his diary 'still expressed some hope' of this.[53]

At some point over the week-end or that same Monday morning, Goddard was summoned to the Treasury (Chamberlain's department) to see Sir Horace Wilson (who was at this time combining his work in the Prime Minister's office with the post of Acting Permanent Secretary to the Treasury) and told that the Government would like him to go to Cannes to see Mrs Simpson 'to ascertain from her her real intentions'. Goddard agreed to go. The King, however, got to hear of the plan; and on Monday afternoon he summoned Goddard to the Fort, where 'the matter was very frankly discussed'. It is clear both from the King's memoirs and Peacock's diary that the King tried to forbid Goddard going to Cannes.[54]

Meanwhile, Mrs Simpson herself had spent that Monday planning a statement to the press; and this was finally issued by Brownlow at seven o'clock in the evening from a hotel in Cannes:

> Mrs Simpson throughout the last few weeks has invariably wished to avoid any action or proposal which would hurt or damage His Majesty or the Throne.
> Today her attitude is unchanged, and she is willing, if such action would solve the problem, to withdraw from a situation which has become both unhappy and untenable.

This was far from being an unconditional renunciation, and Brownlow thought the wording insufficiently strong. But Mrs Simpson 'shrank from dealing him so cruel a blow'; she also feared that, if she went the full way, the King would either refuse to believe her or take some foolish action such as flying out to join her. Her intention seems to have been to give him a way out while his friends worked on him to drop the marriage, at least for the time being. As it happened, the King welcomed the statement for the very different reason, as Peacock noted, that it 'would to some extent divert criticism from her to him, the very thing he wanted'.[55]

The statement quickly reached London, where it was broadcast by the BBC on the nine o'clock news. This caused great excitement, and the *Mail* and the *Express* prepared editions proclaiming the crisis was over. That evening, Goddard went to see Wilson at the Travellers Club to tell of his meeting with the King. Wilson produced the statement (which Goddard had not seen) and asked whether it represented a sincere desire on the part of Mrs Simpson to renounce the marriage. Goddard replied that 'from what he knew of the lady it was undoubtedly her intention'. Wilson then arranged for Goddard to see the Prime Minister, who told him: 'I want you to go to Cannes and find out what is really behind this . . . Immediately — tonight.' Baldwin offered to put a Government plane at Goddard's disposal. Goddard agreed to go, on the condition that he could take a doctor with him as he had never flown before and suffered from a heart condition.[56]

Goddard's journey to Cannes has been regarded hitherto as one of the great mysteries of the Abdication Crisis, and many odd reasons for it have been suggested. When it was discovered by the press twenty-four hours later, one story which gained credence was that the doctor who accompanied the solicitor was a gynaecologist or even abortionist and that the motive for their visit was Mrs Simpson's pregnancy. And even such supposedly well-informed sources as Lord Davidson and Frances Donaldson have seriously suggested that Goddard was sent out to recover royal jewels which Edward VIII is supposed improperly to have given Mrs Simpson.[57]* There can be little doubt, however, that the simple explanation is the true one, and that senior circles of Government and administration were making a somewhat muddled and half-hearted last-minute effort to prevent the marriage and stop the abdication. Baldwin later claimed in conversation with various people,† that Goddard wished to see Mrs Simpson anyway in connection with the threatened intervention against her divorce; that he appealed to the Prime Minister to protect him in face of the King's attempted ban on his journey; and that Baldwin did no more than urge him 'to do his duty to his client' and help him on his way. This, however, was a mere cover story to protect the Prime Minister; for in strict terms it was obviously most improper for the Government to put pressure on a citizen through that citizen's own solicitor. That Goddard went not on Mrs Simpson's business but the Government's is evident from the fact that, when he eventually submitted a bill for five hundred guineas as the fee for his journey, it was presented not to Mrs Simpson but to the Treasury.‡

The idea was that Goddard should leave on Monday night and work on his client throughout Tuesday; for on Tuesday evening Baldwin planned to make a final

---

* Receipts for the jewellery he gave her were kept by the King and prove that he bought it all himself.

† Such as his niece Monica (quoted in Frances Donaldson, *Edward VIII*, p. 286), Sir Edward Peacock (quoted in Lord Birkenhead, *Walter Monckton*, p. 146), and Victor Cazalet (quoted in R. Rhodes James, *Victor Cazalet*, p. 190).

‡ This is apparent from a letter sent by George Allen to Ulick Alexander on 3 February 1937, an original copy of which is in the archives of Maître Suzanne Blum. Allen writes that Goddard had told him he would be charging the Treasury five hundred guineas for his mission to Cannes; and that Allen therefore proposed to charge the Government the same sum for his firm's work in connection with the formal business of the Abdication.

appeal to the King to give up his marriage. But bad weather conditions postponed Goddard's departure until Tuesday morning; and owing to engine failure he did not reach Cannes until Wednesday morning. Meanwhile the King, who learned of Goddard's departure from Allen, telephoned Mrs Simpson in some agitation asking her not to be influenced by anything the solicitor said, or, better still, not to see him at all.[58]

On Tuesday 8 December, Ramsay MacDonald wrote in his diary:

> Knew this to be the decisive day & I had known the King too long to doubt what his decision would be. All his gifts, all his genius, all his opportunities would be submerged in his fascination [for Mrs Simpson]. Apart from her he was still promising to be a great King. His relations with his Ministers were admirable & so were his thoughts of his people & his Empire. His answer that he was to abdicate came today.[59]

At the Fort, the King had now re-established contact with his family. Early on Monday evening he had seen the Duke of York, whom he informed that he had definitely decided to abdicate. The Duke returned to his house to dine but later reappeared at the Fort as the King was 'my eldest brother [and] I had to be there to try & help him in his hour of need'.[60] The King recalled that they discussed 'the disposition of family property, heirlooms and so forth, for, in the process of stepping down from the Throne, I should also abdicate, for legal purposes, the position of head of the House of Windsor'.[61] It is highly probable that they also discussed the question of Mrs Simpson's divorce following the failure of the Two Bills proposal; at all events, by the time he abdicated the King had received a promise from his brother that as future sovereign he would do all in his power to promote the smooth passage of the divorce.[62]

At eleven o'clock on Tuesday morning the Duke of Kent turned up at the Fort and spent the whole day with the King, talking with him 'for hours on end'.[63] This is described by the King in his memoirs as a 'brotherly reunion'[64]; but the Duke of Kent was in a desperate state, 'trying by every means in his power to persuade [the King] to stay'. The King (as the Duchess of Kent told Chips Channon) assured his brother that it was all for the best that he should abdicate. Before coming to the throne, 'while he knew he was an excellent Prince of Wales and liked his job, he nevertheless felt that he could never "stick" being King . . . he was afraid of being a bad one. He could never tolerate the restrictions; the loneliness; the etiquette . . . '[65] Only Mrs Simpson made it tolerable, he seemed to be saying; and marriage to her had been denied him as King. Baldwin later heard that, when the Duke of Kent begged the King to change his mind, the King had replied: 'I made it up long ago. Why should I change it now?'[66]

These conversations with the Duke of Kent continued until Tuesday evening, when Baldwin made a further visit to the Fort for what was to be his eighth and last interview that autumn in order (whether out of motives of personal humanity or political wisdom) to make a final appeal to Edward VIII. He told Dugdale and Monckton, with whom he motored down: 'He must wrestle with himself in a way he has never done before, and if he will let me, I will help him. We may even have to see the night through together.' In this, Baldwin's biographer saw 'something of the old Wesleyan strain'.[67] On the journey Baldwin seemed very nervous; he puffed compulsively at his pipe and fidgeted incessantly.[68] The King was speaking on the telephone to Mrs Simpson when they arrived, and when he joined them he said: 'She is indeed a wonderful woman, and all this has brought us much closer together than ever before.'[69] As Monckton feared, the King seemed 'worn out' and was alarmed at the sight of the Prime Minister's suitcase with its implications that the premier proposed to stay overnight. ('I did not propose to have him on my hands that night, snapping his fingers, storing up homely little touches for his report to Parliament.'[70]) Peacock was therefore prevailed upon to ask Baldwin to stay at his house nearby, but the Prime Minister decided to return to London after dinner.

At the formal audience in the drawing room, Baldwin made a further impassioned plea to the King to give up his marriage project for the sake of the country. When he had finished, the King replied quietly that his mind was made up and he wished to be spared any further advice on the subject. To the astonishment of Monckton (who was present), Baldwin 'returned to the charge with renewed vigour and, I thought, put the position even better than before. He asked me immediately afterwards if I thought he had said all he could, and when I explained I thought he had done even more, it was plain that he had not heard the King's request to desist.'[71]

The King now retired to his room in an apparent state of total exhaustion. The Duke of Kent was still at the Fort, the Duke of York had arrived, and Baldwin and Dugdale had been invited to stay for dinner; but it was assumed that their host was in no state to join them and so, along with Monckton, Allen, Peacock and Alexander, they were preparing to dine on their own when, to the general astonishment, the King entered the dining room wearing his white kilt and sat down at the head of the table with Baldwin on his right. 'That dinner party was, I think, his *tour de force*', wrote Monckton. 'In that quiet, panelled room he sat at the head of the table with his boyish face and smile, with a good fresh colour while the rest of us were as white as sheets, rippling over with bright conversation, and with a careful eye to see that his guests were looked after.' It was a brilliant performance yet curiously strange and unreal, for their host ensured that the matter which had brought them together was never once mentioned. The Duke of York noted that, while the rest of them were plunged in gloom, 'my brother was the life and soul of the party, telling the PM things I am sure he had never heard before about unemployment centres etc. . . . I whispered to Walter Monckton "& this is the man we are going to lose". One couldn't, nobody could believe it.'[72]

As he prepared to leave, Baldwin said: 'Can I take it for certain, Sir, that if the Archangel Gabriel came down from Heaven and asked you to change your mind, it would have no effect on you?' None at all, said the King, adding: 'I quite understand why you and Mrs Baldwin do not approve of my action, it is the view of another generation.' Baldwin replied: 'It is quite true that there are no two people among your subjects who are more grieved at what has happened than we are, but you must also remember that there are no two people who hope more sincerely that you may find happiness where you believe it may be found.' The King thanked Baldwin, saying that these were the first good wishes he had received for his future happiness.[73]

The following morning, Wednesday 9 December, Baldwin told the Cabinet of his final efforts to reason with the sovereign and of the ensuing dinner party, which had been 'like a madhouse'.[74] The King, he said, was the only person during the evening 'who seemed natural, cheerful and completely at his ease . . . He seemed like an ordinary young man happily engaged and looking forward to his honeymoon.'[75] His determination to go had been unshakable. Nevertheless, the Cabinet agreed they must protect themselves by sending the King a final message, which read:

> Ministers are reluctant to believe that Your Majesty's resolve is irrevocable and still venture to hope that before Your Majesty pronounces any formal decision, Your Majesty may be pleased to reconsider an intention which must so deeply distress and vitally affect all Your Majesty's subjects.

('SB would have destroyed himself', Hoare noted, 'if the Cabinet had not sent this last request for reconsideration.'[76]) The King replied promptly: 'His Majesty has given the matter his further consideration but regrets he is unable to alter his decision.'

Meanwhile, Theodore Goddard had belatedly reached Cannes and Mrs Simpson on Wednesday morning, and immediately proposed to her that she abandon her divorce as the only means whereby abdication might still be avoided. Mrs Simpson declared that she was willing to do anything to keep the King on the throne; and Goddard telephoned the following message to 10 Downing Street:

> I have today discussed the whole position with Mrs Simpson . . . Mrs Simpson tells me she was, and still is, perfectly willing to instruct me to withdraw her petition for divorce and willing to do anything to prevent the King from abdicating. I am satisfied that this is Mrs Simpson's genuine and honest desire. I read this note over to Mrs Simpson who in every way confirmed it.[77]

At noon Mrs Simpson managed to reach the King on the telephone to tell him of her decision. The King replied that matters had gone too far for such a gesture to make any difference: he was already in the process of abdicating. This was confirmed by Allen, who advised Mrs Simpson not to withdraw her petition as it could now only mean that the King would lose both his throne and the prospect of marrying her. Mrs Simpson was shattered.[78] Goddard admitted defeat and returned to London, stopping at the British Embassy in Paris to call and report to Sir Horace Wilson, who already seemed to know everything, the lines to Cannes having presumably been tapped by Government interceptors.[79]

In the letter she had sent the King on 6 December Mrs Simpson had wisely advised him that, if he was bent on abdication, he should not commit himself before first settling three questions which were vital to his future: divorce, pension and title ' – all those 3 things must be bound up impossible to find a flaw'.[80] But only now, when the King had formally communicated his decision and there remained to him less than two days on the throne, did he and his little circle of advisers direct their exhausted minds to these subjects. On Wednesday afternoon Monckton and Peacock went to London to discuss them with cabinet ministers, senior administrators and the Duke of York, whom they visited at 145 Piccadilly, but who was at this time in a state of mental prostration and completely under the influence of a group of Conservative senior courtiers, including Hardinge and his predecessor Wigram. The hasty and confused manner in which these issues were considered was to cause endless trouble in the years ahead and much pain to the Duke of Windsor, who came to feel that having played the game and abdicated in the trust that he would be fairly treated by his successor he had been deceived and cheated.* The full story of Monckton's and Peacock's consultations on 9 December has yet to be revealed, but they certainly received oral guarantees from the Duke of York concerning the divorce, the ex-King's royal rank and his future right to live at Fort Belvedere. They also discussed the financial provision which would be made for the King on his giving up all that he had inherited at his father's death, and obtained assurances from Chamberlain and Simon that they would recommend the ex-sovereign's inclusion in the new Civil List provided he had stayed apart from the as yet undivorced Mrs Simpson, and from the Duke of York that he would provide a pension of £25,000 a year in the event of Parliament failing to do so. (This promise, solemnized in a private agreement signed by the two brothers at the Fort on Thursday evening after a conference with their advisers, was later repudiated by George VI.[81]) There was also some discussion, both with the Cabinet and the Duke of York, as to whether the King in his turn would give assurances that he would not return to England after the Abdication except by the consent of his successor;

* This unhappy story is the subject of Michael Bloch, *The Secret File of the Duke of Windsor* (1988).

and while Monckton and Peacock appear to have taken the line that the King would certainly not wish to take any future action which might embarrass his successor, George Allen, who was with the King constantly during those last days, later confirmed that the abdicating sovereign, though certainly expressing his intention to go abroad and stay out of the way for a period, never gave any such assurances or in any sense consented to indefinite exile.

That Wednesday afternoon the King emerged from his seclusion at the Fort for the first time since his withdrawal from the capital, and motored the three miles to Royal Lodge, the Duke of York's house in Windsor Great Park, to see his mother who had gone there to meet him. The King wrote: 'I gave her a full account of all that had passed between Mr Baldwin and myself during the six days since our last meeting . . . She still disapproved of and was bewildered by my action, but now that it was over, her heart went out to her hard-pressed son, prompting her to say with tenderness: "And to me, the worst thing is that you won't be able to see her for so long."'[82] Queen Mary's compassion was overborne by other sentiments, however: a few days later she 'indignantly' reproved Lord Salisbury for expressing sympathy for the ex-King, saying that it was only her second son who deserved sympathy or had made a sacrifice.[83]

On his return to the Fort, the King learned that Esmond Harmsworth had now seen Mrs Simpson, who was trying to make a further last effort at renunciation. He spoke to her on the telephone and appealed to her by reading out a single sentence drafted by Allen: 'The only conditions on which I can stay here are if I renounce you for all time.' Mrs Simpson capitulated. She had even conceived a desperate final plan with Brownlow whereby the two of them would disappear to the Far East: but the King assured her that wherever she went he would follow her.[84]

Nothing remained of the reign but the legal formalities required to bring it to an end. That night,

Monckton returned from London bearing the draft texts of two documents. One was the Instrument of Abdication:

> I, Edward the Eighth, of Great Britain, Ireland and the British Dominions beyond the Seas, King, Emperor of India, do hereby declare my irrevocable determination to renounce the Throne for Myself and My descendants, and My desire that effect should be given to this Instrument of Abdication immediately.
>
> In token whereof I have hereunto set My hand this tenth day of December, nineteen hundred and thirty-six, in the presence of the witnesses whose signatures are subscribed.

The other (in which Monckton's own hand is visible) was a message to the parliaments of the Empire:

> After long and anxious consideration, I have determined to renounce the Throne to which I succeeded on the death of My father, and I am now communicating this, My final and irrevocable decision. Realising as I do the gravity of this step, I can only hope that I shall have the understanding of My peoples in the decision I have taken and the reasons which have led Me to take it. I will not enter now into My private feelings, but I would beg that it should be remembered that the burden which constantly rests upon the shoulders of the Sovereign is so heavy that it can only be borne in circumstances different from those in which I now find Myself. I conceive that I am not overlooking the duty that rests on Me to place in the forefront the public interest, when I declare that I am conscious that I can no longer discharge this heavy task with efficiency and satisfaction to myself . . . *

---

* It will be noticed that this says the same thing, in indirect language, as the most famous sentence of the Abdication broadcast.

The King approved the drafts and declared he would sign them in the presence of his three brothers the next morning. And so it was, in the octagonal drawing room at Fort Belvedere at ten o'clock in the morning of Thursday 10 December, that Edward the Eighth, watched by the Dukes of York, Gloucester and Kent, put his name to six copies of the legislative instrument which would imminently bring his reign to a close and seven copies of the message explaining his intention to the representatives of his peoples.

Five hours later, the message was read out by the Speaker in a quavering voice in a hushed House of Commons, and Baldwin opened the debate on the Abdication Bill with what is generally acknowledged to be one of the great speeches of British parliamentary history, its rhetorical force deriving from the contrast between the tragic drama of its subject and the matter-of-fact nature of its content. Harold Nicolson described it thus:

> The Prime Minister then rises. He tells the whole story. He has a blue handkerchief in the breast-pocket of his tail coat . . . His papers are in a confused state . . . and he hesitates somewhat . . . He confuses dates . . . There is no moment when he overstates emotion or indulges in oratory. There is intense silence . . . I suppose that in after-centuries men will read the words of that speech and exclaim, 'What an opportunity wasted!' They will never know the tragic force of its simplicity . . . It was Sophoclean and almost unbearable . . . When it was over [Attlee] asked that the sitting be adjourned until 6 p.m. We file out broken in body and soul, conscious that we have heard the best speech that we shall ever hear in our lives. There was no question of applause. It was the silence of Gettysburg.[85]

Baldwin spoke of the departing monarch with warm sympathy and paid him many tributes. The King, he said, had constantly stressed the following points in their discussions:

229

That if he went he would go with dignity. He would not allow a situation to arise in which he could not do that. He wanted to go with as little disturbance to his Ministers and his people as possible. He wished to go in circumstances that would make the succession of his brother as little difficult for his brother as possible; and I may say that any idea of what might be called a King's Party was abhorrent. He stayed down at Fort Belvedere because he said that he was not coming to London while these things were in dispute, because of the cheering crowds. I honour and respect him for the way in which he behaved . . .

The speech, however, left the King with a grievance. That morning, he had received (through Monckton) a communication from Baldwin asking if there were any personal messages which he would like included in the speech. He submitted two such messages, one to say that he and the Duke of York had always been on the best of terms and he was confident his brother would receive the support of the Empire, the other to stress that Mrs Simpson had done everything possible to dissuade him from abdication. Baldwin read out the first of these messages but omitted the second. This marked the beginning of the King's cold hostility to Baldwin, which was to lead him, in his memoirs published fifteen years later, to suggest that he had always been wary of the Prime Minister, which (though it was understandable in many ways that he should afterwards feel himself to have been the victim of guile) was not really the case.*

A further cause of anxiety that Thursday afternoon was a threat from the Home Secretary to withdraw

---

* During that final week, the King remarked to Peacock and Godfrey Thomas, and doubtless to others, that he felt lucky to have so sympathetic a prime minister to deal with as Stanley Baldwin (Lord Birkenhead, *Walter Monckton*, p. 144; Charles Stuart (ed.), *The Reith Diaries*, p. 190).

the protection of the royal detective Inspector Evans from Mrs Simpson – a threat which was revoked after a humanitarian appeal from the King made through Monckton. The King, indeed, was greatly concerned for Mrs Simpson's security and asked Vansittart, the head of the Foreign Office, if the French Government could be persuaded to give her police protection.[86]

The questions of where the King would go after abdicating and what he would call himself remained to be settled; but the matter which absorbed him for the remaining hours of his reign was the broadcast which, in exercise of his right as a private citizen, he finally intended to deliver on Friday evening, directly before leaving the country. As he wrote: 'Some in the Government looked coldly upon the idea of my supplying an epilogue to a drama upon which the curtain had already descended. And even my mother tried to dissuade me. But I was determined to speak. I did not propose to leave my country like a fugitive in the night.'[87] If Baldwin's address to the House of Commons is generally considered one of the finest parliamentary speeches of the inter-war period, the Duke of Windsor's words to his ex-subjects may be regarded as the most celebrated ever to have been heard over the air in the history of broadcasting. They were basically his own, though he received some help from Monckton, and antecedents may be found both in the abortive broadcast of a week earlier and the King's message to his parliaments which Monckton had drafted. He had 'found it impossible to carry the heavy burdens of responsibility and to discharge my duties as King as I would wish to do without the help and support of the woman I love'; the 'other person most nearly concerned' had 'tried up to the last to persuade me to take a different course'; he had made his decision 'upon a single thought of what would in the end be best for all'. On Friday he asked Winston Churchill to lunch with him at the Fort in order to show him the draft, to which the veteran orator added a few final touches. As Churchill took his leave, there were tears in his eyes; and he quoted the lines of Andrew Marvell on the beheading of Charles I:

> He nothing common did or mean
> Upon that memorable scene.[88]

While the King was lunching with Churchill, the Abdication Bill passed its third reading in the House of Commons and was hurried through all its stages in the House of Lords in a matter of minutes. As it was to take effect immediately, the King's consent had to be given on his behalf in the Upper House by three Lords Commissioners. It was a traditional ceremony, which did not fail to move the few who were present to witness it. The Commissioners doffed their cocked hats; all the King's titles were solemnly read out; there was a reference to it being the first year of his reign; and the clerk proclaimed *le roy le veult* with tragic emphasis. Thus, at eight minutes to two on the afternoon of Friday the eleventh of December 1936, ended the reign of Edward the Eighth.

Notes

The designation 'Paris Papers' refers to those unpublished archives of the Duke and Duchess of Windsor in the possession of Maître Suzanne Blum in Paris.

Chapter One: Edward VIII

1. Paris Papers.
2. HRH the Duke of Windsor, *A King's Story* (1951), p. 258.
3. J. G. Lockhart, *Cosmo Gordon Lang* (1949), pp. 389—90.
4. Clement Attlee, *As It Happened* (1954), p. 85.
5. Tom Jones, *A Diary With Letters, 1931—1950* (1954), pp. 163—4.
6. John Vincent (ed.), *The Crawford Papers* (1984), p. 566.
7. Geoffrey Dennis, *Coronation Commentary* (1937), pp. 232—4.
8. Sir Harold Nicolson's Diary, Balliol College, Oxford, 14 December 1936.
9. Viscount Templewood, *Nine Troubled Years* (1954), p. 223.
10. John Barnes and David Nicholson (ed.), *The Empire at Bay: The Leo Amery Diaries 1929—1945* (1988), p. 434.
11. Sir Donald Somervell's Memoir of the Abdication,

reproduced as an appendix in H. Montgomery-Hyde, *Baldwin* (1973).

12. *A King's Story*, p. 278.
13. *Ibid.*, p. 274.
14. *Ibid.*
15. Lord Birkenhead, *Walter Monckton* (1969), p. 127.
16. Barnes and Nicholson, p. 406.
17. Ramsay MacDonald's Diary, Public Record Office, London (PRO 30/69 1753).
18. Duff Cooper, *Old Men Forget* (1953), p. 202.
19. Vincent, p. 568.
20. Charles Stuart (ed.), *The Reith Diaries* (1975), pp. 187–8.
21. *A King's Story*, p. 277.
22. See Michael Bloch, *The Secret File of the Duke of Windsor* (1988), pp. 171–205.
23. Nigel Nicolson (ed.), *Harold Nicolson, Letters and Diaries 1930–1939* (1966), p. 232.
24. Robert Rhodes James (ed.), *Victor Cazalet: A Portrait* (1976), p. 209.
25. *The Memoirs of Marshal Mannerheim* (1953), pp. 286–7.
26. *Documents on German Foreign Policy*, Series C, Vol. IV.
27. Robert Rhodes James (ed.), *Chips: The Diaries of Sir Henry Channon* (1967), p. 84.
28. Quoted in *The Secret File*, pp. 175–9.
29. Lockhart, p. 395.
30. *A King's Story*, pp. 280–1.
31. Papers of Philip Guedalla in author's possession.
32. Attlee, p. 86.
33. Paris Papers: Sir John Simon to King Edward VIII, 16 July 1936.
34. *A King's Story*, p. 299.

Chapter Two: The Growing Unease

1. Birkenhead, pp. 125–6.
2. Francis Watson, *Dawson of Penn* (1950), p. 296.

3. Martin Gilbert, *Winston S. Churchill*, Vol. V (1976), p. 810.
4. Michael Bloch (ed.), *Wallis & Edward, Letters 1931–1937: the Intimate Correspondence of the Duke and Duchess of Windsor* (1986), p. 139.
5. *Ibid.*, pp. 118–20.
6. *Ibid.*, p. 145.
7. *Ibid.*, p. 148.
8. *Ibid.*, pp. 156–7.
9. *Ibid.*, pp. 159–60.
10. *Ibid.*, p. 158.
11. Kenneth Young (ed), *The Diaries of Sir Robert Bruce-Lockhart, 1915–1918* (1973), p. 357.
12. Nicolson, p. 238.
13. *Victor Cazalet*, p. 186.
14. Kenneth Young, p. 346.
15. *Chips*, p. 60.
16. Birkenhead, p. 128.
17. *Wallis & Edward*, p. 167.
18. *Ibid.*, pp. 173–7.
19. *Ibid.*, p. 180.
20. Ramsay MacDonald's Diary, 2 December 1936.
21. See *Wallis & Edward*, p. 166.
22. Ramsay MacDonald's Diary, 13 February 1936.
23. G. M. Young, *Stanley Baldwin* (1952), p. 233.
24. Nicolson, pp. 247 and 269.
25. Vincent, p. 569.
26. Quoted in H. Montgomery Hyde, *Baldwin*, p. 422.
27. HRH the Duchess of Windsor, *The Heart Has Its Reasons* (1956), p. 225.
28. G. M. Young, p. 233.
29. Stuart, p. 188.
30. *Chips*, p. 69.
31. Gilbert, p. 811.
32. *Chips*, pp. 45–6.
33. Vincent, p. 569.
34. Paris Papers.
35. Nicolson MS Diary, 14 December 1936.
36. Conversation with Robert Egerton, articled to Theodore Goddard in 1936.

37. FO 954/1 f. 91.
38. *A King's Story*, p. 310.

Chapter Three: The King at his Worst

1. *Wallis & Edward*, pp. 193–4.
2. *Ibid.*, pp. 194–6.
3. *The Heart Has Its Reasons*, pp. 246–7.
4. Birkenhead, p. 126.
5. *A King's Story*.
6. *Wallis & Edward*, p. 198.
7. Gilbert, p. 811.
8. See Michael Thornton, *Royal Feud* (1985), pp. 112–14.
9. Sir John Wheeler-Bennett, *The Life and Reign of George VI* (1958), p. 273.
10. Susan Lowndes (ed.), *Diaries and Letters of Marie Belloc Lowndes* (1971), pp. 148, 152.
11. *Chips*, p. 79.
12. Stuart, p. 189; John Evelyn Wrench, *Geoffrey Dawson and Our Times* (1955), p. 338.
13. *A King's Story*, pp. 313–14.
14. Birkenhead, p. 127.
15. Stuart, p. 187.
16. Vincent, p. 573.
17. Oliver Warner, *Admiral of the Fleet* (1969).
18. *Wallis & Edward*, p. 200.
19. *Ibid.*, p. 203.
20. Lord Beaverbrook, *The Abdication of Edward VIII* (1966), pp. 30–33.
21. Anthony Eden, *Facing the Dictators*, p. 410.
22. Keith Middlemas and John Barnes, *Baldwin* (1969), p. 983.
23. Helen Hardinge, *Loyal to Three Kings* (1967), p. 117.
24. Templewood, pp. 217–18.
25. G. M. Young, p. 234.
26. Neville Chamberlain Papers, Birmingham University Library, NC 1/26/523.

27. *A King's Story*, p. 316.
28. Warner, p. 62.
29. Tom Jones, pp. 284–5; Lord Citrine, *Men and Work* (1964), pp. 325–6; G. M. Young, pp. 234–5; Montgomery Hyde, pp. 450–54; Middlemas and Barnes, pp. 984–6 (based on Mrs Baldwin's Diary); A. W. Baldwin, *My Father: The True Story* (1955), pp. 299–300.
30. *A King's Story*, pp. 316–18.
31. Warner, p. 63.
32. Birkenhead, p. 132.
33. *A King's Story*, pp. 318–19.
34. Hardinge, p. 119.
35. Ramsay MacDonald's Diary, 5 December 1936.
36. *The Heart Has Its Reasons*, p. 240.
37. Paris Papers.

Chapter Four: The King at his Best

1. Ramsay MacDonald's Diary, 27 October 1936.
2. *Ibid.*, 30 October 1936; Wrench, p. 343.
3. Lowndes, pp. 177–8.
4. *The Heart Has Its Reasons*, pp. 241–2.
5. Nicolson, p. 276.
6. Ramsay MacDonald's Diary.
7. Stuart, p. 189.
8. Kenneth Young, p. 357.
9. Raymond A. Jones, *Arthur Ponsonby* (1989), p. 216.
10. *Victor Cazalet*, p. 184.
11. *Chips*, p. 74.
12. Tom Jones, p. 280.
13. Vincent, pp. 572–3.
14. Tom Jones, p. 280.
15. Philip Guedalla, *The Hundredth Year* (1939), pp. 241–6.
16. Nicolson, p. 277.
17. *Chips*, pp. 74–5.
18. *A King's Story*, pp. 322–5.

19. Nicolson, p. 277.
20. *Chips*, p. 75.
21. Ramsay MacDonald's Diary, 3 November 1936.
22. Warner, p. 65.
23. Vincent, p. 572.
24. Beaverbrook, pp. 34–5.
25. *Chips*, pp. 75–6.
26. *Wallis & Edward*, p. 208.
27. Paris Papers: Lady Oxford to Mrs Simpson, 6 November 1936.
28. Paris Papers (also quoted in H. Montgomery Hyde's article in *Vogue*, July 1980, pp. 187–8).
29. Warner, pp. 63–6.
30. *Ibid.*, p. 66.
31. Nicolson, pp. 279–80; Kenneth Young, p. 360; Barnes and Nicholson, p. 431.
32. Birkenhead, pp. 132–3.
33. Conversation with Count Edward Raczyński.
34. *A King's Story*, p. 325.
35. Warner, pp. 66–7.
36. *A King's Story*, pp. 325–6.
37. Warner, p. 67.
38. Templewood, pp. 218–19.

Chapter Five: The Decision to Abdicate

1. *A King's Story*, p. 326.
2. See *Wallis & Edward*, pp. 199, 207.
3. *The Heart Has Its Reasons*, p. 243.
4. *Ibid.*, pp. 244–5; Hardinge, p. 133.
5. *A King's Story*, pp. 326–77.
6. *Ibid.*, pp. 328–9; Birkenhead, pp. 124–5, 133–4.
7. *The Heart Has Its Reasons*, pp. 244–7.
8. *Wallis & Edward*, p. 200.
9. Hardinge, p. 138.
10. Attlee, p. 86.
11. Citrine, p. 327.
12. Wrench, p. 344.
13. Middlemas and Barnes, p. 991.

14. Ramsay MacDonald's Diary, 13 November 1936.
15. Middlemas and Barnes, pp. 987–8.
16. *Ibid.*, p. 991.
17. Ramsay MacDonald's Diary, 13 November 1936.
18. Middlemas and Barnes, p. 993.
19. *Ibid.*, pp. 991–2.
20. *Ibid.*, p. 993; Ramsay MacDonald's Diary, 29 October 1936; Tom Jones, pp. 286, 288; Nicolson, p. 280.
21. Middlemas and Barnes, p. 990.
22. *Ibid.*
23. *A King's Story*, p. 330.
24. *Ibid.*
25. Middlemas and Barnes, p. 994.
26. Hansard, 10 December 1936.
27. Raymond A. Jones, p. 217.
28. *A King's Story*, p. 332.
29. Hansard, 10 December 1936.
30. Middlemas and Barnes, p. 995.
31. *Ibid.*
32. *Ibid.*
33. Ramsay MacDonald's Diary, 16 November 1936.
34. Duff Cooper's Memoir of the Abdication, in possession of Dr John Charmley.
35. Hardinge, p. 139.
36. Raymond A. Jones, p. 218.

Chapter Six: After the Decision

1. *A King's Story*, pp. 332–3.
2. Mabel, Countess of Airlie, *Thatched with Gold* (1962), p. 198.
3. *Ibid.*, p. 200.
4. *Chips*, p. 91.
5. Hardinge, p. 116.
6. Lowndes, p. 151.
7. *A King's Story*, pp. 333–4.
8. *The Secret File*, p. 277.
9. Charles J. V. Murphy, *The Windsor Story* (1979), p. 220.

8. *The Secret File*, p. 277.
9. Charles J. V. Murphy, *The Windsor Story* (1979), p. 220.
10. *A King's Story*, p. 335.
11. Conversation with Kenneth Rose.
12. Airlie, p. 197.
13. Hardinge, p. 116; Middlemas and Barnes, p. 987.
14. *A King's Story*, p. 319.
15. *Ibid.*, pp. 339–40.
16. Sir Samuel Hoare's Notes of the Abdication, Templewood Papers, Cambridge University Library, IX/7.
17. Duff Cooper's Memoir.
18. Cooper, *Old Men Forget*, p. 201.
19. *A King's Story*, p. 340.
20. Hardinge, p. 145.
21. *A King's Story*, p. 338.
22. Warner, p. 69.
23. *Ibid.*, pp. 68–9; Brian Inglis, *Abdication* (1966), p. 234.
24. *Ibid.*
25. Warner, p. 69.
26. Middlemas and Barnes, p. 996.
27. *A King's Story*, p. 338.
28. Inglis, p. 235.
29. *The Times*, 19 November 1936.
30. James Agate, *Ego 3* (1938), p. 58.
31. Ramsay MacDonald's Diary, 21 November 1936.
32. *Chips*, p. 91.
33. *Ibid.*; Duff Cooper's Memoir; *Victor Cazalet*, pp. 186–7.
34. Birkenhead, pp. 135–6.
35. Montgomery Hyde, pp. 469–70.
36. Cecil Beaton, *The Wandering Years* (1961), pp. 300–303.

Chapter Seven: Morganatic Marriage

1. *The Heart Has Its Reasons*.
2. *A King's Story*, p. 342.
3. Beaverbrook, p. 50 (editorial footnote).

4. Barnes and Nicholson, p. 432.
5. *A King's Story*, pp. 341–2.
6. *Ibid.*
7. *Ibid.*
8. Paris Papers: Walter Monckton to Edward VIII, 24 November 1936.
9. Paris Papers.
10. Paris Papers.
11. Tom Jones, pp. 267–8; Duff Cooper's Memoir.
12. *Chips*, p. 85.
13. Tom Jones, p. 288.
14. Robert Rhodes James (ed.), *Memoirs of a Conservative* (1969), p. 416.
15. Quoted in Frances Donaldson, *Edward VIII* (1974), p. 258.
16. *Memoirs of a Conservative*, p. 417.
17. Tom Jones, pp. 287–8; Duff Cooper's Memoir.
18. Neville Chamberlain's Diary, quoted in Middlemas and Barnes, p. 999.
19. *A King's Story*, p. 342.
20. Neville Chamberlain's Diary; Ramsay MacDonald's Diary, 25–6 November 1936.
21. *A King's Story*, p. 343.
22. Zetland to Linlithgow, 27 November 1936, India Office Records.
23. G. M. Young, p. 237.
24. See for instance Guedalla, op. cit.; Compton Mackenzie, *Windsor Tapestry*(1938); Winston Churchill, *The Gathering Storm*; Beaverbrook, op. cit.
25. *A King's Story*, pp. 343–4.
26. *Ibid.*, p. 342; Birkenhead, p. 140.
27. Beaverbrook, p. 109.
28. *The Secret File*, pp. 311–12.

Chapter Eight: An Official Matter

1. *A King's Story*, p. 345.
2. Kenneth Young, p. 361.
3. *A King's Story*, p. 345.

5. Gilbert, pp. 338—9.
6. Beaverbrook, p. 53; Sir Samuel Hoare's Notes.
7. *A King's Story*, p. 345.
8. Beaverbrook, p. 57.
9. Duff Cooper's Memoir.
10. Zetland letter, 27 November 1936, India Office Records.
11. Ramsay MacDonald's Diary.
12. Duff Cooper's Memoir.
13. Zetland letter.
14. Duff Cooper's Memoir.
15. Ramsay MacDonald's Diary.
16. Neville Chamberlain's Diary, quoted in Iain Macleod, *Neville Chamberlain* (1961), p. 197.
17. Sir Samuel Hoare's Notes.
18. Duff Cooper's Memoir.
19. Ramsay MacDonald's Diary.
20. Duff Cooper's Memoir.
21. For a discussion of the constitutional aspect, see Nicholas Mansergh, *Survey of British Commonwealth Affairs*, Vol. III (1952), pp. 41—6.
22. Sir Samuel Hoare's Notes.
23. DO 127/21, quoted in Sarah Bradford, *King George VI* (1989), pp. 185—6.
24. Quoted in Montgomery Hyde, p. 568.
25. Malcolm MacDonald, *People and Places* (1969), p. 124.
26. Beaverbrook, p. 61.
27. *A King's Story*, pp. 346—7.
28. Beaverbrook, pp. 61—2.
29. *A King's Story*, p. 347.
30. Lowndes, p. 151.
31. *Chips*, pp. 85—6.
32. *The Heart Has Its Reasons*, p. 252; *A King's Story*, pp. 347—8.
33. *Chips*, pp. 86—7.
34. *Wallis & Edward*, pp. 213—14.
35. *A King's Story*, p. 348; Beaverbrook, p. 66.
36. Beaverbrook, pp. 64—5.
37. *Chips*, p. 88.

38. Wrench, p. 349.
39. For Cockburn, *The Bedside Lilliput* (1950), pp. 220–24, and Claud Cockburn, *In Time of Trouble* (1956), pp. 248–52; for Martin, D. N. Pritt, *From Right to Left* (1965), p. 94.
40. Blunt's apology is published in his biography, John Peart-Binns, *Blunt* (1969), pp. 150–62.
41. Owen Chadwick, *Hensley Henson* (1983), p. 226.
42. Peart-Binns, p. 154.
43. Duff Cooper's Memoir.
44. Wrench, p. 347.
45. Peart-Binns, pp. 155–6.
46. *A King's Story*, pp. 349–50; Beaverbrook, pp. 65–7.
47. *A King's Story*, p. 354.
48. See Mansergh, op. cit.; Bradford, pp. 187–8; Cecil Edwards, *Bruce of Melbourne* (1965), pp. 254–5; Janet Adam Smith, *John Buchan* (1965), pp. 401–3; Vincent Massey, *What's Past is Prologue* (1963), p. 250; Lockhart, *Cosmo Gordon Lang*, pp. 401–2; *Victor Cazalet*, pp. 189–90.
49. Duff Cooper's Memoir.
50. Ramsay MacDonald's Diary.
51. *A King's Story*, p. 353.
52. G. M. Young, p. 238.
53. Quoted in Kenneth Young, *Baldwin*, p. 137.
54. G. M. Young, p. 238.
55. Quoted in Kenneth Young, *Baldwin*, p. 137.
56. Wrench, p. 349.
57. Mrs Baldwin's Diary, quoted by Middlemas and Barnes, p. 1005.

Chapter Nine: The Broadcast Proposal

1. *The Heart Has Its Reasons*, p. 254; *A King's Story*, p. 355.
2. *The Heart Has Its Reasons*, p. 254; *A King's Story*, pp. 356–7.

3. Birkenhead, p. 143.
4. *A King's Story*, p. 356.
5. Nicolson, p. 281.
6. *Memoirs of a Conservative*, pp. 414–15.
7. Duff Cooper's Memoir.
8. *A King's Story*, pp. 358–9; *The Heart Has Its Reasons*, pp. 254–5.
9. *Wallis & Edward*, pp. 208–9.
10. Paris Papers.
11. *The Heart Has Its Reasons*, pp. 254–6; *A King's Story*, pp. 359–63.
12. *Chips*, pp. 89–90.
13. Nicolson, p. 281.
14. *A King's Story*, pp. 361–2; *The Heart Has Its Reasons*, p. 259; Gilbert, p. 815.
15. Paris Papers.
16. Stuart, pp. 189–91.
17. Wheeler-Bennett, pp. 284–5.
18. *A King's Story*, pp. 364–5.
19. G. M. Young, pp. 239–40.
20. *A King's Story*, p. 365.
21. Stuart, p. 191.
22. Duff Cooper's Memoir.
23. Neil Balfour, *Paul of Yugoslavia* (1980), p. 136.
24. *A King's Story*, p. 365; Wheeler-Bennett, p. 285.
25. Beaverbrook, pp. 70–71; *A King's Story*, p. 366.
26. Vincent, p. 574.
27. *A King's Story*, pp. 366–72.
28. *The Heart Has Its Reasons*, p. 259; Duff Cooper's Memoir (6 December).
29. Stuart, p. 191.
30. Duff Cooper's Memoir.
31. Ramsay MacDonald's Diary.
32. Duff Cooper's Memoir.
33. Middlemas and Barnes, p. 1008.
34. Duff Cooper's Memoir.
35. Quoted in MacLeod, p. 198.
36. Zetland to Linlithgow, quoted in Montgomery Hyde, pp. 486–7.
37. Duff Cooper's Memoir.

38. *The Heart Has Its Reasons*, pp. 257–60.
39. *Chips*, p. 92.
40. Paris Papers.
41. Ramsay MacDonald's Diary.
42. *A King's Story*, p. 379.
43. Beaverbrook, p. 74.
44. Peacock's Diary, quoted by Donaldson, p. 275.
45. Gilbert, p. 815.
46. G. M. Young, p. 242.
47. Duff Cooper's Memoir; Ramsay MacDonald's Diary (5 December).

Chapter Ten: The Final Week

1. Winston Churchill's Memoir of the Abdication, quoted in full in Martin Gilbert, *Winston S. Churchill*, Companion Volume V, Part III (1982), pp. 452–4.
2. *Ibid*.
3. Salisbury to Churchill, 5 December 1936, quoted in Gilbert, Companion Volume, pp. 456–7.
4. Duff Cooper's Memoir.
5. *Ibid*.
6. Barnes and Nicholson, p. 431.
7. Winston Churchill's Memoir.
8. *Ibid*.
9. *A King's Story*, p. 381.
10. Winston Churchill's Memoir.
11. Birkenhead, p. 144.
12. *A King's Story*, pp. 381–3.
13. Birkenhead, p. 144.
14. Beaverbrook, pp. 77–8.
15. *A King's Story*, p. 345.
16. Quoted in Birkenhead, p. 144.
17. *A King's Story*, pp. 385–6.
18. *Ibid*., pp. 386–7.
19. G. M. Young, p. 240.
20. Birkenhead, pp. 144–5.
21. *A King's Story*, p. 387.

22. Quoted in Montgomery Hyde, pp. 488—9.
23. Beaverbrook, pp. 79—80.
24. Gilbert, Companion Volume, p. 455.
25. *Ibid.*, pp. 455—6.
26. *Ibid.*, pp. 457—8.
27. *Chips*, p. 92.
28. Beaverbrook, p. 80.
29. Middlemas and Barnes, p. 1010; Birkenhead, p. 145.
30. *Ibid.*
31. *Ibid.*
32. *A King's Story*, p. 391.
33. *Ibid.*, p. 392.
34. Middlemas and Barnes, p. 1010.
35. *The Heart Has Its Reasons*, pp. 264—9.
36. *Chips*, pp. 93—4.
37. *Wallis & Edward*, pp. 219—22.
38. Sir Samuel Hoare's Notes; *A King's Story*, p. 392; Beaverbrook, pp. 80—81.
39. Ramsay MacDonald's Diary.
40. Birkenhead, p. 145.
41. *A King's Story*, pp. 392—3.
42. Birkenhead, p. 146.
43. Duff Cooper's Memoir; Ramsay MacDonald's Diary.
44. Gilbert, pp. 820—1.
45. *Chips*, p. 95.
46. Churchill to Boothby, 12 December 1936, quoted in Gilbert, Companion Volume, p. 486.
47. Paris Papers.
48. Barnes and Nicholson, p. 432.
49. G. M. Young, p. 242.
50. Ramsay MacDonald's Diary.
51. *Chips*, pp. 93—4; Duff Cooper's Memoir.
52. *Ibid.*
53. Macleod, p. 198.
54. Theodore Goddard's Memoir, in Beaverbrook, pp. 116—20; *A King's Story*, p. 398; Peacock quoted in Birkenhead, p. 146.
55. *The Heart Has Its Reasons*, p. 273; *A King's Story*, p. 397; Birkenhead, p. 147.

56. See Goddard's Memoir and the fuller account in *A King's Story*: the latter derives from the recollections of George Allen and may be regarded as reliable.
57. Donaldson, p. 287.
58. *A King's Story*, p. 399; *The Heart Has Its Reasons*, p. 273.
59. Ramsay MacDonald's Diary.
60. Wheeler-Bennett, p. 285.
61. *A King's Story*, p. 399.
62. See *The Secret File*, Chapters 1–2.
63. Diary of Princess Paul of Yugoslavia, quoted in Balfour, p. 136.
64. *A King's Story*, p. 400.
65. *Chips*, pp. 96–7.
66. G. M. Young, p. 243.
67. *Ibid*.
68. Birkenhead, p. 148.
69. Duff Cooper's Memoir.
70. *A King's Story*, pp. 400–401.
71. Birkenhead, p. 148.
72. Birkenhead, p. 149; *A King's Story*, pp. 400–401; Wheeler-Bennett, p. 286.
73. Duff Cooper's Memoir; Mrs Baldwin's Diary, quoted in Middlemas and Barnes, p. 1015; *Victor Cazalet*, p. 190.
74. Sir Samuel Hoare's Notes.
75. Duff Cooper's Memoir.
76. Sir Samuel Hoare's Notes.
77. Paris Papers.
78. *A King's Story*, pp. 402–3; *The Heart Has Its Reasons*, pp. 275–6.
79. Theodore Goddard's Memoir.
80. *Wallis & Edward*, p. 220.
81. See *The Secret File*, Chapter 2.
82. *A King's Story*, p. 404.
83. Airlie, p. 200.
84. *The Heart Has Its Reasons*, pp. 266–7; *A King's Story*, pp. 402, 404–5.
85. Nicolson, pp. 285–6.

86. *Victor Cazalet*, p. 190.
87. *A King's Story*, p. 409.
88. *Ibid*.

As a condition of consulting the diaries of Ramsay MacDonald in the Public Record Office, I am enjoined to declare that their author kept them only as 'notes to guide and revive memory' without intending them to be used as a general historical source. In common with other scholars who have made use of them, however, I have found them both vivid and reliable.

Index

253

Rites of Spring
The Great War and the Birth of the Modern Age
Modris Eksteins

On May 29, 1913, near riot broke out in the Parisian audience for the first performance of *The Rite of Spring*. Stravinsky's powerful, discordant music and Nijinsky's frenzied, almost brutal choreography were intended to shock, and shock they did like no other artistic event before or since. *The Rite of Spring* shook the Establishment and started an urgent and irrevocable movement towards newness and purification in Art and intellectual life. Yet more shocking, however, was the Great War, which began only fifteen months later. The horrifying and unprecedented scale of its carnage resulted in almost universal revulsion and reinforced the overwhelming urge for change and renewal.

In *Rites of Spring*, Modris Eksteins has written a dazzlingly original and penetrating work of cultural history showing how these two momentous events have shaped our contemporary sense of self. He argues that the Great War's slaughter swept away the old order and ushered in the individualism, collective violence and mass culture of our age, and he identifies, in Stravinsky's dance of death, a potent symbol for the world today in which the struggle for freedom has paradoxically produced the power of ultimate destruction.

Rites of Spring avoids the linearity of conventional histories to offer startling new insights. Concluding in Spring 1945 with the suicide of Hitler in his bunker beneath Berlin, it takes the significant political, cultural and social events of those times and links them together in a symbolic chain to sum up the whole of our turbulent century and to reveal to us who we are, what values we adhere to and how we came to be.

BLACK SWAN

A SELECTED LIST OF NON-FICTION
FROM BLACK SWAN

THE PRICES SHOWN BELOW WERE CORRECT AT THE TIME OF GOING
TO PRESS. HOWEVER TRANSWORLD PUBLISHERS RESERVE THE RIGHT
TO SHOW NEW RETAIL PRICES ON COVERS WHICH MAY DIFFER FROM
THOSE PREVIOUSLY ADVERTISED IN THE TEXT OR ELSEWHERE.

☐	90100 0	FIRE FROM WITHIN	*Carlos Castaneda*	£4.99
☐	99332 8	THE POWER OF SILENCE	*Carlos Castaneda*	£3.95
☐	99406 5	RITES OF SPRING	*Modris Eksteins*	£6.99
☐	99450 2	HOTHOUSE EARTH	*John Gribbin*	£5.99
☐	99443 X	COSMIC COINCIDENCES	*John Gribbin and Martin Rees*	£4.99
☐	99364 6	VIDEO NIGHT IN KATHMANDU	*Pico Iyer*	£4.99
☐	99243 7	CONFESSIONS OF A FAILED SOUTHERN LADY	*Florence King*	£3.99
☐	99376 X	REFLECTIONS IN A JAUNDICED EYE	*Florence King*	£3.99
☐	99337 9	SOUTHERN LADIES AND GENTLEMEN	*Florence King*	£3.99
☐	99377 8	WASP WHERE IS THY STING?	*Florence King*	£4.99
☐	99105 7	1933	*Philip Metcalfe*	£5.99
☐	99404 9	EXTRAORDINARY PEOPLE	*Darold Treffert*	£4.99
☐	90143 0	CELTIC DAWN	*Ulick O'Connor*	£4.45
☐	99158 9	BRENDAN BEHAN	*Ulick O'Connor*	£5.99
☐	99367 0	THE RIGHT STUFF	*Tom Wolfe*	£5.99
☐	99366 2	THE ELECTRIC KOOL-AID ACID TEST	*Tom Wolfe*	£4.99
☐	99370 0	THE PAINTED WORD	*Tom Wolfe*	£3.50
☐	99371 9	THE PUMP HOUSE GANG	*Tom Wolfe*	£4.99

All Black Swan books are available at your bookshop or newsagent, or can be ordered from the following address:

Corgi/Bantam Books,
Cash Sales Department,
P.O. Box 11, Falmouth, Cornwall TR10 9EN

Please send a cheque or postal order (no currency) and allow 80p for postage and packing for the first book plus 20p for each additional book ordered up to a maximum charge of £2.00 in UK.

B.F.P.O. customers please allow £1.50 for postage and packing for the first book, £1.00 for the second book, and 30p for each subsequent title ordered.

NAME (Block Letters) ....

ADDRESS ....

....